JOURNEYS TO ENGLAND AND IRELAND

Happy –

Happy B.day

I can promise you that this will be one of the best you will have read in quite some time

Johnny, Teddy,

J. Thomas, Mom,

and Katie

ALEXIS DE TOCQUEVILLE

Journeys to England and
Ireland

Translated by
GEORGE LAWRENCE AND K. P. MAYER

edited by
J. P. MAYER

Transaction Publishers
New Brunswick (U.S.A.) and London (U.K.)

Second printing 2003

New material this edition copyright © 1988 by Transaction Publishers, New Brunswick, New Jersey. Originally published in 1979 by Arno Press.

Library of Congress Catalog Number: 87-30234
ISBN: 0-88738-716-0
Printed in the United States of America

Library of Congress Cataloging-in-Publication Data

Tocqueville, Alexis de, 1805-1859.
    Journeys to England and Ireland.

    Translation from French.
    Originally published: New York: Arno Press, 1979.
        1. Great Britain—Description and travel—1801-1900.
        2. Tocqueville, Alexis de, 1805-1859. I. Title.
DA 625.T63   1987   914.1'0475   87-30234
ISBN 0-88738-716-0

IN MEMORIAM
Madame la Comtesse Christian de Tocqueville
(1875–1954)

Contents

INTRODUCTION TO THE TRANSACTION EDITION

These pages are perhaps the most penetrating writings on the spirit of British politics. In effect, as indicated by John Stuart Mill, Tocqueville was the Montesquieu of the nineteenth century, above all if one thinks of the present Irish situation.

His political observations reach out into the future, now our present.

J. P. Mayer
31 May 1987

The Grey House
Stoke Poges
Buckinghamshire
England

FOREWORD TO THE ARNO PRESS EDITION

Once again this book has found another publisher. The Anchor edition
has been out of print for several years and by friendly agreement between
Doubleday and the Arno Press the book is now again available for the
student and the general reader.

I have corrected a few minor misprints and added as Appendix 7 two
letters by Tocqueville which appear here for the first time in English.
They put Tocqueville's masterly analysis of English life and
institutions into the wider framework of his political sociology.

I am grateful to the Arno Press for making this book accessible again.
Tocqueville's observations on English and particularly Irish problems,
have lost nothing of their validity for today - on the contrary.

With regard to note 1 on p. 21, the note should now read:
See now Alexis de Tocqueville, Œuvres Complètes, ed. J.P. Mayer,
Volume VIII, 1, pp. 47ff, where the complete letter by Tocqueville to
Beaumont has now been published.

With regard to p. 92, there should now be a note on Sutton Sharpe [sic]:
Sutton Sharpe (1797-1843) was a member of the British Radical circle,
a friend of George Grote, the historian of Greece. Cf. S. Drescher,
Tocqueville and England, Cambridge, Mass., 1964. Drescher's book is quite
informative, but his 'own' translations from Tocqueville's French are
rather loose. He draws our attention, among other 'discoveries', to
Cottu's Administration de la Justice criminelle en Angleterre (1822),
assuming that no other scholar will have read our edition of Tocqueville's
Journey to America, where on pp. 317f. the reference to Cottu has been given.

University of Reading
Tocqueville Research Centre   J.P. Mayer
December 1976

FOREWORD TO THE ANCHOR EDITION

The present book was published by the Yale University Press in 1958
and by Faber's in London in the same year. By friendly agreement with both
firms it is now reprinted in this series. I have taken the opportunity to
add as Appendix 6 an important text by Tocqueville on certain aspects of
British local government which was omitted from the previous edition. My
colleague André Jardin, while preparing the Tocqueville-Beaumont correspondence for the Œuvres Completes, found these pages among some Tocqueville
letters at the University Library at Yale. They belong to the Tocqueville
Archives.

This section of the text has been previously published in French;
cf. Contrat Social, Vol. VII, 6, Paris, November 1963.

The Grey House, Stoke Poges   J.P. Mayer
May 1964

Preface

Alexis de Tocqueville's notebooks on England and Ireland appear in this volume for the first time in English. The text is based on Volume V, 2 of Tocqueville's *Œuvres Complètes* which I am directing. My colleague M. André Jardin has collaborated with me in establishing the French text from the manuscript.

I have added to Tocqueville's notebooks a long extract from an unpublished letter to his friend Gustave de Beaumont which shows his remarkable understanding of English social and constitutional history five years before his visit to England. The document on *Bribery at Elections* is reprinted from a House of Commons Report by kind permission of the Speaker of the House. I thank the Editor of *The Times* for allowing me to reproduce an article of mine published in his paper in 1955 in commemoration of Tocqueville's 150th anniversary. As this article uses material from the Royal Archives at Windsor Castle, it is my duty to thank Her Majesty the Queen for her gracious permission to republish these pages in the context of this book.

Finally, I wish to thank the Comte Jean de Tocqueville, who has permitted me to dedicate this volume to the memory of his mother to whose kind generosity and deep understanding I owe so much.

Editor's notes have been added to Tocqueville's text.

With the publication of this book I have perhaps fulfilled what I set out to do in 1938 when I began working on Tocqueville: to define through him the principles underlying British politics, which he analysed against the background of the American and the French political mind.

J. P. MAYER

Stoke Poges, Buckinghamshire
16th December 1957

So many of my thoughts and feelings are shared by the English, that England has turned into a second native land of the mind for me.

Tocqueville to Nassau Senior
(*27th July* 1851)

Introduction

Tocqueville left New York for Havre on the 20th February 1832. He had stayed in America for nine months. Back in France, he and his friend Gustave de Beaumont, who had travelled with him through the United States, wrote their joint work on the *Penitentiary System in the United States* which had been the pretext of their journey. This task completed, Tocqueville began to write his *Democracy in America*. But before putting the finishing touches to this work, he decided to visit England.

He had private reasons, too, for visiting the United Kingdom. He had become attached to Mary Mottley, an English middleclass girl, whom he had met at Versailles in 1828 where he had been a judge, and, no doubt, felt in 1833 that it would be well to make the acquaintance of her family in England. He married Mary Mottley in 1836. But that private reason apart, while working on the *Democracy in America*, Tocqueville probably felt that he could not fully understand American political and social institutions without some experience of British political practice. With British constitutional history he was familiar as the long extract we print from a letter to his friend Beaumont proves.

He stayed in England for five weeks. It was the England of the first Reform Bill which had become law on 7th June 1832. The age of Democracy had begun. Nassau Senior, the well-known economist, describes how Tocqueville came to see him in 1833 saying: 'I am Alexis de Tocqueville and I have just made your acquaintance.' They became close friends until Tocqueville died in 1859. He visited the House of Commons, as

13

Introduction

Montesquieu had done before him, attended election meetings, and watched the proceedings of a magistrate's Court where Lord Radnor was a Justice of the Peace. He went to Oxford and noted the importance of that ancient university as a recruiting ground for the English political élite.

After a general survey of English political and social life, Tocqueville made a sketch of the political sociology of the country. Here are some of his salient points: 'Decentralisation, like Liberty, is something which the leaders of the people always promise and never give. To get it and to keep it the people must rely on its own efforts, and, if they have not the taste for it, there is no cure for the ill.' The close connection between centralisation, decentralisation, and liberty is for Tocqueville the crucial question. All his works turn on that. He observed, too, that the English aristocracy was open to recruits: 'The difference in this matter is clear from the use of one word in each language; *gentleman* and *gentilhomme* have the same origin; but *gentleman* in English applies to any well-educated man, regardless of birth, whereas in France *gentil-homme* can only be used of a noble by birth. The meaning of these two words of common derivation has been so changed by the different social climate of the peoples, that they are quite untranslatable, at least without recourse to a periphrasis. This grammatical observation is more illuminating than the longest argument. . . . The English aristocracy has a hand in everything; it is open to all; and anyone who wished to abolish it or attack it as a body, would find it very hard to define the object of his onslaught. . . .' Nevertheless Tocqueville thought one could say that the English aristocracy was losing daily some of the scope of its power. 'The immediate future of European society', he notes, 'lies with democracy. . . . In England the people are beginning to get the idea that they, too, could take part in government. So the gradual development of democratic principles must follow the irresistible march of events. Daily some new privilege of the aristocracy comes under attack. It is a slow war waged against one little point after another, but in time it will certainly bring the whole edifice down.' From what he could learn from his radical guides or observe himself of the political and social tensions of England in 1833, he felt that a violent revolution was 'something possible but not probable

14

Introduction

. . . if things follow their natural course, I don't think there will be a revolution, and I see a good chance for the English to succeed in modifying the social and political set-up, with sharp growing pains no doubt, but without convulsions, and without civil war.' Tocqueville was a penetrating observer; he discovered gradualism long before the Fabians.

Eighteen months later—from May to September 1835—Tocqueville paid his second visit to England. He was no longer the unknown magistrate, but the famous author of the *Democracy in America* of which the first two volumes had just been published in Paris and in Reeve's translation in London. His circle of friends had grown much larger: to Senior, Lord Radnor, Bulwer, Dr. Bowring now were added John Stuart Mill, Hallam, the historian, Roebuck, and most important his devoted translator Henry Reeve, not to mention many others. He met the historian of Greece, George Grote, who was then a member of the Commission on Electoral Corruption, before which Tocqueville was invited to give evidence. We reprint this evidence which gives a masterly analysis of the party system under the July Monarchy in France. Lady Holland gave him the *entrée* to her salon, a brilliant centre of London political society, and he was received at Lansdowne House on the strength of a letter of introduction from Count Molé. The groundwork of 1833 now leads to achievement. Tocqueville is evidently more sure of himself. One sees how he is struggling with the problems dealt with in the second two volumes of his *Democracy in America*, which, however, he was not to finish for another five years: they were published in 1840.

Tocqueville touches one of the most subtle and for the continental observer perhaps the most puzzling trait of the political animal in the British Isles. He terms this attitude tentatively the spirit of association and the spirit of exclusion. 'I can't completely understand', he writes, 'how the spirit of association and the spirit of exclusion came to be so highly developed in the same people, and often to be so intimately combined. Example, a club: what better example of association than the union of individuals who form the club? What is more exclusive than the corporate personality represented by the club? The same applies to almost all civil and political associations, the corporations. . . . See how families divide up when the birds

15

are able to leave the nest.' Perhaps Tocqueville might have carried the argument a little further. The adaptability of the spirit of association explains to some extent the simplicity of the British parliamentary system. There are so many clubs and other associations to deal with specific problems that the organised political parties can concentrate on big questions of national policy. Indeed, this strange combination of the spirit of association and the spirit of individualism nourishes and sustains the Englishman's political capacity. Many of Tocqueville's observations refer to the structure of the British legal system. 'The English', he notes, 'are the first people who ever thought of centralising the administration of justice. This innovation, which dates from the Norman period, should be reckoned one of the reasons for the quicker progress that this nation has made in civilisation and liberty.' On the other hand Tocqueville is aware of the archaic nature of certain features of criminal justice during this epoch. Moreover, he is not blind to the evil effects of the administration of justice favouring the rich.

He reflects on the distinctive feature of centralisation in England. 'Legislation and not administration, government more than administration.' His brilliant analysis of the new Poor Law Act (14th August 1834) goes to the very roots of the principles of British administration. 'Let us stop a moment', he writes in his account of the Poor Law, 'to say a word about that organisation which is characteristic of the English race and which we will find again in almost all the institutions which it has brought into being in the new world. There are three elements there: 1. Choice of the executive power. 2. Election. 3. Control by the Judicial power. These three elements are combined so as to establish an administration which is active but not tyrannical.' Comparing this structure of administration with France, Tocqueville comes to this conclusion: 'Impossibility of having an elected power working side by side with a nominated administrative power without recourse to the arbitration of the judicial power. What happens in France proves it. We are working either towards complete independence or complete subordination of the provinces and the destruction of municipal life.'

But no one should imagine that in the admiration for the spirit of English politics Tocqueville forgot to note the deep social crisis caused by the rapid industrialisation of those years. His pages dealing with the poverty of the working classes in Manchester recall in style and in depth of analysis the remarks of La Bruyère on the conditions of the seventeenth-century peasants in *Les Caractères*. They herald Friedrich Engels' *Conditions of the Working Class in England*, one of the source-books of Marxism. Although Tocqueville had been struck by the unhappy conditions of the English working people, he does not seem to have been in touch with Chartist activities in those years. On the other hand, he was continually impressed by the importance of the social rôle of wealth in England. Thus he wrote from London to his fiancée: 'The respect paid to wealth in England is enough to make one despair.'

In a note on a conversation with his friend Henry Reeve Tocqueville comes back to the problem of centralisation: 'Why', he asks, 'is centralisation especially a habit of Democracy? That is a great question to explore in the third volume of my work, if I can fit it in there. Question of first importance. Centralisation, instinct of democracy, instinct of a society which has managed to extricate itself from the individualistic system of the Middle Ages. Preparation for despotism.' It is evident from these jottings that Tocqueville did not look forward to our own age without deep apprehensions. Here he anticipates the fourth part of the second volume of the *Democracy in America*, which is the crowning achievement of his sociology.

Did he mean to write a book on England? He denies it though the form of his notes makes his denial not quite convincing. In any case, on his return to France, he wrote to Count Molé: 'I agree with you, Sir, that after a book which has had some success, one should not be in a hurry to take up the pen again. So I never intended when I went to England (whatever my publisher may have said without my knowledge in the *Journal des Débats*) to collect the material for a new work. In undertaking that journey my only object was to regain my health, which was troubling me a little, and at the same time to give myself the intellectual pleasure of watching a great people in the throes of revolutionary change. That was the object, and that will be the result of my journey. I think I have picked up some ideas in England, which, for me, are new, and may be useful later on; but I have never thought of writing a book

B   17

about the country I hurried through. If the idea did enter my head as I started out, I have quite dropped it since my return. It would take a very fatuous philosopher to imagine that he could understand England in six months. A year has ever seemed to me too short a time for a proper appreciation of the United States, and it is infinitely easier to form clear ideas and precise conceptions about America than about Great Britain. In America all laws originate more or less from the same idea. The whole of society, so to say, is based on just one fact: everything follows from one underlying principle. One could compare America to a great forest cut through by a large number of roads which all end in the same place. Once you have found the central point, you can see the whole plan in one glance. But in England the roads cross, and you have to follow along each one of them to get a clear idea of the whole.' These sentences give an admirable synthesis of the cardinal thoughts Tocqueville was formulating in his mind during his two journeys to England.

In July and August 1835 Tocqueville was in Ireland. Again he travelled with his friend Gustave de Beaumont who in 1839 published his book *L'Irlande sociale, politique et religieuse* whereas Tocqueville's notes on Ireland remained largely unpublished. He does not hide his contempt for the British aristocracy and its instruments which treated the Irish as conquered people. With patient and sympathetic understanding he disentangles Irish social and political institutions. He studies the land question, the problem of a poor law for Ireland, the administration of justice; he analyses the moral and political attitudes against the background of the class stratification of the Irish people. His account of the deep religious feeling he meets everywhere reveals how this sharp observer and analyst was moved to his very depth. 'It is the people', an Irish priest told him, 'that believes firmly in another world because they are unhappy in this one.' In Ireland it is the poor who save the poor from dying of hunger. 'What does the Lord do meanwhile ?' Tocqueville notes. 'He goes for walks inside his huge domains surrounded by high walls. Within the park all is splendid; poverty groans without, but he does not see it; it is his doorman's job to keep the poor out of sight, but should he by chance meet a poor man, he answers his prayers by saying: "I make it a duty not to encourage begging." His dogs are large and fat and fellow beings are dying at his door. Not only does he never help the poor in their need, he profits by their necessities to extract enormous rents and goes to France or Italy to spend the money he has so gained. . . .'

It is the contrast between Tocqueville's English and Irish impressions which makes these pages so fascinating. What he admires in British politics in England, he abhors in Ireland. He has never served a class; he always upheld the sanctity of the human soul, so infinitely threatened by the modern State structure which he analysed in its historical beginnings. These pages contain invaluable lessons for those who wish to learn them: he discovered in 1828, influenced by Guizot, the egalitarian tendency in the democratic development of our constitutional history; he dissects British administrative practices into their formative elements; he reveals the two essentially British contributions to politics: the openness of our aristocracy and the spirit of association combined with the spirit of individualism.

I know of no more penetrating book written on the British political mind. Tocqueville was indeed the Montesquieu of the nineteenth century and his interpretations reach far into the future which has become our present.

J. P. MAYER

I

Reflections on English History[1]

Tocqueville (5th October 1828)

. . . Well, here I am at Tocqueville, in my old family ruin. A
league away is the harbour[2] from which William set out to conquer England. I am surrounded by Normans whose names figure
in the lists of the conquerors. All that, I must admit, 'flatters the
proud weakness of my heart', and sometimes stirs a childish
enthusiasm of which afterwards I am ashamed. However all that
brings me round to a subject I had quite forgotten about, and
puts me in mind to write to you my musings about English history, which I must do much more shortly than I could wish as I
have so little time here. I will write haphazard what I think for
you to put in order if you can or will. But on my soul and conscience I warn you that I don't yet know what I am going to
say.

I don't think you like the beginnings, and I can well believe
it. I could never read about them without yawning, and could
never remember the sequence of events narrated. But still I
think that when I, as you too, studied the matter, had our reading been better directed, we might have found it interesting and
the source of some pregnant thoughts. As for facts, I have given
up all hope of remembering the names of the kings of the Hept-
archy and all that muddle of obscure happenings whose cause
and whose results no one knows. But I should like to get a clear
picture of the movements of peoples spreading over on top of
each other and getting continually mixed up, but each still keeping something that it had from the beginning. There is hardly

[1] Letter by Tocqueville, addressed very probably to his friend Gustave de
Beaumont. The document is slightly cut in the beginning where Tocqueville
reports on some intimate details of his private life which are irrelevant here. It
is published here for the first time.
[2] Tocqueville refers to Barfleur.

anywhere better than England for studying the underlying factors and the details of the armed emigrations which overturned
the Roman Empire, because there were more of them there and
they lasted into a time when the barbarians in the rest of Europe
were already refinding civilisation. But besides that there is
something in the broad picture which strikes the imagination;
revolution after revolution compared to which those of our own
time are trifles: the driving back of the British tribes by the
Scots: the Saxons coming and driving all before them: the battles
of the Saxons against the Danes, a third race of conquerors still
coming from the same part of the world, but keeping more of the
savage energy of the Northern peoples; battles which lasted
until the Normans, coming from the North, too, but endowed
both with the impetuous energy of the Danes and with a higher
civilisation than the Saxons, united them all under one yoke.
One thinks with horror of the inconceivable sufferings of
humanity at that time. Don't you think that an account which
disregarded individuals and told of the march of peoples, a short,
staccato account, would paint a terrible picture but one from
which much could be learnt? But I'm a fool to let my imagination
run. Back please. I was saying that one could find pregnant
thoughts in the study of early English history. I must work that
out more: It has always surprised me that so many sensible,
thoughtful people should suppose that the feudal system in
France originated from the troubles of the second race and the
weakness of the third. That seems to me much as if a doctor
should attribute a malignant fever of which one might be cured
or die three months later, to the exhaustion of a day's hunting.
I think just one observation is enough to destroy that theory. If
the feudal system is due to chance in France, by what odd
coincidence does it turn up again among the Germans, among
the Poles where it still exists, among the Goths in Spain, and
even in Italy, the Southern extremity of Europe? Clearly the
feudal system of the twelfth century is but the result of an underlying cause. It sprang fully armed from the peoples of the North,
like Minerva from the head of Jupiter, needing only the hatchet's
blow. Do you see what I want to get at? This is it: if you want
to understand the first underlying principles of the feudal system,
and you need to understand them to see how the wheels work in
the finished machine, you cannot do better than study the time

before the Norman conquest, because, as I said before, we know of no people nearer to their primitive state than the Saxons and the Danes. No other people show a clearer record of their institutions, and I am sure that deep research into those times would enable us to explain many things which cannot now be explained in the history of other peoples, as for instance certain maxims of legal procedure which have become laws throughout Europe, but of which we can neither trace the origin, nor account for the reason why people are so obstinately attached to them. Besides that, the customs of the Saxons are interesting in themselves and especially interesting in the context of English history. Their legal procedure is the oddest which has ever existed, and one can find in it all the elements of the present-day procedure, some parts of which we have adopted ourselves.

To conclude, I always come back to the view that the Saxons, coming later and farther from the ancient Roman hearth of civilisation, are precious as a type of the peoples from whom we all, such as we are, are sprung. Perhaps one could make something of that idea.

But I admit that that won't help you much at present. So let us go on to the history of England after the conquest. As I have no book of any sort in front of me, I am sure to make many mistakes about men, dates and sometimes even events, but at least I feel sure that I am right about the basic trends.

There were many reasons why William's conquest was both easy and lasting. The differences which still existed between the various races inhabiting the island, the size of the capital and the absence of all fortifications in the provinces, the vast intellectual superiority of the Normans at that time (a superiority which I cannot explain, but which surely existed), these are what facilitated the conquest. What made it last was the change in the ownership of land and the introduction of the fully developed feudal system. But be sure that if no notion of this had existed before, no power on earth could have established it at once in a form to last. However that may be, it was established and the system made a more coherent whole than in any other country, because one head had thought out all the machinery and so each wheel fitted better. I admire that creation of William and cannot resist stopping a moment to talk about it. There are two great drawbacks to avoid in organising a country. Either the whole strength of social organisation is centred on one point, or it is spread over the country. Either alternative has its advantages and its drawbacks. If all is tied into one bundle, and the bundle gets undone, everything falls apart and there is no nation left. Where power is dispersed, action is clearly hindered, but there is strength everywhere. So it is safe to say that in the first case a people will do greater things and have a more active life than in the second case, but its life will be poorer. I don't know if a mean between these extremes can be found, but it would seem that William did find it. Wherever it was established these were the principles of the feudal system: the grant of land and of power of government in return for a money rent and, more important, the obligation to provide an armed force for a stated time. That is the whole point. It followed therefrom that the right to make extraordinary levies going beyond the original agreement required the consent of the parties concerned. So the King had no other armies but those of his barons, and no revenue but that from his domains. So then if the King was not the richest and by far the most powerful of the feudal lords, his kingship was but a name. That is what happened in France, where the barons went so far as to abolish the right of appeal to the king's courts. That is what did not happen in England. William, master of all, gave lavishly but kept still more. Power was so divided among the ruling class that a handful of Normans could hold down an unwilling country for a century, but the royal power was so strong that it could crush any individual baron who would have wished to break away from the king's general supervision, and could only be brought down by a general combination against him. So then if William's successors had been different from what they were, his work would surely have lasted as he had conceived it, and in spite of the revolutions which followed, his version of the feudal system is nevertheless by and large the one which caused the least harm and left the smallest legacy of hatred.

There have been few worse rulers and, especially, few rulers more inclined to abuse their powers than the Norman kings and the first Plantagenets. William Rufus was like a wild beast; Henry I ruled with ability but with a rod of iron; civil war came; the royal domain was squandered under Stephen, each faction plundering it for its private needs. But seldom has fortune favoured anyone more than Henry II, the founder of the Plantagenets. In his own right Count of Anjou, Poitou and Maine, his marriage to Eleanor brought him Guyenne and Saintonge. So the whole Atlantic coast became English without a sword drawn. Henry II was a hard, autocratic ruler as were all the rest of his family. His son Richard, hero only of romance, was a wild madman; one of those brilliant beings who burn but give no light. His reign exhausted the royal domain. Money was raised by extortion; the poll-tax, a levy, often arbitrary, which the king and the barons exacted from people of the third estate and serfs, became exorbitant, and even the barons' property was subject to confiscation. The provinces won in France only made oppression worse, since each was used to rule the other and so the king was never short of obedient servants.

So you see, my dear friend, that if William's work did not produce the results we might have expected, the bad behaviour of his successors is alone to blame.

However that may be, when John came to the throne the English were in a bad way. The king's power, which for a century had been in the hands of tyrants, weighed heavily both on the barons and on the third estate which was beginning to emerge in Europe at that time and which the kings of France took trouble to encourage in their domains. The pressure must have been severe, for it was at that time that Philip-Augustus met hardly any resistance when he occupied the English provinces in France, even Normandy. John's tyranny grew no less through the loss of those provinces, for it is a law of all dominion, past, present and future, to make greater demands in proportion as power decreases. At last one fine morning, I think it was about the year 1206,[1] the leaders of the English barons realised that, if they united, they would be stronger than the king though each by himself was still weaker than he. John was surrounded and made to sign first Magna Carta and soon afterwards the Forest Charter.

Historians have a passion for decisive events. One must admit that they are very convenient. An event like that makes an excellent starting point; your purpose set once for all, you have only to give a straightforward, frank account of the ensuing

[1] The barons met in 1214 and swore to obtain from the king a confirmation of Henry I's charter. Magna Carta was actually signed in June 1215.

consequences. What could be better? But unfortunately this world's affairs do not always go like that. Many people treat the words 'Magna Carta' as magic. They see the whole English Constitution in it; the two Houses; ministerial responsibility; taxation by vote and a thousand other things that are no more there than in the Bible. Magna Carta served no national purpose, but was devised to serve the private interests of the nobles and to redress some intolerable abuses which harmed them. The few stipulations that affected the common people amount to so little that it is not worth talking about them. But unimportant though it was in some respects, Magna Carta nevertheless brought great things about. It was *decisive*: it gave a clear shape to the opposition. Everything was ready for change. From then onwards a great many men marched under the standard of the Great Charter without knowing or caring what it had enacted. There were more than thirty ratifications of that same charter imposed on kings in the century after it.

Generally any power challenged reacts by finding ways to support itself. So we see Edward I succeed to John.[1] Edward no doubt had just as despotic a disposition as any of his predecessors, but he was a skilful ruler who knew that one has to tack in a storm. He took the measures which are almost always successful after a revolution, when there are a great many private disasters and the first need is for personal safety. He brought back order and made good civil laws which, as you know, often make people forget good political laws. He was largely responsible for the organisation of English judicial procedure. Trade was encouraged. Finally he did all he could to soothe popular passion and succeeded pretty well. He reigned long, firmly and with fair renown. He was a bad man but able, which by and large is better for peoples than an honest but incapable ruler. In his reign began the war between England and Scotland in which later on France took a prominent part.

Nota Bene. This is what happens when one writes quickly without a book. Racking my memory I notice that I have left out a trifle, a reign of fifty years, that of Henry III.

Henry III was the son of John. He succeeded him after the French pretender, *Louis d'Outre Mer*, had been driven out. He was a good enough prince but a nonentity who let the revolution

[1] Henry III succeeded John in 1216 and Edward followed Henry III in 1272.

glide on. One of those people whom one has met since the
thirteenth century, who give up important points and argue
obstinately about small ones, thus annoying without giving in.
Henry fell completely under the guardianship of the barons who
were then led by a Frenchman, Simon de Montfort, Earl of
Leicester. This time is remembered for the first occasion that
the Commons were summoned to Parliament. That was the
result of a general movement occurring over the whole of
Europe. One must stop here and pay careful attention.

The barbarian invasions brought into existence only two
classes of men; noble and serf. The progress of civilisation and
the weakening of the feudal system soon allowed a third class to
appear, but the seeds of this were half smothered by the other
two. The 'Tiers Etat' or the commons come on the scene from
the twelfth century in France and, I think, about the same time
in England. They were composed of all the hard-working people
of independent spirit who were put upon in every sort of way by
the tyranny of barons and king. So communal organisations were
formed in every town where there were enough people to put up
some resistance. As time went on this class became, for that age,
very enlightened and rich, as all commerce had gradually fallen
into its hands. It gained what the others lost, for it was nearer
than the others to the natural state of mankind. The capital was
of little importance in feudal days, so it was possible that, at the
same time as a baron, safe in his corner, struck money, held
court and made war with his serfs and his liegemen, a bowshot
away there might be a town, appointing its magistrates, mana-
ging its finances, and having its armed band under its own flag,
in a word a real republic. And in such republics there were often
heroes worthy to have lived in Rome or Sparta. Such was the
state of Europe in the twelfth and more especially the thirteenth
century. An odd mixture of oppression and liberty, one can see
no unity in its variegated confusion, but everywhere centres of
active life. Now, listen. Suppose that two men have been engaged in a long and determined fight although one of them is a
little weaker than the other. A third man comes up, weaker than
either of the two but who, whichever side he took, would be
sure to tilt the balance that way. But who will think of asking
him for help, who will urge his claim for help most strongly?
It is sure to be he who feels himself weakest. When the two

weak ones join together, the strongest enemy will be defeated. But which of the two allies will have the upper hand? The fight begins again, and ends in full or partial victory for one of them. There, my dear friend, is the whole history of France and of England in the story of those three men, but with this difference that in France it was the king who was the weaker of the first pair and therefore the one to call the Commons to his aid, to join forces with them and lead them, to use their help to destroy the feudal system, and in the end to be swallowed up by them when the two were left face to face in 1789. In England, on the other hand, the feudal nobility started weaker of the two and so was the one to call the third estate to Parliament, year by year to put forward claims in its interest as if they were their own, to build up its strength, promote and sustain it every time. When the king's power was gone, it was the third estate which threw over the nobility in 1640 and established the republic. We will see how it came about that that revolution was not final. But you see that in every case the weakest becomes the strongest, and the ally gets his master down, which goes to show, as I said before, that after all rational equality is the only state natural to man, since nations get there from such various starting points and following such different roads.

So you see it is a crucial point for my argument that it was the barons, with Lord Leicester at their head, who summoned the Commons to Parliament to use as a prop against the royal power. Whereas in France it was Philip the Fair who summoned them to the States General. Others pretend that petty circumstances controlled these events, but I can only see them as the necessary consequence of the state of affairs. The third estate had to be called in to the management of affairs as soon as anything was to be feared or hoped from it. That's the natural way for the world to go.

This innovation was revolutionary. Leicester killed and his faction destroyed, it was some years before there was talk of the Commons again. It was Edward I, of whom I spoke before out of turn, who summoned them in legal form. That prince who, as I said, knew that one had to tack in the storm, saw all the advantage that he could draw from the Commons, if he chose who should represent them and united them under his control. Besides the great feudal maxim 'do not tax the un-

28

willing' was then in full force. Edward needed money; the Commons were rich; the barons would not have allowed them to be trampled on in contravention of accepted principles. So once more the short answer was to bring them together on his side by means of their representatives. So from then onwards Parliament was constituted more or less as it is today, though it was not very like Mr. Canning's Parliament. Here I may be able to help you by explaining how that Parliament is formed, a matter which has always bothered me and which I think I now understand properly.

All the 'freeholders' that is to say, if I am not mistaken, all those in the feudal hierarchy who held direct from the king— and there were a great many of them—had the right to appear in Parliament. I don't know where that law was written, nor indeed if it was written at all, but it sprang from the very nature of the feudal system, since one needed the consent of all that lot of people to do a heap of things, among others the imposition of all extraordinary taxes. At the time of the conquest many of them found this right a burden. In fact the freeholds were very far from equal. There might be a baron holding direct and in that sense the equal of the leaders of the English nobility, whose modest property made him in fact their inferior and who had a sorry part to play in Parliament which only involved him in unwanted expense. This situation was made a great deal worse as time went on and properties were divided up. Then next it was found necessary to impose fines to compel the lesser lords to come to Parliament as with us to jury service. Finally, their numbers multiplying as their patrimonies diminished, after persistent requests they were permitted only to send 'representatives' to appear for them. Follow all this carefully, please. So Parliament came to be composed of two different sorts of men, the leaders of the higher nobility or the lords, and the representatives of the inferior nobility or 'gentry'. First of all, these two sorts of men claimed equal status, but soon the hereditary members came to be accepted as more important than the elected ones and little by little the Lords shut the representatives of the gentry or the counties out from the management of affairs. It was then that the Commons became strong enough and rich enough for others to have an interest in summoning them to Parliament. They, too, sent representatives to appear for them under the name of deputies for the boroughs. At first this new element in Parliament was deeply distrusted by the other two. They sat separately, only voted taxes, and when they tried to play a part in government, the lords and the representatives of the counties roughly repulsed them. The borough members themselves feeling their own inferiority often said that questions of government did not concern them at all. We will soon see how all that changed in time. All you need to know for the moment is that as the borough members gained in importance, those for the counties lost theirs. Finally the two classes of men found themselves on a level and then formed what was afterwards called the English House of Commons. Now that explains our neighbours' complicated electoral system and gives you the key to it. Each county elects two members. Those members represent the lower nobility, or, if you like it better, the landed interest. There is a fairly high property qualification for the electors and a higher one for the elected. That is the principle of a French election. For the boroughs it is quite a different matter. Every borough has been granted by some old charter the right to send one or more members to Parliament; it can choose them as it likes, that is its affair. So the form of election varies from place to place. Many towns, not knowing where to draw the line, summoned all the inhabitants. Hence the 'hustings'; shouting speakers, stones and fisticuffs and all the orgies we witness of English liberty. I think you understand now how Parliament is formed. Back to the main theme; I can't give you dates but will try not to lose the thread again. I forgot to speak of the clergy. For reasons easy to discover but which are questions of general history, the Catholic clergy throughout Europe had become both a religious and a political body. Almost all the bishops and many abbots held fiefs on the same terms as the barons, subject to military service and feudal dues. Like them they took their places as of right in Parliament. The clergy also met separately to raise its own taxes. After the Reformation these meetings, which had already become very infrequent, ceased altogether, and only the more important bishops kept their seats in the House of Lords.

There then is Parliament in being. It is composed of turbulent Lords and weak and timid Commons, themselves surprised at the part they have been called on to play. Nothing made the summoning of Parliament obligatory, so a skilful king would take pride in getting on without it as long as possible. But that did not often happen, since Parliament on its side was careful only to vote taxes for a short period. When the king wanted to summon it, he dispatched 'Writs' to the counties and boroughs, which both ordered the election and generally named the candidate. That was a strange form of election. Yet, once together these same men were almost always brave opponents, so great is the strength of assemblies. Besides, once Parliament had come together, the Lords almost always spurred the Commons on and backed them up every time, which helped considerably to unite these two orders of men who, in the rest of Europe, have been irreconcilable enemies, and which soon encouraged the Commons to go their own way, relying on their own strength.

The Commons' first step was to declare that no tax could be levied on them unless it had been agreed by *them*. Before that a tax thrown out by the Commons, could be passed by the Lords, and then became binding on all. Lords and clergy joined with the Commons to gain this point. Each thought that the principle would be good for its own order. Once in control of taxation it was plain that the Commons would soon infiltrate into all branches of government. That is what happened, but it happened slowly on account of the jealousy of the Lords about this and the lack of grasp of general principles at that time.

It was through the right of petition that the Commons gradually gained ground. The king asked for a tax; the Commons put the bill on the Speaker's table and in their turn asked to have grievances redressed which affected them *particularly*. Sometimes the king agreed, but often he was annoyed, ordered the Commons to pass the bill, and even imprisoned some who opposed him. These measures were long successful and were never entirely given up; but they became continually less effective and at last several times the Commons bluntly declared that they would not vote a tax until their wrongs had been righted, and it was done.

I have just been looking over your letters again, my dear friend; your ostensible epistle is very funny. There is every thing needed there and nothing unnecessary. My brother and I laughed to tears over it. I am going to show it and think that it will produce its full effect. As for your second letter where you complain of living with so much friendship and so pleasantly, here is the answer to it; I hope that this in-folio will plead my cause better than any discourse. Back to business.

I was saying that from the moment when the Commons were legally summoned to Parliament, that is to say under Edward I, they steadily gained in power and importance; and going on to the period when the wars of the Roses began, we will find them mixed up with all the operations of government, only granting subsidies when they knew how they would be used, addressing fiery speeches to the king, and bringing accusations against the ministers. That certainly fits together into an established system. Extreme liberty jostled with extreme oppression, and one side or the other would often adopt measures that cannot be reconciled with the spirit of a monarchy; but one must put the blame for that on the ignorance of the times, and the absence of definite limits mutually accepted by all the parties. Particular circumstances played, and had to play, an important part. However, one must admit that there is much to admire in the English people at that time. Their *constitution* was famous already and was thought to be different from that of other countries. Nowhere else in Europe as yet was there a better organised system of free government. No other country had profited so much from feudal organisation. I have stopped here and I point that out, because I believe it is the dividing line between two very distinct epochs. Now I will carry you on to the next epoch, following up events. Again please forgive anachronisms.

About the year 1300[1] Edward II succeeded Edward I. Edward married the daughter of Philip the Fair, king of France. Few beings have ever brought so much ill to the human race. She threw England into confusion and had her husband assassinated; she brought the Plantagenets what they afterwards called their 'cross' to the Crown of France and so started that war of more than a hundred years which is believed to have cost humanity eighteen million lives. Edward III, one of the greatest of England's kings, sat on his father's throne much as Alexander after the death of Philip, that is to say without clear proof that he had no part in the assassination.

At this same time France gave a fine example to the world. While the house of Plantagenet showed what terrible crimes am-

[1] It was in 1307.

bition will lead men to commit, the descendants of Hugh Capet showed exemplary and astonishing moderation. The last son of Philip the Fair at his death left his wife pregnant; Philip of Valois showed his respect for the principle of legitimacy even in this embryo king. The States General appointed him Regent; the Queen being brought to bed of a son, he had him recognised and was himself the first to do so. The baby died soon afterwards, but the loyalty of the Valois was so well known that no one in that age of violence suspected that he had met a violent end. The great question of the salic law then arose. Philip was the only male representative of the house of Capet, but Edward III had a closer blood relationship. The nation was assembled and the French prince declared King by acclamation and the sequel showed that the acclamation was no futile shout.

Then began the most heroic, the most brilliant and the most unhappy time in our history. Such, dear friend, was the first history book that fell into my hands, and I cannot convey the impression it made on me; every event is engraved on my memory, and thence derives that often unreflecting instinct of hate which rouses me against the English. Time and time again when I came to those disastrous battles in which valour was always crushed by superior discipline, I have skipped the pages and left out whole passages to which nonetheless irresistible curiosity would later drive me intermittently back. But forgive me, I am running off talking about myself which is not the subject in hand.

The energy shown by the English people in going off to conquer France proves two things: the sovereign's ability and the unity of the different sections of the nation when their common interests were at stake, which in its turn shows that by that time the constitution was already strong and stable. Edward III was clever at adapting means to end, but he had not the ability to conceive a comprehensive plan. He was one of those men of the second rank who perform great deeds, but do not achieve great things. I don't know if you understand me, but have not the time to develop my thought. He attacked Wales at the same time as France. In France he waged a war of devastation, he who wanted to rule there. He divided his forces. But his troops were excellent, his courage stood any test, and his son was the Black Prince, the hero of that brilliant century. He defeated

C   33

Philip of Valois at Crécy, and at Poitiers the Black Prince defeated King John and took him prisoner. Almost the whole of the French nobility fell into the power of the English in those two days. The French commons and serfs who had nursed an implacable hatred against that order, took this chance to seize power. A most terrible civil war was added to that against the foreigner. The English were before Paris. Finally it looked as if everything would fall to bits when Charles V took up the reins of power and Duguesclin the command of the armies. Never was there better proof that no blind force directs this world, but incapacity or wisdom. In less than ten years all the possessions, surrendered at the shameful treaty of Bretigny, had been taken from the English. It is true that the Black Prince was dead and that the stirring of the whole nation to turn the foreigner out of France wonderfully abetted the skill of king and general.

Perhaps you will ask me what I think constituted the superiority of the English troops over our own in those unhappy wars. This is it: Geographical position and freedom had already made England the richest country in Europe. Throughout the war Parliament put her wealth at the king's disposal. By this means Edward was able to maintain a paid army, that is to say an army of men who had to obey all his orders, which he could keep in being as long as he wanted and use as he wanted. Whereas the French king, not so provided, had to put the great feudal machine in motion. The barons were only bound to give forty days' service, they were on an equality between each other and would obey the king only; chance alone decided which men they assembled, so that they were but an impetuous ill-disciplined mass. You will see the picture when I say that the battle of Crécy was started without an order. Every one wanted to put his own standard on the same line; thus they advanced so close to the English that finally blind courage seized the crowd and they charged head down without any order of battle against a prepared enemy whom it was not intended to attack until the next day. It was only when bitter sufferings had taught the nobility to obey, when the people had been toughened by all manner of affliction, and above all when the money provided by the States General had enabled Charles V to buy the courage of plenty of brave and disciplined adventurers, that the odds became

34

even and the English quitted France leaving nothing but their bones behind.

At one moment Edward III was the arbiter of Europe, but, like almost all men, he could not die at the right moment. Like Louis XIV he outlived his glory and his family, only leaving as his heir his grandson, the unlucky Richard II.

Richard was received with wild delight when he came to the throne. All hearts rejoiced at the glorious memory of his father, the Black Prince. His minority was stormy. When he was old enough to take personal charge of affairs, he thought of the turbulence of the Commons, of the insolence of the Lords; he decided at once, or perhaps was led on little by little, to try to destroy that dangerous constitution, as yet ill defined, which made the strength of skilful princes, but which threw the unskilful from the throne. The manner in which he set about this deserves your full attention. There are few more instructive pages in history. He reassembled Parliament and, before dissolving it, made it choose from its body commissioners to represent it when it was not assembled, just as Parliament itself represented the nation. He had the same powers granted to this restricted assembly as the whole of Parliament enjoyed. That done, one can see that he could easily dominate this small group of men put under his hand. National representation was then only a name. Richard ruled without control. All went well for some time. Perfect calm seemed to reign over England; hearts seemed benumbed and no doubt there were young people at that time who wondered anxiously whether they had not been born into an age of soft lethargy that had succeeded the age of marvels. They soon had a chance to change their minds. Richard wanted to do the very thing that was most contrary to the spirit of feudal constitutions and to that of England in particular, to raise a tax which had not been voted. It was paid, but proved the drop of water which makes a glass overflow. While the king complacently contemplated his power, his cousin Henry of Lancaster landed with a few friends on the English coast and raised the standard of revolt. In a few days a hundred thousand men were following his banner. The king was captured without a fight. One night terrible cries were heard in the castle of Pontefract where he had been imprisoned, and the next day he was found assassinated. A parliament had already declared him deposed from the throne and had put Lancaster in his place under the name of Henry IV.

As I think about all this, my dear friend, and about the fearful consequences of these events, I feel that the history of this time should be written in huge letters in all public places and in the palaces of all kings. Perhaps the peoples would realise what it costs to sacrifice the principle of legitimacy, and doubtless their rulers too would learn that one cannot make sport of the rights of nations unpunished, and that triumphs of that sort do not always last long.

All seemed to go well for the usurper. Henry IV was an able man. Moreover he was chosen by the people. He kept his position, although with some difficulty, and his son's renown seemed to make the fortunes of his family certain.

That son was Henry V whom the English regard as the hero of their history. Henry V made use of the best means of distracting the restless energy of a people still shaken by the after-effects of a revolution; he decided to break the truce with France and profit from the internal disturbances which were again rending our unhappy country. Charles V and Duguesclin were dead. The Burgundians and the Armagnacs were quarrelling for power. Henry V landed in Normandy, won the decisive battle of Agincourt, marched on Paris, was received by one faction, had himself crowned king of France and recognised as such by a Parliament. In appearance every one submitted. But Henry died at the height of his fame at the castle of Vincennes. Soon after that comes the incredible story of Joan of Arc, which one cannot understand but can still less question. The English, attacked on all sides, began to retreat and for the second and last time France was saved.

When Henry V was dead,[1] a few years after 1400, the most savage civil war which has ever stained the annals of a country broke out in England. It is known as the Wars of the Roses, and was due to the ambitions of the houses of York and Lancaster who fought for the throne through fifty years of unparalleled bitterness. I will not go into the details of that bloodstained time; it would be pointless and besides the shifts of fortune were so sudden that I could hardly follow the thread. The only man whose figure stands out imposing amidst the horrors of the

---

[1] He died in 1422.

time is Warwick who, ever changing from one side to the other, always brought victory with him, and smashed the work of his hands as easily as he had set it up. All the others are just frightful criminals whose only merit is the one common in times of troubles, to know how to die. One could make a terrible picture of this time in English history, a picture that would make the hairs of the staunchest stand on end. But Lingard[1] is at his most phlegmatic on these occasions. It is enough for you to know that during these civil wars each party triumphed in turn more than ten times, and each time the vanquished suffered all manner of punishments and confiscations. Eighty princes and lords of the Royal House met a violent death, land changed hands quickly, and finally that scourge of God, like a great fire, stopped only when it could find no more to burn. The whole tyrannical and cruel race of the Plantagenets vanished from this world. Surely without being superstitious one can see in that something like the finger of God. Henry Tudor, Duke of Richmond, who was descended through his mother from the house of Lancaster, married the heiress of the house of York and finally occupied in peace the place made vacant by the family whose children had thus devoured one another.

There are many people, both among those who have studied English history and those who have not, who suppose that the English constitution has passed through various regular, successive stages until it has reached the point where it now is. According to them it is a fruit which every age has helped to ripen. That is not my view and I shall be very surprised if it is yours when you have read all English history carefully. No doubt you will agree with me that there comes a moment when the forward movement is not only stopped but gives way to a most marked retrogression. That is the time to which we have now come. I stopped in 'the history of the constitution' at the outbreak of the Wars of the Roses. I pointed out that at that period the English constitution formed a complete whole, that all free tendencies had been developed and that those anomalies which still existed had their roots in particular

---

[1] Here Tocqueville refers to his source in spite of the fact that he had claimed previously to write without referring to books. Cf. *Abrégé de l'histoire d'Angleterre de John Lingard* (Paris 1827). On Lingard see the valuable study by Th. L. Coonan in *Some Modern Historians of Britain*, Essays in honour of R. L. Schuyler, New York, 1951, pp. 1 ff.

causes. During the civil wars Parliament was merely an instrument of factions. On the arrival of the Tudors one sees something like a general agreement by all orders in the state to throw themselves into servitude. A word about this strange tendency of their minds. If a wise man had looked at England after the extinction of the Plantagenets, he would have been surprised at the incredible changes which had come about in less than fifty years. The nobility seemed reduced almost to nothing, almost all the descendants of the Normans were dead or ruined, and new unstable families without roots in the nation had risen in their place. The members of the Commons, deprived of the support of the Lords which they had never lacked when it was a question of restraining the royal power, and not feeling themselves strong enough yet to act by themselves and for themselves, had lost all that republican energy which had marked their fathers. The spirit of both these orders was bruised and bent by the series of private and public disasters. They only hoped that what they lost in freedom, they had gained in security. Add that a similar movement was taking place all over Europe. At that time all monarchies were tending to become absolute. One man's standard replaced the oligarchic liberty which had been enjoyed for two centuries. This was the first fruit of the civilisation which had made men more vividly aware of the vices of the feudal system, and led all the peoples to throw themselves, bound hand and foot, into the power of their rulers to correct its defects.

This movement was more marked in England than anywhere else. Special reasons gave it peculiar strength. Nowhere in Europe was despotism more terrible, because nowhere else was it more 'legal'. Note that well; nothing gives more food for thought. When a despot forces his way to sovereignty, his power, however great, will have limits, be they only those imposed by *fear*. But a sovereign clothed in power to do everything in the name of law is far more to be feared and fears nothing. So when one of the Tudors asked the people for an exorbitant tax, it was the people themselves who granted it, for Parliament had voted it; when the blood of the highest fell on the scaffold, who was responsible? The sentence was signed by the hand of all the Lords. Thus its own instrument was turned against liberty. So in England obedience to a master soon took on that

38

servile air which is characteristic of all states once free but no longer so, so different from France where the subject will give money or life to his prince while seeming to act entirely from his own free will. My dear friend, I have often wanted to clap my hands at seeing these English so proud today of their independence, so free from the old prejudices of the continent, to see these same English bow their heads beneath a yoke ten times more humiliating than any other, to hear the humble language of the Commons and axioms of despotism on every mouth, to think of those rotten Parliaments which never refused a man's life to the king's will and ended under Henry VIII by condemning men unheard. That is what are called 'Bills of Attainder', a diabolical invention which even the Tribunal of the Revolution never revived. Finally, my dear friend, when I see the English people change their religion four times to please their masters, and when I think that almost in our own day we have seen the French clergy nearly in mass prefer exile, poverty and death to the mere appearance of a schism, when I see that, I am prouder to be born on this side of the channel than I should be to claim that the blood of Plantagenets and Tudors ran in my veins.

I don't know who can see in this time an advance towards the Revolution of 1688. But what was able to raise the English people from that state of degradation? The same thing as had thrown them down. The spirit of the constitution had been broken, but the forms remained: it was like the corpse of a free government. When spirits stupefied by the disasters of the civil wars began little by little to revive, when numbed hearts beat again, when the passage of time had given the Commons the strength they lacked or thought they lacked, in a word, when the nation awoke, it found the tools for regeneration to hand, and with the spirit of its ancestors all the means to be like them. Attention was naturally drawn to and fixed on something which had happened before, a circumstance which is a wonderful help to popular movements.

The Tudors reigned for about a hundred years. The founder of the family who took the name of Henry VII was of a hard, despotic temperament, but as a new arrival he was still held within some limits. I know of no more complete tyrant in history than his son Henry VIII. He has given us his own picture on his death-bed, when he said that he had never been able to refuse a woman's honour to his passions, or a man's life to his anger. A prop of Catholicism then under attack, for its unity appealed to his love of dominion, he soon became its bitterest enemy because the Pope would not let him marry his mistress whom, by the by, he later had beheaded. But the instincts of a tyrant warned him that sooner or later the new theories of the reformers would lead on to republican ideas. So he struck on the strange idea of preserving the doctrines, beliefs and hierarchy of the Roman Church, and only taking away its head. He was the English Pope. The strange events that follow paint a sad picture of the human species. Should a man in renouncing obedience to the Pope also deviate from the principles of Catholicism, he was burnt in grand style, for that was the church's punishment for heretics. But should another combine obedience to the Pope with the same Catholic doctrines, they slashed his stomach open good and proper to snatch out his heart and beat his cheeks with it, for that was a man who had refused the king one of his rights, he was guilty of high treason and should suffer the death of traitors. Poor humanity! That shows you at once the overweening power of the Tudors. You will easily understand that the mass of the people could not come to terms with this political religion, a halfway house which pleased no one entirely. However that religion established itself and its domestic forms have lasted till our day.

After Henry VIII comes Edward VI of whom one can say nothing, as he died too young and his ministers were solely responsible for what happened under him. He established the reformed religion in almost all respects.

His reign delightfully proves how men need *authority* in questions of religion, and how far they go astray when they lose a sure basis and appeal to their reason alone. One finds them then discussing various questions of belief as if they were so many paragraphs in a Bill, and a simple majority would decide what was or was not so in spiritual matters, determining what one must believe or answer to be saved in the next world and not to be hanged in this.

Mary arrives and the scene changes. Catholicism raises its head in the most intolerant guise it has ever shown. The Queen was Catholic. Parliament declared that any other religion was false and decreed penalties against dissidents. One hung under

Edward, one burnt under Mary. Then as before the masses submitted. If there was any popular agitation it was suppressed at once.

Mary died. Her sister Elizabeth re-established the religion of Henry VIII and Parliament imposed the death penalty on anyone who resisted that belief.

Elizabeth's rule was arbitrary but glorious. Commerce increased, but commercial activity was the prelude to a more dangerous development. When the Tudor dynasty came to an end, the huge edifice of tyranny which they had built up still seemed to be standing, but it had lost its foundations in the hearts of Englishmen. The spirit of argument introduced by the Reformation began to bear fruit: the Commons already began proudly to take thought of their power and their wealth. The revolution was silently ripening under the protection of despotism itself. Just at that moment a new family came to the throne impregnated with all the old traditions of the former ruling house, but coming to reign over a people where everything had changed. Never had there been greater pretensions to absolute power than just at that moment when the foundations on which it rested were going to collapse.

I stop here. The age of the Stuarts would need another letter all to itself. This one which I have written by fits and starts is sure to be an indigestible muddle. I do not know about that and probably never shall know, as I must leave you now without re-reading it. So please forgive the anachronisms, the mistakes in French, and the mistakes in spelling too which are sure to be numerous; forgive me too for the professorial manner which I think I have put on sometimes.

I leave here on the 15th; I shall be in Paris on the 17th. Be a good chap and come and see me on the 18th before one o'clock or for dinner, which would be much better. Unless you do that, I shall think you are cross with me for being so slow in writing to you. That reminds me that my letter will arrive like mustard after dinner. What of it? Nothing comes at the right moment in this world!

Good-bye then, Sir and dear future collaborator, I am burning to escape to your cloister. Meanwhile I embrace you with all my heart.

II

Journey to England (1833)

Notes, Ideas and Observations which I gathered in England during the five weeks which I passed there in 1833

---

1. REFLECTIONS

A Sitting of the House of Lords (15th August 1833)

The room is largish, rectangular and hung with scarlet cloth. It is well lighted by three or four beautiful chandeliers full of candles.

That evening the Lords were debating various amendments of detail to the Slavery Bill.[1] There were hardly more than about fifty members present. They were sitting round a large table at the far end of the room, or nonchalantly leaning on the cushions which cover all the benches. They had kept on their morning dress. Most of them were in frock-coats and boots. Many kept their hats on. There was nothing pompous, but a general air of good manners, an easy good taste and, so to say, an *aroma* of aristocracy. Amidst these negligently dressed peers there were several bishops in full dress, and Lord Brougham[2] buried under a monstrous white powdered wig. The clerks too had wigs.

Why are wigs retained in this assembly and on the Judge's Bench? I could just believe that one must appear in the House of Lords in medieval costume in order to show the unchanging continuity of the English constitution. But why from all our ancestors' clothes have they chosen the *wig* which brings no age of heroes to mind and which is neither ancient nor modern, dating only from the eighteenth century? But let us carry on.

On a question of detail Lord (*sic*) Wellington stood up.

[1] The bill became law on 29th August 1833.
[2] Lord Brougham was then Lord Chancellor.

Journey to England (1833)

Glory clothes a man in such magic that seeing him in the flesh and hearing him speak I felt as if a shudder ran through my veins. There must, I thought, be something extraordinary in every word of this man who had made the sound of his name reverberate so far; but I was far off the mark. The Duke began his speech with difficulty and hesitation and was never completely at ease. It was the strangest sight to see the man, who had won so many battles and defeated Bonaparte, as embarrassed as a child reciting its lesson before a pitiless pedagogue. The hero of Waterloo did not know where to put his arms or legs, nor how to balance his long body. He picked up and put down his hat, turned to the left and the right, ceaselessly buttoned and unbuttoned the pocket of his breeches as if he wanted to seek his words there, words to be sure that did not flow easily from his mind. Never have I seen a more direct application of this line of La Fontaine:

Let us not force our talent . . .

*   *   *

An Election in London (15th August 1833)

. . . It was the last day of the Poll. I could not get to the Guildhall, the place where the election was taking place, till a little before four o'clock. The result was to be announced at that hour. All the adjacent streets were full of common people carrying poles with posters bearing a candidate's name with a slogan, for instance, 'Kemble for the City of London! Kemble for ever! Crawford and Reform!' Some slogans offered a crude bait to the passions of the people. Thus on a poster in favour of Crawford, the Liberal candidate, one read: 'Poor laws in Ireland! Better wages in England!'

On the bottom of the posters carried by the supporters of the candidate who had the best chance, were written the results of the Poll as far as they were known, in the hope of attracting the indifferent by the near certainty of their victory. So I learnt that the Whig had gained more than twice the votes cast for the Tory.

As one approached the Guildhall the number of poster carriers increased. In front of the building there were about fifty. There were placards too on all surrounding walls.

The Guildhall is a vast gothic chamber decorated with statues in honour of the great men that England has produced. It was there that the election took place. All along the walls there were small tables at which clerks sat.

The hall was packed with an inquisitive crowd, most of them clearly of the lowest classes. Their very faces were stamped with those signs of degradation only to be found in the people of big towns. But there were a certain number of black suits among them. The general look of the assembly contrasted most grotesquely with the feudal majesty of the place they were in. It was through this crowd that the electors passed to go and vote. I think the vote was given publicly (I was too far away to be sure), for all the time there were cheers or whistles and shouts as the supporters of the two candidates kept up their regular cries. In short it was a very turbulent and rather disgusting spectacle. At the moment the clock struck four, there was a general cry of satisfaction and then a deep silence, and an official of the city, coming up on to a platform, proclaimed Mr. Crawford the Member. At once there was a thunder of applause, for the Whigs were in great majority in the assembly, and Mr. Crawford spoke. He spoke for about ten minutes. His style seemed to me generally as vulgar as the people who listened to him. He allowed himself jokes about his opponent which would have seemed in very bad taste in France, but they were greeted there with acclamation. Most of the time the assembly continuously interrupted the orator. It was a sort of conversation between it and him.

However amidst this electoral farce there were signs of some manly customs which deserve admiration. Thus it was evident that victory did not in the least make the beaten party disappear as so often happens. On the contrary the defeated braved the storm with remarkable constancy. Kemble, the Tory candidate, although he was certain of his defeat since the morning, nevertheless appeared at the poll with several of his friends. After Crawford had spoken, he in his turn stood up and braving the insults hurled at him, maintained his principles, attacked his adversaries, and reproached them for their shifts and the ill means they had used. While listening to him I could not help thinking of those savages in North America who keep their spirits up by insulting their enemies while they are being burnt. The people quite welcomed the grit of the candidate and he got away with a few hoots. After his speech the assembly broke up; Crawford was triumphantly escorted to the nearest tavern by an almost ragged crowd, and the rest drifted away in peace. There was not a single soldier, but many policemen. (These wear uniform, but do not carry arms. It seemed to me that the feeling of the populace towards them was more or less the same as that of the French populace towards the gendarmes and the sergeants-at-arms.)

The impression that this saturnalia of English liberty had on me was one of disgust rather than fear. I concede that such scenes in *ordinary times* present no danger. It is only the lowest classes of the people who take part in them. In the eyes of all others it harms the cause of the people more than it helps it. But the lower class, by itself alone, is generally incapable of a revolution. It is a very rare exception for this to happen and such a revolution is never lasting. I should not be surprised if this licence given to the lower classes in England has not up to the present contributed more than anything else in maintaining the aristocracy, by giving the middle classes a horror of purely democratic forms, which they see only under such a frightening and hideous aspect. This reminded me of the Spartans who made a slave drunk to give free men a horror of wine.

*   *   *

A Meeting (*19th August 1833*)

Mr. Bulwer,[1] a distinguished member of the House of Commons, and a Radical, though he is one of the more moderate of that party, suggested today that I should go with him to a meeting in support of the Poles (those who, having left France for Switzerland, found themselves destitute). The meeting took place in a magnificent hall capable of holding about twelve hundred people as near as I could judge. On a very high platform were the chairman, the people who were going to speak, and a

---

[1] Lytton, Edward George Earl Lytton, Bulwer Lytton, M.P. for Lincoln in 1832 He published in 1833 his book *England and the English* which Tocqueville has read

certain number of spectators. Bulwer had me sit with him in the front row. The chair was given to Lord Dudley Stuart[1] who earned this honour more by his rank than by his merit, to judge by the opening speech which he gave, a fundamentally mediocre speech delivered with strange hesitation. But the audience was all in favour of His Lordship and applauded every utterance provided that it made some sense and that he played just a little on the passions of the day. In the middle of his improvisation he broke off short, but the audience made the hall echo with a thunder of applause so that the speaker appeared to have been interrupted by them; and he had time to find the thread of his ideas. One could easily have taken this artificial enthusiasm as ironic, but it was not so at all. We shall see later that the meeting was wise to be grateful to a Lord for presiding over it.

After Lord Dudley came Lord Morpeth,[2] who made a most pompous speech full of rhetoric on the Poles and liberty. Then came Mr. Hume[3] of the House of Commons. All these speakers uttered commonplaces, used big words and produced those banal ideas by which the people in France are generally stirred up. When Mr. Hume had finished, a man of the people stood up in the middle of the assembly and asked to be heard. The chairman hesitated, but there were cries from everywhere of *Hear him!* The speaker stood on a bench. He was a small man, rather badly made and with an undistinguished face. Nobody knew him; but word soon passed round that he was called Duffey and belonged to the Political Union of the Working Classes. He started by addressing the chairman with respect, calling him *My Lord*. He expressed himself without diffidence, his stance was firm and assured, and his voice made the air vibrate in all parts of the hall. In short we heard an orator. His first bound broke away from the commonplaces which the heroism of Poland and the cause of the liberty of peoples could provide. . . . He took his stand on completely English ground. He showed with peerless energy what sacred bonds England had contracted with Poland at the Congress of Vienna. He showed that her interest and her honour were involved in maintaining Polish

[1] Lord Stuart was an ardent supporter of the Polish cause. Cf. *Dictionary of National Biography*.

[2] Lord Morpeth was a leading Whig figure. Lord Privy Seal in Grey's Cabinet in June 1834.

[3] Joseph Hume, prominent radical in the House of Commons.

independence. He maintained that this engagement did not only bind the English government but Englishmen of all ranks: 'And me,' he cried out finally, 'I too find that my honour is engaged in the Polish cause, although I am only a simple worker.' At these words frenzied applause broke out from all sides of the hall. Encouraged and, so to speak, carried on by the enthusiasm around him, the speaker tackled his subject from a new point of view. Instead of congratulating his fellow citizens on the interest which they took in Poland as had those who had spoken before him he was angry that English people could be content with such insignificant results, and 'give charity to those whom it is our duty to defend'. This part of his speech could have been regarded as trenchant irony, directed not only against the government but even more against the members of the two Houses present at the meeting, who, in effect, limited themselves to asking for alms for Poland instead of protecting her effectively in Parliament. When the speaker sat down again the cries of enthusiasm were so violent that the meeting remained quasi-suspended for five minutes. The rest of the meeting was insignificant. This was the salient and capital episode of the evening.

Rarely in my life have I been so won over by words as I was that evening while listening to this man of the people. I was carried away, body and soul, by the irresistible torrent of his oratory, so strongly was I affected by the real warmth of his feelings and the energy of his delivery. Besides there was something else which I felt the whole time while he was speaking. In him I saw the precursor of those revolutionaries who are destined at no distant date to change the face of England. The old and the new English society seemed face to face here and ready to fight it out hand to hand. It was a lord who was presiding. It was lords or rich landowners who addressed this democratic assembly. This war between the past and the present showed in the very words he used. His speech, addressed to the upper classes of society, maintained those formulas of respect that ancient usage had consecrated. But what immense and rebellious pride in those simple words which followed his noble sentiments: 'However, I am just a simple worker!' With what satisfaction and superb humility he continued to add, 'A worker in the lower grades of industry.' When men appear so happy and so proud in their lowliness, those above them should take alarm.

It was strange, too, to see the aristocracy present obliged to let itself be put in the background without a word to say; or rather being actually driven to flatter the prejudices and passions of democracy to buy its indulgence and to win its cheers.

*   *   *

Oxford (*August 1833*)

Oxford is now one of the most remarkable towns existing in Europe. It gives one a very good idea of the feudal cities of the middle ages. There are in a very confined space gathered nineteen colleges, most of which preserve their gothic architecture. Not that all of them date from the time of their foundation. Indeed there is not even one, I think, that is built of the materials actually used in the middle ages; but care has been taken always to restore them in the same style and keep the illusion complete. I should even say here in parentheses that gothic architecture seems to me as suited to palaces as to churches, and that by and large it seems far better, to me at least, than our modern architecture, if not than that of the ancient. Besides it has the merit of being original.

One's first feeling on visiting Oxford is of unforced admiration for the men of old who founded such immense establishments to aid the development of the human spirit, and for the political institutions of the people who have preserved them intact through the ages. But when one examines these things closely and gets below the surface of this imposing show, admiration almost vanishes and one sees a host of abuses which are not at first sight obvious.

The colleges that together make up the university of Oxford were originally to make available instruction in all knowledge then known to man.

They were richly endowed so as to draw the best teachers there and to enable the best possible education to be given free of charge. Such is clearly the aim and spirit of these foundations, some of which date back to the fourteenth and fifteenth centuries. As at that time land was the only form of wealth properly understood or valued, an immense amount of land was given to the colleges as inalienable property. Let us see how that has worked out.

The principal study at the university of Oxford is that of Latin and Greek, as in the Middle Ages. I should see no harm in that if the studies of the nineteenth century had been added to those of the fourteenth. But that is only done very incompletely. It is true that the exact sciences have been introduced into the university courses but I have heard no claim that they have been developed as far as possible, and the study of living languages is excluded.

The immense riches with which the colleges are endowed (I have been assured that Magdalen College alone has a revenue of forty thousand pounds) were originally intended, as I have said above, to enable the university to get the best teachers and give instruction free.

Today the property of the colleges does not belong to the teachers but to a corporate body. This body is composed of Fellows (Magdalen College has forty of them) who recruit themselves by election. To be elected it is necessary to fulfil certain conditions, such as having taken a degree. The revenue of the college is in the first place used for the upkeep of the establishment and the salaries of the teachers. The rest, which is considerable, is distributed among the Fellows who receive the money without fulfilling any function. This is just the same story as the ancient abbeys, whose incumbents were often not priests. There are Fellows who get £500 a year as their share.

University education is not in the least free of charge.

As its property has remained territorial, it has come to hold an immense stretch of land from which private enterprise can only profit very incompletely. All the town of Oxford and nearly all the county belongs to the university. So the whole establishment is an abuse, both in the mode of getting the revenue and in its employment.

If the State ever took over these lands (it could do so legally and peacefully by not permitting the Fellows to vote for further recruits and profiting from each successive vacancy among them), I am sure it would maintain at a hundredth of the cost a university much richer in talent and more useful than present Oxford.

D

Journey to England (1833)

Oxford with its twenty-two[1] colleges has no more than 1,500 students a year; so on the average each of these immense colleges does not have more than sixty-eight students. Each one of them has several rooms, and the rich are allowed to enjoy all the pleasures of luxury.

All of them have *six* months of vacations.

Oxford at the present time is menaced with reform. Thus all the secondary abuses upon which the aristocracy leans, are falling. After its fall will England be happier? I think so. As great? I doubt it.

*   *   *

New information given by Mr. Wilson, one of the Fellows of Queen's College

It is important to be clear about the guiding principle with regard to the foundation of the colleges of Oxford.

They were founded for two distinct aims. Because during the Middle Ages war and the cares of Government took up all the time of the landowners (there were no 'owners' of anything else then) so that none of them would or could devote himself to the sciences or to letters. On the other hand poverty prevented men of the other classes from doing so.

The religious and enlightened men who founded the English colleges wished to create places where education was given free of charge and where at the same time educated people could devote themselves to their studious tastes. They wanted the revenues of the establishments which they had founded to go to: (1) A certain number of intelligent and learned men who took the name of 'Fellows' and who would find the college funds sufficient to enable them to pursue their career of study. (2) To the education of a certain number of children who were to be brought up for nothing.

The Fellows were not necessarily the teachers of the children, although they often were. I was mistaken above.

This state of things was excellent for society as it was when the colleges were founded. But it is a strange thing to see how

[1] Cf. p. 48, where Tocqueville gives this number as nineteen. The figure of nineteen is correct.

50

these principles work out now. In this enlightened century when science and literature lead as quickly to riches as did arms in feudal times, the riches of these foundations are not given to famous scholars and writers, but to those who in most cases have no other merit than that of having taken their degree at the university or of being friends or relations of *existing* Fellows. (It is they who elect the new Fellows, as I said above.) To tell the truth it is a communal purse open to the younger branches of the aristocracy. While the number of Fellows has remained the same as it was in the Middle Ages, and introduction into their number is governed by the same rules, the number of children educated gratis has decreased, and paying students have been admitted, so that the Fellows' incomes have increased as subsidies to students became less needed. Furthermore the studies consecrated by medieval usage have been retained; and while a man's whole life is scarcely long enough to keep abreast of modern knowledge, at Oxford there are still the same six months of vacations which were given without disadvantage to pupils in the fourteenth century.

When one asks the present generation why all these things are not changed even a little, they say, 'The founders' wishes should be respected.' 'But then, please, why do you own property which was given to these institutions when they were monastic as well as educational, you who have rejected catholicism?'

It is true that by a very English compromise, after driving out the monks, the Fellows have been obliged not to marry.

* * *

A Sitting of the Justices of the Peace (Petty Sessions) (3rd September 1833)

Note: Justices of the Peace are nominated by the King on presentation by the Lord Lieutenant of the county.

The law requires that they must have £100 of income. But this rule is not observed in the least and it is sufficient that they are landlords. The Justices of the Peace are competent to deal with the affairs of the whole county, but generally they only take part in those of their own district. Their competence is wide and ill-defined. They are at the same time the judges of all petty offences and the administrators of the country.

Generally speaking most places do not have corporate municipal bodies, or at least the municipal body only manages very few things. It is the Justices of the Peace who administrate. In that capacity they are absolute masters. As Judges one can appeal against their sentence.

Lord Radnor who is one of the Justices of the Peace in the county of Wiltshire in the south of England, yesterday suggested that I should accompany him to the neighbouring town of Salisbury to watch a sitting of the Justices of the Peace of the county. I accepted with great pleasure. Together we entered a vast hall divided into two by a wooden bar. Behind the bar there was a small table around which were seated three gentlemen. Lord Radnor took his place among them. He explained to me who they were. One of them was an attorney of Salisbury who was present as clerk and made the law known to the others. The other two were local landowners.

The first case which came up was that of two young people accused of breaking windows by throwing stones. The Justices of the Peace heard two witnesses under oath. There was no defence, and the delinquents were fined and had damages awarded against them, failing payment of which they had a sentence of two months in prison.

After that came an old man dressed in an excellent black suit and wearing a wig. He decidedly had the appearance of a landlord. But he approached the bar and stated that the vestry of his parish assembly (charged with the distribution of the revenue brought in by the Poor Tax) had without reason diminished the portion which he received from public charity. The case was suspended to hear the reasons of the vestry.

After this there appeared a young pregnant woman, an inhabitant of Salisbury, who came to complain that the overseer of the poor refused to assist her. The overseer appeared; he gave several reasons, among others that the father-in-law of this woman was a well-off tradesman of Salisbury and it was to be hoped that he was completely willing to take care of his daughter-in-law. The father-in-law was made to attend; they attempted to make him ashamed of his conduct. But it was impossible to force him to take care of his daughter-in-law, and the case was adjourned to obtain information on the young woman's means.

After her there came five or six big, vigorous young men. They pleaded that the vestry of their village did not want them to work at the expense of the community and would not distribute aid to them. They addressed themselves to the Justices of the Peace to ask for work or money. I cannot remember any more what was decided.

Lord Radnor said to me, 'You have here, just on a small scale, a part of the numberless abuses which the Poor Law has produced. The old man who came first probably has enough to live on. But he believes that he has a right to ask to be kept in comfort and he did not blush in claiming public charity, which has lost its degrading character in the eyes of the people.

'That young woman who seemed honest and unlucky would certainly be helped by her father-in-law if the Poor Law did not exist. But the hope of gain has stripped him of shame, and he leaves to the public a duty which he should perform.

'Finally those young people who appeared last. I know them. They come from my district. They are detestable characters. They spend what they earn in the public house, because they know that afterwards the State will come to their aid. Also you see that at the first difficulty for which they are to blame they come to us.'

The sitting continued. A young woman appeared at the bar; she carried a child in her arms, and came up without the least sign of hesitation or of shyness. The overseer of the poor of her village said accusingly that the child in her arms was illegitimate, and to this she agreed quite freely. Then she was made to swear to tell the truth and to kiss the Bible, and was asked who was the father. She named a countryman who was beside her, and he very calmly confirmed the fact. He was condemned to pay a pension and they both retired. This incident did not seem to make the slightest impression on an audience used to such things.

After this young woman there came another. This one was pregnant. Nothing forced her to appear before the magistrates; it is only after the birth of the child that the mother is obliged to name the father. But she came of her free will, and with the same detachment as the first declared what was the position and named the father of the unborn child. As this person was not present, the case was suspended for another day to cite him.

Lord Radnor said to me, 'You see again the harmful results of one of our laws.

'We have made immorality for the women of the lower classes as advantageous as possible. If they become pregnant due to their own fault, instead of their material situation getting worse, due to this legislation it improves. They can attribute a rich father to their child and make him pay a considerable pension. And in any case the Poor Law is there to come to their aid. Thus you have seen how far the women who came before us today have lost all instinct of shame and how little moral sense now has the public which surrounds us. This sort of event has become so frequent that nobody is shocked any more.'

The sitting was suspended at that moment and we returned to Longford Castle.[1]

2. CONVERSATIONS

Portsmouth (9th August 1833)

Mr. Clark is a Catholic priest at Portsmouth. There are two churches at Portsmouth; Mr. Clark's has about 300 parishioners.

Q. Is the number of Catholics in England increasing?

A. Yes. We often have converts. But on the other hand the number of those who do not believe in Christianity is growing. The sect of Unitarians has made decided progress.

Q. Is religious indifference on the increase?

A. Yes, but slowly. The English are a naturally religious people. With them religion is seldom a passion engendering enthusiasm. But it is a deep, persistent feeling which does not easily slacken its hold.

Q. You are not paid at all by the Government?

A. No, God forbid! All the strength of the Catholics is in their independence. The English Government would like nothing better than to pay the Irish priest very generously. But they have stubbornly refused. They answered, 'Now we are men of the people; paid, we should be agents of the Government.' I

[1] The home of Lord Radnor.

think France, with regard to religion, is in an almost desperate position. The only remedy would be the emancipation of the clergy and their independence from the Government, but there are those who say that this remedy would absolutely destroy religion, because there would not be enough zeal to support religious observances of any sort . . .[1]

The same day a Protestant clergyman told me that indifference was increasing and that it was not rare for parents not to have their children baptised.

* * *

Bulwer[2] (*August 1833*)

It should not be forgotten that Bulwer, because of his position and, above all, the opinions of his constituents, is a member of the Radical Party, although by birth and tastes he belongs to the aristocracy.

'The aristocracy still has considerable strength with us. None-the-less I think its fall will be complete, though perhaps slow. There has been an immense revolution in the minds of Englishmen during the last half century. Our aristocracy was great; it wanted to be fashionable, and that is one of the chief causes of its ruin. A line has been drawn between the upper and the middle aristocracy which, until then, had been united. The high nobility has set a tone and conventions of its own; it has flaunted this superiority of convention, treated the middle aristocracy with arrogance and alienated it. This is much the same, I think, as what happened in your country at the time of the French Revolution. The result of this is that our peers, instead of forming the centre and kernel of a large aristocratic body revolving around them, are isolated and therefore almost powerless. That became very clear when the question of Reform arose. The House of Lords found itself alone in the struggle. I am convinced that a time will come when the middle aristocracy will join up again with the upper, realising that they face a common danger, but then, I think, it will be too late for resistance.'

Q. However it seems to me that aristocratic ideas and instincts have firm roots with you. This shows itself in the smallest

---

[1] The dots are Tocqueville's.　　　　[2] Cf. our note, p. 45.

things. Thus I have not yet found an Englishman who seems to understand that a law of inheritance could be made favouring the division of properties, so completely has inequality of wealth come to seem a natural part of your customs.

A. The English have only a very slight capacity for appreciating general ideas. They see very clearly around their feet but their circle of vision is restricted. They have not yet reached the point you mention, but they are moving in that direction. Already one can discuss the advantages and disadvantages of an hereditary peerage. By and large there is an immense intellectual revolution taking place. In olden times the English thought that everything about their constitution was perfect, both advantages and abuses. Today everybody is looking for what needs mending. Sometimes it is one thing, sometimes another, but the process never stops. Moreover real, deep wrongs give daily cause or pretext for such restlessness. I believe that the next election will give a formidable impulse to Reform and that the Whig Party will almost completely disappear from the House, which will then be divided into Tories and Radicals. I admit that I think England very sick, and believe that we 'gentlemen', whatever our opinions, will all end up by being driven out. I do not believe that the middle classes are nearly as powerful in England as in France. Here the groups that really count are the aristocracy and the people, but among the people there are men of surprising ability and energy who could well take the lead.

*　*　*

Conversation with Lord Radnor at Longford Castle (1 September 1833)

Lord Radnor belongs to the most extreme wing of the Whig Party. Indeed he is generally reckoned as a Radical. His general ideas are in fact radical but it is easy to see that he does not wish to apply them completely or immediately to England. In any case my *impression* is that Lord Radnor is a man of good faith and often an enlightened man. But, as with all the other *evidence which I hear*, one must accept what he says with reserve when he cites facts to his opinions. This rule should never be forgotten, *whatever* confidence my informants inspire.

Journey to England (1833)

Q. What is the state of morals among the people?

A. In my experience the state of morals among the country people is very bad. The small neighbouring town of Salisbury is full of prostitutes and on market days there are frequent brawls. Furthermore many country women become pregnant before marriage. One might almost say that this is the natural order of things. The number of bastards is continually increasing and the laws are specially to blame for this. It is easy to prove that here it is much to a girl's advantage to have an illegitimate child:

(i) Her oath is accepted designating whom she wishes as the father, and he is obliged to pay her an allowance.

(ii) If she cannot or does not wish to name the father, the Poor Law is there to take care of her illegitimate family, and, as the help given by the parish is generally more than is necessary for the child, a girl who has several illegitimate children is in a very good position. I have heard it said that in Scotland and Ireland morals are better. The morality of our upper classes is just as bad. (I believed Lord Radnor on all these points because his theory is that morals should improve with enlightenment, and the above-mentioned facts contradict it.)

Q. What is the state of religion? (Lord Radnor is very religious, and strongly attached to the Anglican Church, although he wishes for reform.)

A. Religion is running great risks at the moment due to the fault of its ministers. The clergy of the Established Church seem to do all in their power to alienate the goodwill of the people; it becomes the cynosure of many hatreds and I fear that in the end religion itself will suffer. Generally our clergy leads a regular life but it fulfils its duties lazily and without zeal. Here, for example, we have a clergyman who does not reside, his pretext being that his health does not permit him to do so. He lives in the neighbouring town, leaving all the care of the parish to a poor devil encumbered with a young wife and six children, and to whom he gives perhaps only a tenth of his stipend. It is the same in a great many places; the resident clergy are generally young people who take all the responsibilities of the apostolic ministry, but have hardly enough to live on. Tithes are beginning to cause great hatred against the clergy. The number of dissenters is rapidly increasing; sects are multiplying infinitely. That accounts, I think, for the continually increasing number of

Catholics in England. Your dogmas do not seem to me reasonable, but they are precise and give rest to minds tired with controversy.

Q. How are the provinces administered?

A. By the Justices of the Peace. We have towns like Salisbury for example which have an independent administration called a 'Corporation'. But apart from the *incorporated* towns there is no local assembly or administrative organ; the villages sometimes have what is called a 'vestry', which is an assembly responsible for some details of communal life, for example the Poor Rate, but the decisions of a vestry are submitted to the assembly of the Justices of the Peace, which is certainly the great administrative authority of the county.

Q. Is there an administrative authority superior to the Justices of the Peace?

A. No, the Justices of the Peace as a *court* are subject to appeal, but as an administrative body they are sovereign. The central government has nothing to do with provincial matters, nor even their supervision.

Q. The Justices of the Peace are nominated by the King and exclusively chosen from among the landowners. Does this state of things not cause complaint? Do the counties not ask for an elected body to watch over their affairs?

A. Up to now these questions have been raised very little. Democratic jealousies have not been much roused on this point. But I do not doubt that the growing movement of reform will lead to that.

Q. Does the class of lawyers and business men already exert great influence?

A. Yes. One might almost say that England is in the hands of lawyers. The country lawyers have great influence.

Q. What happens to the younger sons of aristocratic families under the present law of inheritance?

A. They take up lucrative careers. We were four in my family. As I was the eldest I inherited almost the whole fortune and am a member of the House of Lords. One of my brothers is a Canon of Salisbury cathedral, another is a captain in the navy, and the fourth is a banker in London.

Q. If the number of lucrative positions easily available to the younger members of the aristocracy were diminished, do you think inequalities in the division of property would arouse more criticism and become hard to maintain?

A. Yes, I think so.

3. ALPHABETIC NOTEBOOK[1]

A

ARISTOCRACY

(*21 August 1833*)

The English aristocracy has been adroit in more than one respect.

First of all it has always been involved in public affairs; it has taken the initiative in protecting its rights; it has talked a great deal about liberty.

But what distinguishes it from all others is the ease with which it has opened its ranks. It is often said that in England men of all social ranks could rise to [important] positions. This was, I believe, much less true than was thought: what was taken for a rule, was in fact a rare exception. In general the aristocracy had everything at its disposal. But, with great riches, anybody could hope to enter into the ranks of the aristocracy. Furthermore since everybody could hope to become rich, especially in such a mercantile country as England, a peculiar position arose in that their privileges, which raised such feeling against the aristocrats of other countries, were the thing that most attached the English to theirs. As everybody had the hope of being among the privileged, the privileges made the aristocracy, not more hated, but more valued. The reason why the French nobles were the butt of all hatreds, was not chiefly that only the nobles had the right to everything, but because nobody could become a noble. It is this happy combination which made and still makes the power of the aristocracy in England. The English aristocracy in feelings and prejudices resembles all the aristocracies of the world, but it is not in the least founded on birth, that inaccessible thing, but on wealth that everyone can acquire, and this one difference

---

[1] Tocqueville had already applied his alphabetic method in his notes during his journey in America. (Cf. *Œuvres Complètes* (ed. Mayer), v, 1.) See also our Introduction.

makes it stand, while the others succumb either to the people or to the King.

The aristocracy in England has thus even in our time a power and a force of resistance which it is very difficult for a Frenchman to understand. Those general conceptions which he has formed in his own country or in many others concerning the strength or weakness of aristocracy, must be forgotten here, where he finds himself on entirely new ground.

However the English aristocracy now seems to me to be exposed to dangers to which it will finally succumb.

I remarked earlier that the strength of the English aristocracy did not depend only on itself, but on the feelings of all classes who hope to enter into its ranks. This applied most strongly the nearer a man approached it and so the better were his chances of sharing its privileges. Thus the banker who was a millionaire already and would soon be a great landowner, supported the aristocracy more than did an ordinary London merchant, and the latter more than a shopkeeper, and he in his turn more than a worker.

But in our time the classes who have almost no hope of sharing the privileges of the aristocracy, have become more numerous than they ever were before; they are more enlightened and see more clearly what I have just said. In the classes which have a chance of gaining the privileges of the aristocracy, there is a crowd of people who realise that they can reach this position more quickly by another way. That democratic spirit which in Europe one calls the French spirit, has made startling progress among them.

In any case I believe that the English aristocracy would be in a good position to fight the general difficulties of its present situation, based as it is on the riches and the *instincts* of the nation, if it could provide, as before, material prosperity for the lower classes. For the man of the people to be satisfied in a sphere from which it is almost impossible for him to escape, he must be fairly well-off there. This is more especially true in such a time of intellectual ferment and moral restlessness as ours. But the English people are afflicted by real and profound hardships.

A Frenchman on seeing England for the first time is struck by the apparent comfort and cannot imagine why people complain. But under this brilliant surface are hidden very deep distresses. Moreover one should judge by comparisons here; experience proves that people demand factitious necessities almost as imperiously as natural ones. So it comes about that so many people kill themselves for evils which seem imaginary to their neighbours. In the same way, for the English the lack of certain superfluities to which they have become accustomed by long habit, is as grave as a lack of food or clothing for a Russian. It stirs up in him a feeling of irritation and impatience at least as great.

The aristocracy has thus not only to fight against the difficulties common to all aristocracies in our time, but also against passions aroused by suffering or at least by lack of comfort.

I still persist in believing that if the aristocracy could form a compact body with all the other classes who have some hope of sharing their privileges, it would succeed in holding out, for nothing is more difficult than for a people to make a revolution all by itself.

But that is not how things are. With every increase in the power of democracy the number of people will grow greater who prefer the quicker chances of advancement which it can give, to the more distant ones which the aristocracy offers. Thus up to the present the people enjoy the support of many men whose birth or position should put them on the side of the aristocracy.

Furthermore the first ranks of the nobility have contrived to alienate the second ranks, with the result that the latter no longer support the former as they always did in the past. The fact is that for three years now the House of Lords has seemed isolated in the country. A time will no doubt come when, the danger becoming imminent for the whole aristocracy, the second rank will rally to the first, but by then the revolution will be too far advanced to be stopped.

C

CENTRALISATION

(*24th August 1833*)

Dr. Bowring[1] said to me today (24th August 1833), 'England is the country of decentralisation. We have got a government, but

---

[1] Sir John Bowring (1792–1872). Philologian and economist; influenced by Bentham; editor of the *Westminster Review* in 1825; Member of Parliament in 1835.

we have not got a central administration. Each county, each
town, each parish looks after its own interests. Industry is left to
itself; so you will not see an unfinished undertaking in England,
for since everything is done with a view to private profit, nothing is undertaken without the necessary capital, and while the
project is unfinished, the capital is idle. In your country industry
is subject to endless interference; here it is infinitely more free.
I consider that nothing is more difficult than to accustom men to
govern themselves. There however is the great problem of your
future. Your centralisation is a magnificent idea, but it cannot
be carried out. It is not in the nature of things that a central
government should be able to watch over all the needs of a great
nation. Decentralisation is the chief cause of the substantial progress we have made in civilisation. You will never be able to
decentralise. Centralisation is too good a bait for the greed of
the rulers; even those who once preached decentralisation, always abandon their doctrine on coming into power. You can be
sure of that.'

E[1]

ILLEGITIMATE CHILDREN

(*3rd September 1833*)

Enquiry of paternity. For a long time I held the view that the
French law forbidding this favoured bad morals. Now I am of a
diametrically opposite opinion.

Good morals in a people depend almost always on the women
and not on the men. One can never stop men attacking. The
point is therefore to make things so that they will be resisted;
this goes back to what I have said above. All the laws which make
the position of a woman who falls more comfortable are therefore eminently immoral; for example laws such as ours relating
to foundlings. Further, the law which permits enquiry of
paternity, might well serve to restrain the men, but it greatly
diminishes the strength of resistance among the women, which
must be avoided at all costs. Any people which permits the
enquiry of paternity is forced to believe the woman on oath, for
how else can a fact of this nature be proved? The woman thus

---

[1] In French: *Enfants naturels.*

has an infallible way of diminishing the consequences of her error and even has a way of making it profitable. Thus in England a girl of the people who has illegitimate children generally marries more easily than a chaste girl.

PARLIAMENTARY ENQUIRIES[1]

(3rd September 1833)

Their utility, their frequency, their forms. It may be possible to write a very interesting article on this subject.

P

POLICE

It is impossible to imagine anything more detestable than the criminal investigation police in England.

Its defects can be listed as follows:

(1) No central control whatever of its efforts. There is no hierarchy among its officials. Each is master in his own district to such an extent that not only does no one know how to get information passed from one place to another, but that it is even almost impossible to get orders carried out.

(2) Officers of the police are paid so little by the State that the interested parties are allowed to pay them themselves, so that justice is only within the means of the rich, which, in criminal cases, is a great social evil. This state of affairs also has the great disadvantage that it gives those who should suppress crime an interest in seeing that many crimes are committed and that those crimes should be serious rather than trivial.

(3) There is no official charged with a duty to prosecute, which both makes worse the defect mentioned above, that of placing justice out of reach of the poor, and means that the criminal law is never enforced continuously or firmly.

CRIMINAL PROCEDURE

English criminal procedure, preferable to ours in a few points, has several enormous defects; here are a few:

---

[1] *Engnêtes parlementaires* in French.

Journey to England (1833)

(1) The English have multiplied the number of grounds for quashing a case to an absurd extent. Thus the mere form of the accusation can give rise to a swarm of grounds for quashing a case on grounds which make almost no difference to the good administration of justice, such as an error in the first name of the accused, or the district where the crime was committed. . . .[1]

(2) Not only are the reasons for quashing infinitely multiplied, but, whatever is quashed, the accused is acquitted, instead of an annulment of the procedure up to the mistake being permitted; all this by virtue of the Gothic maxim, which has no useful application in our times, that the life or liberty of a man should not be in jeopardy twice.

(3) The tribunal of the place where the crime was committed is the only one competent to judge it, a rule which insures impunity for many crimes, especially in England where, as I remarked about the police, it is difficult to communicate from one judicial district to another.

R

RELIGION

The state of religion in England seems to me such as to cause some anxiety. The majority of the English, as one knows, profess the Anglican religion which is called 'The Established Church'. Now this church finds itself much in the position of the Catholic Church in France before the revolution of 1789. It is immensely rich, very badly organised and full of great abuses; moreover, it is a political power—three great causes of ruin of spiritual powers, the National Church has become in England a political party; it defends itself and is attacked as such. In this respect it sustains an unequal struggle, having against it the passions and interests of the majority. So nothing is more popular at the moment than to attack and outrage the clergy. The newspapers are full of diatribes. The day after my arrival in London a meeting took place to get certain restrictions abolished which, it seemed, stood in the way of the development of dramatic art. The bishops in the House of Lords had opposed a Bill on the subject, and from the point of view of public morality I believe they were right. None-the-less they were attacked at the meeting in the strongest language. They were

---

[1] The dots are Tocquevilles.

64

belaboured with sarcasms and mockery. One might have been at a similar French gathering.

But experience has proved that even the doctrine of a religion whose ministers are an object of hatred or distrust, is in danger. Men's minds, taken generally, are incapable of separating the man from the teaching.

The spirit of irreligion, or at least that of indifference, therefore is making and will make great progress in England.

However I do not think that it will for a long time come to a state so unfortunate as that prevailing in France today. And this for several reasons:

(1) It is only the Established Church which is being attacked, and the sects, which are very numerous, gain from its losses. In France every manifestation of the religious spirit was attacked along with Catholicism.

(2) The English are a people with less passion and imagination than ourselves. They can more easily separate the priest from the religion.

(3) The English people are more serious than ours, and serious characters are more susceptible to religious ideas than are others.

U[1]

UNIFORMITY

England illustrates a truth I had often noticed before; that the uniformity of petty legislation instead of being an advantage is almost always a great evil, for there are few countries all of whose parts can put up with legislation which is the same right down to its details. Beneath this apparent diversity which strikes the view of the superficial observer and shocks him so strongly, is to be found real political harmony derived from government appropriate to the needs of each locality.

But in France this is not appreciated in the least. The French genius demands uniformity even in the smallest details, much as the music-loving Germans need the order and harmonic relationship of sounds. We should thank heaven for being free, for we have all the passions needed to smooth the path to tyranny. . . .[2]

[1] Note by Tocqueville: *Hic.* Advantage of a federal Government of better lending itself to diversity than any other. Note for my work on America . . .

[2] The dots are Tocqueville's.

Journey to England (1833)

To return to England. 'One of the great difficulties one finds when one wishes to describe its institutions lies in their extreme diversity', Mr. Bowring said to me today (24th August). 'Westminster where we are at the moment, has municipal laws and practices which are completely different from those that are found two miles from here in the city. I do not hold that in the present case we reap great advantage from this lack of uniformity, but the principle, that municipal laws should be adapted to localities and not localities to municipal laws, is excellent. What most prevents you from decentralising administration in France is that you feel obliged to apply the same rule at the same time to the whole of your vast territory, to those parts which can already govern themselves and to those which cannot. If you did not hold to uniformity so much, your legislation could accord liberty to each according to its degree of civilisation.'

4. LAST IMPRESSIONS OF ENGLAND

(*London, 7th September* 1833)

Trying to sum up my various impressions gathered during the month I have been in this country, mixing as far as possible with all classes, listening to men of all parties, here is what stands clear and precise.

I arrived in England under the impression that the country was on the point of being thrown into the troubles of a great revolution. My opinion is in part changed on this point.

If any fundamental change in the law, or any social transformation, or any substitution of one regulating principle for another is called a revolution, then England assuredly is in a state of revolution. For the aristocratic principle which was the vital one of the English constitution, is losing strength every day, and it is probable that in due time the democratic one will have taken its place. But if one understands by a revolution a violent and sudden change, then England does not seem ripe for such an event, and I see many reasons for thinking that it will never be so. But I must explain my reasons for thinking this.

In England an illustrious name is a great advantage and a

cause of much pride to him who bears it, but in general one can say that the aristocracy is founded on wealth, a thing which may be *acquired*, and not on birth which cannot. From this it results that one can clearly see in England where the aristocracy begins, but it is impossible to say where it ends. It could be compared to the Rhine whose source is to be found on the peak of a high mountain, but which divides into a thousand little streams and, in a manner of speaking, disappears before it reaches the sea. The difference between England and France in this matter turns on the examination of a single word in each language. 'Gentleman' and 'gentilhomme' evidently have the same derivation, but 'gentleman' in England is applied to every well-educated man whatever his birth, while in France *gentilhomme* applies only to a noble by birth. The meaning of these two words of common origin has been so transformed by the different social climates of the two countries that today they simply cannot be translated, at least without recourse to a periphrasis. This grammatical observation is more illuminating than many long arguments.

The English aristocracy can therefore never arouse those violent hatreds felt by the middle and lower classes against the nobility in France where the nobility is an exclusive caste, which while monopolising all privileges and hurting everybody's feelings, offers no hope of ever entering into its ranks.

The English aristocracy has a hand in everything; it is open to everyone; and anyone who wishes to abolish it or attack it as a body, would have a hard task to define the object of his onslaught.

The power of the aristocracy in England, which could be called the domination of the richer classes, is however losing its scope. This is due to several reasons.

The first results from the general movement common to humanity the world over in our time. The century is primarily democratic. Democracy is like a rising tide; it only recoils to come back with greater force, and soon one sees that for all its fluctuations it is always gaining ground. The immediate future of European society is completely democratic; this can in no way be doubted. Thus the common people in England are beginning to get the idea that they, too, can take a part in government. The class placed immediately above it, but which has not yet played a notable part in the course of events, especially shows this ill-defined urge for growth and for power, and is becoming more numerous and more restless day by day. Furthermore the discomforts and real poverty suffered in England in our time, give birth to ideas and excite passions which would perhaps have long continued to sleep if the State had been prosperous.

So a gradual development of the democratic principle must follow from the irresistible march of events. Daily some further privilege of the aristocracy comes under attack; it is a slow war waged about details, but infallibly in time it will bring the whole edifice down.

Moreover the same cause now increases the strength of democracy in England as it once helped to maintain the long domination of the aristocracy; for there is no absolute truth or good in human affairs.

When a body is composed of a limited number of members, clearly defined and exclusively possessing certain privileges, like the nobility in France, such a body makes itself prey to frightful hatreds, but when attacked it defends itself like a single man, all its members having a clear and certain interest in defending the whole body.

Thus at the time of the French Revolution all the nobles took a common line. If the effort had been as well organised as it was great, their resistance might perhaps have been successful.

But in England where the limits of the aristocracy are unknown, there are many of its members who share democratic ideas up to a point, or see advantage to themselves in extending popular power. It thus happens that on many questions the House of Lords is of one opinion, but all the rest of the aristocracy is with the people. On one side there is continual attack, and on the other divided and often weak resistance.

Therefore the English aristocracy will fall more slowly and less violently than the French, but I think that it will fall as inevitably.

These are the general reasons that make me believe that England is not threatened, as is generally believed in France, by a violent and rapid change in its social state.

Now here are the symptoms which I have noted and which, to whatever cause they are attributed, seem to me to show that the revolution which we await is still far away.

When a people has been kept away for centuries from all

political activity and in ignorance of everything relating to the government of society, and suddenly the light shines on it, it is impossible to predict what will be the course of its ideas. Some thought which had been barely entertained even by the most heated brain, could become an article of faith for such a people in the course of a single year; and then nothing could be more dangerous than to judge from what people think today what they will think tomorrow.

But that remark is not applicable to England. Freedom of the press has existed in England for more than a century. All questions relating to the government of society, even if they have not been treated in detail, have at least been raised. There is no theory so destructive of the present order that it has not found an echo among those bold spirits who, like the pioneers in America, advance into the wilderness and are often very far ahead of the mass of the people who follow them.

So if the English people are not yet convinced of an idea, one can be sure that it will take some time for them to become so.

It is easy to notice one alarming symptom in England; it is a spirit of innovation spread through all classes, which announces the weakening of the aristocratic principle more than does any other thing. In past times what most distinguished the English people from any other was its satisfaction with itself; then everything about its laws and its customs was good in its eyes. It was drunk in those days with the incense of flattery which it lavished on itself, and sanctified even its prejudices and sorrows. This proud disposition was even further increased by the French writers of the eighteenth century, who all took the English at their word and carried their praises even further than they.

Today everything has changed. In the England of our times a spirit of discontent with the present and hatred of the past shows itself everywhere. The human spirit has fallen into the opposite extreme. It only looks for what is wrong around it, and is much more bent on correcting what is wrong than in preserving what is good.

The English are thus on a dangerous road; but they are taking one small thing after another, and have not in any way conceived one of those general principles which announce the approach of the total subversion of the existing order.

The privileges of the aristocracy are being attacked; it is easy

69

to see that at each step they are losing something of their strength. But it is an indirect attack that is being made against them. Public opinion is far from having taken a stand about the utility of an aristocracy in principle. I even believe that in the present state of opinion the majority are decidedly in favour of the aristocratic principle to a greater or less extent according to the disposition of the individual.

I explained earlier what has made the aristocracy so strong in England. This strength, although it is shaken, is still very great. I was singularly struck during my stay in this country by the extent to which the aristocratic principle affected manners. This is what struck me most in what I saw. I think the following notes prove the point completely.

Talk with a man of the people or with a member of the middle classes and you will see that he has a vague feeling of discomfort. He will complain of such-and-such a Lord, or the course which the House of Lords has adopted, but it does not seem to have entered his head that one could do without Lords. His anger will be brought to bear against some individual, but you will only very rarely notice in him that violent feeling, full of hatred and envy, which incites the lower classes in France against all those who are above them. These feelings, it is true, are germinating among the English, but they are not yet developed and perhaps it will be a long time before they are so if the aristocracy avoids a head-on collision with the people.

Listen to the same man on the subject of government; he sees clearly that he should take part in the government, but the idea that government belongs to the people does not strike his imagination.

So, too, if you speak to a member of the middle classes; you will find he hates some aristocrats but not the aristocracy. On the contrary he himself is full of aristocratic prejudices. He deeply distrusts the people; he loves noise, territorial possessions, carriages: he lives in the hope of attaining all this by means of the democratic varnish with which he covers himself, and meanwhile gives a livery to his one servant whom he calls a footman, talks of his dealings with the Duke of——, and his very distant family links with the house of another noble Lord.

The whole of English society is still clearly based on an aristocratic footing, and has contracted habits that only a violent

70

revolution or the slow and continual action of new laws can destroy. Luxury and the joys of pride have become necessities of life here. Many still prefer the chance of procuring them in their entirety to the establishment of a universal equality around them in which nothing would come to humiliate them.

There are several positive observations that convinced me of what I am saying. I will note them here.

It is known that England is administered by the Justices of the Peace who are nominated by the King. These magistrates are all taken from the landowning class. In this arrangement there are two things which particularly shock our democratic habits:

The first is exclusively to put provincial affairs into the hands of great landowners, the second that they are nominated by the King. This state of things shocks us not only because it is contrary to our customs, but because it is contrary to a certain general theory of democracy which is generally accepted in our country. But it is not in the least so accepted in England. There are in fact complaints against the order of things I have described. The Justices of the Peace are attacked indirectly and on certain points of detail in various political writings, but there is no great current of opinion against them. The need for change does not make itself generally felt, and the people quite quietly lets itself be taxed and governed by men it does not nominate and who are not taken from its ranks. If democratic ideas and passions were as developed in England as is presumed, this would certainly not be so.

Here is another even more conclusive observation.

It is not rare to hear an Englishman complain of the extension of aristocratic privileges and to speak with bitterness of those who exploit them; but come to tell him the one way to destroy the aristocracy, which is to change the law of inheritance, and he will draw back at once. I have not yet met one person who did not seem frightened by such an idea. Thus it is true that there is hatred of the aristocrats, but public opinion is far from cold-bloodedly envisaging the destruction of the aristocracy. Moreover, this law of inheritance which is, as it were, the cornerstone of the aristocracy, this law has entered into the customs of all classes. In France the code permits a father to leave one child's share extra to the eldest, but it is very rarely that he does so. In England hardly anyone is obliged by law to make a settlement,

71

but there are few rich men who do not do so; to such an extent has this system of unequal fortunes and the preservation of the family become an accepted habit! Indeed, here as elsewhere, the foundations are unsettled; but the attack is indirect and not open; one thing leads to another without general or defined principles. Each day sees the disappearance of one of the lucrative sinecures which used to go to those younger sons whom their fathers' aristocratic instincts had disinherited. When it will become difficult for younger sons to get anything to live on, the eldest sons will have to divide the inheritance. So here, too, the revolution is on the move, but it goes slowly.

The state of the poor is the deepest trouble of England. The number of paupers is increasing here at an alarming rate, a fact which should to some extent be attributed to the defects of the law. But in my view the first and permanent cause of the evil is the way landed property is not divided up. In England the number of people who possess land is tending to decrease rather than increase, and the number of the proletarians grows ceaselessly with the population. Such conditions tie up with the increase in taxation which means that the rich man cannot employ the poor as he would have been able to, if a large part of his money did not go into the State coffers; such a state of things cannot but indefinitely stimulate poverty. Well then! . . . and what struck me most of all, was that this truth, so far from being generally realised, is not understood except by a few. The thought of even a gradual sharing of the land has not in the least occurred to the public imagination. Some speculators think of it, some agitators seek to exploit it, but to my extreme surprise the masses have not yet got the idea at all. The English are still imbued with that doctrine, which is at least debatable, that great properties are necessary for the improvement of agriculture, and they seem still convinced that extreme inequality of wealth is the natural order of things. Notice that it is not of the rich I am speaking here at all, but of the middle classes and a great part of the poor. As long as the imagination of the English has not broken this fetter, and does not follow another chain of ideas, the chances of a violent revolution are few, for, whatever anyone says, it is ideas that stir the world and not blind needs. Certainly when the French Revolution broke out, French imaginations had already gone far beyond these limits.

Journey to England (1833)

To sum up, England seems to me in a critical state in that certain events, which it is possible to predict, can from one moment to another throw her into a state of violent revolution. But if things follow their natural course, I do not think that this revolution will come, and I see many chances of the English being able to modify their political and social condition, with much trouble no doubt, but without a convulsion and without civil war.

I have said that a violent revolution was something possible although not probable. In fact when the human spirit begins to move in a people, it is almost impossible to say beforehand where it will end up. Furthermore England, apart from the dangers of Reform, is exposed to other dangers which greatly intensify those; a great financial crisis caused by bankruptcy, an increase in poverty caused by the prolongation of the present Poor Laws coming in the middle of the agitation for Reform, could no doubt give popular passions an impulse which it is very hard to foresee.

But the greatest danger could come from the conduct of the aristocracy. At the moment the House of Lords is isolated in the country and it is very difficult for it efficiently to oppose Reform. But there will come a time when the popular party will gain ground, movement will become more rapid and the final result of the revolution will be clear to all eyes. Then the Lords will find the support they now lack in the country; all the second rank of the aristocracy and all those who have a positive interest in maintaining the old order, will see that they have to make common cause with the high nobility. It is to be feared that the aristocracy may try to oppose the irresistible current of the new ideas. Once the fight is on, it is impossible to say where the winning party will stop, for the English are a violent, although a deliberate, people.

Moreover the blind strength of the lower classes would find a guide in the enlightened ideas of the middle classes, who, at this moment, turn from them in terror and disgust.

In Ireland there is a bridge called 'Carrick Horn'[1] made of

[1] Carrick Horn is no doubt Carrick-a-rede on the Antrim coast. An illustration and description of the rope-bridge are given in Mr. and Mrs. S. C. Hall's *Ireland, its scenery, character etc.* Vol. III, p. 152 (London, 1843). See also S. Lewis's *Topographical Dictionary of Ireland*, London, 1837, Vol. I, p. 119.

rope and suspended more than a hundred feet above the ocean. Hardly anyone, except the fishermen of the district, dares to risk his neck on this trembling bridge, and strangers who see a man high in the air like that over the sea, can hardly convince themselves that he will not certainly be killed. It is however very probable that he will arrive on the other side safe and sound. But if during his dangerous crossing, the fisherman were surprised by a hurricane, or if he lacked skill or a cool head, he would doubtless be thrown into the chasm. The English people at the moment are very much like the fisherman of 'Carrick Horn'.

III

Journey to England (1835)

Ideas, Opinions, Accounts, Conversations

---

1. NOTES MADE DURING MY STAY
IN LONDON
(8th May–24th June 1835)

London (8th May 1835)

The French wish not to have superiors. The English wish to have inferiors. The Frenchman constantly raises his eyes above him with anxiety. The Englishman lowers his beneath him with satisfaction. On both sides there is pride, but it is understood in a different way. . . .

What is the reason for this? Does it not happen because, in a democratic society ranks being no longer defined, everyone, though despairing of placing himself in a recognisable position in the hierarchy and rising above everyone else, at least wants nobody to rise above him. If this was so, the English form of pride would be natural to man, and the French form would be attributable to a particular cause; it would be pride not achieving what it wishes, but reduced to a makeshift. That is a question to dig into.

Does this effect not arise from the fact that the Englishman was used to the idea that he could advance himself, but the Frenchman could not? The one to be something had to destroy what was above him, the other had to seek to raise himself to this higher rank.

* * *

Journey to England (1835)

Sharp.[1] *Lawyer and Radical (8th May 1835)*

Q. What do the common people in England do with their money when they have any to spare?

A. They spend it in orgies or they put it into business.

Q. Have they the idea of buying land?

A. Not at all. Such an idea would never enter the head of an English peasant.

Q. Why is that?

A. Partly because the English countryman never sees small landed properties, and also because commerce offers many more openings here than in France.

Q. Thus everyone who rises above the working classes goes into commerce or industry?

A. Yes.

Q. Thus when the poor man sees before him a landowner who himself alone possesses half a county, the idea does not strike him that this immense property divided between all the inhabitants of the neighbourhood, could give comfort to each one of them, and he does not regard this great landowner as a sort of common enemy?

A. No. That feeling has not yet been born. I repeat that the taste for real estate is a taste of the rich man. When one becomes a millionaire by trade, one buys a large estate which brings in hardly 2 per cent, and which entails much showy expenditure, but at the same time gives you a high social position.

* * *

Hampstead. Conversation with Reeve[2] *(11th May 1835)*

Q. What are the openings for the younger branches of the aristocracy?

A. *Firstly* the Established Church; generally the great landowners have rights of nomination to some well-endowed livings.

Secondly the Bar; one must start by being quite rich to be able to qualify. The rich landowner makes this initial expendi-

[1] According to *Clarke's New Law List* there were six Sharps or Sharpes listed as solicitors in London in 1835. I have been unable to trace the one Tocqueville has met.

[2] Cf. *Œuvres Complètes* (ed. Mayer), vi, 1.

76

ture for his son, and by this means the son finds himself in an
élite body, where competition is necessarily limited as great
means are required to enter into it.

Thirdly the army; commissions are bought; a soldier almost
never becomes an officer.

Fourthly the great resort is India. India offers quite a large
number of positions at enormous salaries, £10,000 for example;
the aristocracy pushes its younger sons in that direction. It is an
inexhaustible resource for it, all the more because the climate is
so deadly that the odds are three to one that an Englishman will
die there; but if he does not die, he is *sure* of getting rich. Thus
India always offers a large number of vacant positions, and all
of them are always in demand.

Q. Do you not think that the most efficient way of destroying
the aristocracy would be to destroy its sources of wealth or make
them accessible to everyone?

A. Yes.

Q. I see democracy represented here by a great army, but
one without a leader. These missing leaders are in the aristocracy itself, but they must be made to come forward. The rearguard of the aristocracy must become the vanguard of democracy,
and so it will be if, without attacking the advantages of the
nobles, you make things difficult for their sons and brothers.

*   *   *

Reeve (11th May 1835)

Centralisation

Q. I think I see a strong tendency to centralisation in this
country. Am I mistaken?

A. No. The tendency exists and is already taking effect. You
have seen our new Poor Law.[1] I am led to believe that the
administration of our prisons will be similarly centralised. . . .[2]

Centralisation, a democratic instinct; instinct of a society
which has succeeded in escaping from the individualistic system
of the Middle Ages. Preparation for despotism.

Why is centralisation dear to the habits of democracy? Great

[1] The Poor Law Amendment Act of 1834.
[2] The dots are Tocqueville's.

questions to *delve into* in the third volume[1] of my work, if I can
fit it in. A *fundamental* question.

* * *

Reeve (*11th May 1835*)

Unpaid Positions

Q. Do you have many paid positions in your administration?

A. Almost all positions are unpaid. In the counties, the Lord
Lieutenants, the High Sheriffs,[2] the Justices of the Peace and the
Overseers of the Poor are unpaid. Only the road surveyors are
paid because they are industrial specialists who give their time
to public service. Here most of those who accept paid positions
lose more than they gain from them. They work from ambition,
not cupidity; the expenses expected from them to keep up their
position always involve spending their own money.

That state of affairs is, as one sees, completely aristocratic.

* * *

[1] Here Tocqueville alludes to the last two volumes of his *Democracy in America*
which he published in 1840. Cf. *Œuvres Complètes* (ed. Mayer), I, 2.

[2] The offices of Lord Lieutenant and Sheriff play an important part in British
constitutional and administrative history. Before the Norman Conquest the sheriff
was a royal officer, appointed by the king and representing royal authority. He was
the royal bailiff, mainly concerned with the king's interests. The Norman Conquest
did not destroy the *shire*, it merely became, in analogy to the equivalent French
district (*comitatus*) a *county*. The sheriff appears in Latin documents as *vicecomus*.
With the increasing power of the kings the power of the sheriff increases as well;
he became a kind of provincial viceroy: all the affairs of the shire (county), fiscal,
military, governmental were under his control; he was also president of the county
court.

The decline in power of the sheriff is a consequence of the fact that under pressure
of parliaments during the fourteenth century they became annual officers. On the
other hand the lord lieutenant is originally a military officer, commanding the county
militia, but he becomes also the honorary head of the justices of the peace whom
he recommends for appointment on the advice of a special committee. The lord
lieutenant's function as commander of the militia was taken away in 1872; he now
keeps certain county records in the capacity of *custos rotulorum*, yet the actual keeper
of these records is the clerk. Both sheriff and lord lieutenant are appointed by the
crown.

Maitland gives an indication of the relation of the two officers in the following
amusing sentence: 'The sheriff . . . falls lower and lower in real power: his cere-
monial dignity he retains—he is the greatest man in the county and should go to
dinner before the lord lieutenant.' Cf. F. W. Maitland, *The Constitutional History
of England*, p. 234, Cambridge, 1920. Tocqueville returns to a discussion of the
office of high sheriff during his second conversation with Sharp. (14th June 1835.)

Journey to England (1835)

Q. Is the number of the Dissenters known?

A. No. One could only obtain this figure with the aid of the Government, and it has been in its interest up to now to hide it.

Q. What causes changes of religion in this country?

A. Several curious facts are relevant to that question. As to Catholicism, one sees men of all classes join that church from weariness of the sect.[1] Their number is increasing rapidly, but changes of religion without Protestantism depend on facts which have nothing to do with religious belief.

One notices that when a family becomes rich, when it reaches an income of five or six thousand pounds, it leaves the *dissenters* to join the Established Church. It is a way of entering the bosom of the high aristocracy, or at least of rubbing shoulders with it. Then one finds oneself in fine churches where there are always carpets, comfortable pews, well-dressed people and well-educated preachers.

The poor man who is born in the bosom of the Established Church, is made uneasy by this very splendour; his feeling of inferiority takes him to a church where he finds his like in the congregation, and in the preacher a man less superior to himself and one who says things within his grasp. A great many poor men (and I give the word a comparative, not an absolute, meaning) leave the Established Church for these reasons and do not take up with any other; although they do not yet march under an enemy banner, they are adversaries not neutrals.

Q. Thus you not only have a political aristocracy and democracy, but also an aristocratic religion and a democratic one. Religious tensions are going in the same direction as political ones; a grim symptom for the future.

* * *

Whigs (22nd May 1835)

Lady Charlemont[2] said to me today (22nd May 1835): 'One should not judge our situation by the fears that are expressed;

---

[1] Note by Tocqueville: Lord Radnor told me the same.

[2] Lady Charlemont was the wife of the second Earl of Charlemont; cf. Hubert Maxwell, *The Creevey Papers*, London 1904, pp. 324 f.

since I have been in the world, I have heard it said each year that we are going to have a revolution, and at the end of the year we always found ourselves in the same place.'

Somebody answered: 'We have heard it said all our lives that we must die, and we do not die. Does this mean that we are immortal?'

I have quoted Lady Charlemont's words because I have heard the same from many *Whigs*. They seem characteristic of their Party. For a century and a half the Whigs have played with the British constitution; they believe that the game can continue, but the machine is worn and should be handled with discretion. They have talked of equality and freedom at a time when the people had a vague instinct, not a clear, practical idea of these two things; they used it to come to power, and then left society almost in the state in which they found it. This experience of the past deceives them, and they believe that they can do the same thing in a century when these same conceptions of freedom and liberty have taken clear shape in the idea of certain laws. After all the *Whigs* are only a fragment of the aristocratic party; they have long used democracy as a tool, but the tool has become stronger than the hand that guides it.

Generally speaking the English seem to me to have great difficulty in getting hold of general and undefined ideas. They judge the facts of today perfectly well, but the tendency of events and their distant consequences escape them. The Whigs seem to me to have more of this characteristic than the others. Besides they need illusions more than all the others.

* * *

Centralisation (*24th May 1835*)

Lord Minto[1] said to me today (24th May 1835): 'You should not try to imitate our administrative system for it is very bad. It rests almost entirely on the Justices of the Peace, magistrates who are responsible to no one and are not paid for the performance of their duties.' He came back several times to this idea which I had already heard expressed by more than one member of the Whig aristocracy: *symptom of democracy and centralisation.*

[1] The second Earl.

Journey to England (1835)

Q. Do you not think that the present tendency of this country is towards centralisation?

A. Yes.

Q. Are you not afraid of this tendency?

A. No, because I hope that it will not lead us on too far. Up to now centralisation has been the thing most foreign to the English temperament:

(1) Our habits or the nature of our temperament do not in the least draw us towards general ideas; but centralisation is based on general ideas; that is the desire for power to attend, in a uniform and general way, to the present and future needs of society. We have never considered government from such a lofty point of view. So we have divided administrative functions up infinitely and have made them independent of one another. We have not done this deliberately, but from our sheer inability to comprehend general ideas on the subject of government or anything else.

(2) The tendency of English politics up to now has been to remain as free as possible to do what was convenient. The taste for making others submit to a way of life which one thinks more useful for them than they do themselves, is not a common taste in England. We are attacking the present parochial and provincial institutions because they serve as tools of the aristocracy. Taking power from our adversaries we naturally hope to vest it in the government, because nothing is prepared within the present institutions for inheriting some of this power. But if democracy was *organised* in our parishes and our counties so that it could take over the tasks of government, I am sure that we would leave them quite independent of the central government. Perhaps we will try to do it too late, and by a compromise the government will be enriched with the chief spoils from the aristocracy.

Q. Could it not be that what you call the English temperament, is the aristocratic temperament? Would it not be part of the aristocratic temperament to isolate oneself and, as each enjoys a fine estate, to be *more* afraid of being disturbed in one's own domain, *than* wishful to extend it over others? Is not the

---

[1] John Stuart Mill. Cf. *Œuvres Complètes* (ed. Mayer), vi, 1, where I have published the complete correspondence between Tocqueville and Mill.

instinct of democracy exactly opposite, and may it not be that the present tendency which you consider as an accident, is an almost necessary consequence of the basic cause?

A. These are ideas which had not occurred to me before, and which deserve to be examined with the greatest care. While admitting their correctness, I believe that they should be modified by what I have said about the English temperament, for the English temperament seems to me somehow something different from the aristocratic temperament.

Religion, Religious Customs

Today, 27th May 1835, I lunched at Lord Radnor's house. Before coming to table Lord Radnor went to his study; Lady Radnor and his daughters went there too; after a moment eleven or twelve women- and eight or ten men-servants came in. They walked in formal order of hierarchic precedence, as was easily seen by the age and dress of each of them. At the head of the women was the children's governess; then the housekeeper and the chambermaid and then the lower servants. The steward came at the head of the men and the grooms at the tail. These twenty people took their places round the room and knelt down looking towards the wall. Near the fireplace Lord and Lady Radnor and Lady Louisa[1] knelt down too, and Lord Radnor read a prayer aloud, the servants giving the responses. This sort of little service lasted six or eight minutes, after which the male and female servants got up and went out in the same order to resume their work.

The Spirit of Legislation

(*About 27th May 1835*)

The spirit of English legislation is an incomprehensible mixture of the spirits of innovation and of routine, which perfects the details of laws without noticing their principles; which always

[1] Sir Lewis Namier sent me this comment on 'Lady Louisa'; 'William, 3rd Earl of Radnor, who succeeded to the peerage in 1828 and died in 1869, had no daughter of the name Louisa, nor a sister. He had, however, a sister—in-law Louisa, the wife of Dunscombe Pleydell Bouverie, a naval officer who married 27th December 1809 Louisa 2nd daughter of Joseph May. She died in 1852, leaving an only daughter called Louisa. Still neither of them had the courtesy title of "Lady", which possibly Tocqueville used by mistake.'

goes ahead in a straight line, taking step after step in the direction it happens to be in, without looking to right or to left to make connections between the different roads it is following; active and contemplative; sometimes wide awake to notice the slightest abuse, and sometimes sound asleep amid the most monstrous ones; which exhausts its skill in mending, and does not create except, so to say, without knowing it and by chance; the most restless for improvement and the well-being of society, but the least systematic seeker for these things; the most impatient and the most patient; the most clear-sighted and the blindest; the most powerful in some things, and the weakest and most embarrassed in some others; which keeps eighty million people under its obedience three thousand leagues away, and does not know how to get out of the smallest administrative difficulties; which excels at taking advantage of the present, but does not know how to foresee the future. Who can find a word to explain all these anomalies?

BRIBERY

Mr. Hallam[1] (*29th May 1835*)

Today, 29th May 1835, I saw Mr. Hallam on his return from an election; he said to me:

'In electoral expenses it is important to distinguish between those which are permissible and those which are not. Even permissible expenses are very considerable; it is the custom for the candidate to go himself or to send his authorised representatives to ask the electors whom he supposes to favour him, for their votes. So some time before the election he forms a sort of administrative office. Its task is to go through the electoral list, to count votes, and to know the names and the dispositions of the electors. That work done, the candidate and his representatives start doing the rounds. Election day arrives. There are a great many electors whom he must send to fetch, and when they have arrived they must generally be fed and housed at the expense of the candidate for whom they vote. He will not be able to get out of that for less than several thousand guineas. However,' Mr. Hallam added, 'there is a clear tendency to cut down these expenses.'

[1] Henry Hallam, author of the well-known *Constitutional History of England.*

Those are the permissible expenses. Many others cannot be admitted. The latter come under the heading of *bribery*.

But one has to make a distinction between several sorts of bribery. The first sort consists in the indirect action a man can take against one or more of the electors, as for instance a great landowner against his tenants or shopkeepers; then there is bribery properly so called because it is a matter of buying votes.

This last is almost unknown in the counties. It hardly exists except in the towns, and not in all of them. It is worth noting that in the towns which have recently received the privilege of sending members to Parliament, the custom of buying votes has hardly been introduced. But it prevails in most of the old boroughs. However it is important to understand correctly how the people in general look on this corruption. The poor among the electors have come to consider the right to vote as a sort of capital from which it is right that they should derive some income; a deplorable idea, but it prevents the *special* form of corruption to which it gives rise from spreading to all the rest of a man's feelings and ideas, which would have been sure to happen if, in accepting the money, the poor felt they were doing wrong.'

RADICAL

(29th May 1835)

Today (29th May 1835) I have seen Mr. Roebuck,[1] one of the most advanced radicals in the House of Commons. He is a man who lives outside almost all the accepted notions of how to live in this country. He is very poor; he became an M.P. by chance and without payment (a letter of recommendation from Mr. Hume of the electoral body at Bath was enough). His only lodging in London is 'chambers' in one of the 'Inns of Court' (Gray's Inn) of the Temple, and he lives there, in complete defiance of convention, with his wife whom he married for love. He is very young (thirty years old), very energetic and very much in earnest. He told me that reform would never go boldly forward until the Whigs had been pushed back among the Tories, since, after all, they were but a modified offshoot of the Tories.

[1] Member of Parliament since 1832; disciple of John Stuart Mill. Cf. *Dictionary of National Biography*.

To that I answered: Allow me to say that I take a different view of the matter. The *immediate* success (for eventual success is, I think, certain) of Reform seems to me to depend on the opposite happening. English society seems to me to be divided into three unequal categories: the first comprises almost the whole aristocracy properly so called and a large proportion of the middle classes, taking them from the top; that is the Tory or Conservative Party.

The second is formed out of the middle classes, taking them from the bottom, and a small section of the aristocracy. These have instincts rather than definite opinions in favour of reform; they let themselves be carried without resistance by the spirit of the age which goes that way. Those are the Whigs; they keep marching day by day without knowing too much about where the road they follow will end.

The third is formed out of the lower classes, the people properly so called. Those, or rather their leaders, know exactly what they want to do; they are destroying all the old structure of the aristocratic society of their country.

It seems to me that in the present state of society and opinion in England, with the hundred thousand ties of habits, tastes, vanity and interest which unite all the classes above the simple people, the reformers ought to feel that it was an unhoped-for piece of luck to find allies, within those very classes, who help on the work of destruction without wishing to bring things down. In every country, and perhaps most of all in this one, to try to carry through a radical revolution with the aid of the people only against a united front of all the rich and enlightened classes, is an almost impossible undertaking whose results have been disastrous. So I consider the union of the Reformers with a section of the conservatives as greatly favouring the slow but steady progress of the former, and I think that Reform would almost certainly be delayed if Whigs and Tories joined forces before the great majority of the Whigs had been carried little by little so far along the road of change that retreat was no longer possible.

To that Mr. Roebuck and Mr. John Mill, who was there too, answered that the Radicals, hiding behind the Whigs, letting themselves get forgotten, and, in a word, not giving a lead to the passions and opinions of those who sent them to Parliament, risked losing their identity to the profit only of the Tories, for there had been enough desertions already to show that the Whigs could not carry on the campaign by themselves, and the Radicals could not support them effectively unless they succeeded *in creating a great excitement*,[1] and that was something they could not do if they just let themselves be carried in tow by the Whigs.[2]

They also added: 'all the upper class and a large part of the middle class, as you said just now, has already gone over to the Tories: one section of the middle class, which is nearest to the people, is daily going over'.

'That being so,' said I, 'a year hence we will probably see Sir Robert Peel in the Ministry,[3] and he will make a temporary delay in the progress of Reform, for you do not seem to be in a position either to seize the government yourselves, or to direct those who hold power in the direction you want.'

They both agreed that that seemed likely to happen.

General characteristics of English Radicals

There are basic analogies between English and French Radicals. But the differences between them are much greater still. These are the most striking as far as I have noticed up to the present.

(1st) Everything I have heard said among Radicals (I speak of the leaders) is permeated with real respect for the principle in whose name they act. I have never caught them showing signs of wishing to impose on the Nation (even for its own good) a political condition not of its own choosing. The whole question is to win a majority: and I have never seen that they had any idea of doing so otherwise than by legal means.

The most characteristic trait of the French Radical is a wish to use the power of some to secure the happiness of the greatest number, and his most important means of government is material force and contempt for the law.

(2nd) Though the Radicals do not join in the Tories' superstitious cult of the rights of property, the respect they profess for

---

[1] The words in italics are in English in Tocqueville's manuscript.

[2] Note by Tocqueville: I still think this argument more subtle than true; the reasoning of a man in a hurry to enjoy, rather than of men whose first care is to make enjoyment sure.

[3] Peel did not return to office until 1841.

them seems very genuine. They do not question that this respect is the essential basis for a civilised society.

The French Radical has the greatest mistrust for property; and, ready to violate it in practice, he attacks it in theory.

(3rd) There are a great many enthusiastic sectarians among English Radicals. One also finds a fair number of men who have been won over by French philosophic ideas: but even those are firmly convinced of the political necessity for religion and have a real respect for it.

One of the principal characteristics of the French Radical Party is the flaunting not only of anti-Christian opinions, but also of the most anti-social philosophical ideas.

(4th) Generally speaking the leaders of the English Radical Party are in easy financial circumstances, for up to now some wealth has been the necessary preliminary to everything else. They have almost all had a careful education, and, though their manners are very different from those of the aristocracy, they are recognised as 'gentlemen'. Almost all of them have some knowledge of political economy, the history of their own country, precedents, political forms. . . .[1] They argue their opinions and are not afraid of discussion.

The French Radical is almost always very poor, often boorish, still more often presumptuous, and profoundly ignorant of political science, who understands nothing but the use of force, and deals in empty words and superficial generalisations.

In brief, at present I think that an enlightened man, of good sense and good will would be a Radical in England. I have never met those three qualities together in a French Radical.

ANOMALIES. SPIRIT OF ASSOCIATION AND SPIRIT OF
EXCLUSION

(*30th May 1835*)

I see many things in this country which I cannot yet completely understand, among others this:

Two spirits which, if not altogether contrary, are at least very diverse, seem to hold equal sway in England.

The one prompts people to pool their efforts to attain ends which in France we would never think of approaching in this

[1] The dots are Tocqueville's.

way. There are associations to further science, politics, pleasure, business. . . .

The other prompts each man and each association to keep all advantages as much as possible to themselves, to close every possible door that would let any outsider come in or look in.

There is a story that a collector owned a very precious antique vase; he heard there was another like it. Having bought it at a very high price, he had it broken before his eyes, so that he could say that he possessed the only marvel of this sort in the world. He must have been an Englishman, exclusive proprietorial jealousy being so far developed here that it counts as one of the main national characteristics.

To come back to the subject of this note. I cannot completely understand how 'the spirit of association' and 'the spirit of exclusion' both came to be so highly developed in the same people, and often to be so intimately combined. Example a club; what better example of association than the union of individuals who form the club? What more exclusive than the corporate personality represented by the club? The same applies to almost all civil and political associations, the corporations. . . .[1] See how families divide up when the birds are able to leave the nest!

On reflection I incline to the view that the spirit of individuality is the basis of the English character. Association is a means suggested by sense and necessity for getting things unattainable by isolated effort. But the spirit of individuality comes in on every side; it recurs in every aspect of things. Perhaps one might suggest that it has indirectly helped the development of the other spirit by inspiring every man with greater ambitions and desires than one finds elsewhere. That being so, the need to club together is more generally felt, because the urge to get things is more general and stronger (a clumsy, obscure sentence, but I think the idea is right and needs looking into again). I suppose that if the French could become more enlightened than they are, they would take to clubbing together more naturally than the English. * * *

Judicial System (*1st June 1835*)

The English are the first people who ever thought of centralising the administration of justice. This innovation, which dates from

[1] The dots are Tocqueville's.

the Norman period, should be reckoned one of the reasons for the quicker progress which this nation has made in civilisation and liberty.

They established some courts which were unique in the kingdom and which only sat in London, such as the Court of Chancery, that, I think, of King's Bench, and others besides. The Courts attracted to themselves, to London, the decision of all cases of a certain nature.

As for the great majority of cases, what are called 'Common Law Suits', they are tried by judges from the Central Court, who go round the country separately every year. So cases are both brought to the Central Court, and the Central Court is brought to the cases. Both courses help the centralisation of justice.

But if one studies the actual state of affairs carefully, one finds that a very large proportion of cases escape the Central Court's net. There are in fact three classes of tribunal which are not subject to this central direction:

(1) Justices of the Peace: the Justices of the Peace individually or assembled together at 'Quarter Sessions' have the right to judge a very large proportion of the offences committed in the countryside. Their jurisdiction extends to all crimes which do not carry the death penalty or transportation for more than fourteen years.[1]

(2) The 'Corporate Courts': these are the tribunals established by royal charters in some boroughs to try civil and criminal cases arising in those boroughs. The jurisdiction of these tribunals 'materiae causa' is in general very wide under the charters. But the Central Courts have little by little attracted to themselves the more important matters.

(3) The 'Local Courts': Parliament which has never much trusted the corporations, at the same time as it established in their midst a public administration foreign to them, also created local tribunals whose duty it was, I believe, particularly to see to the enforcement of the *local* regulations which it ordained. I think the local courts have a rather limited jurisdiction. The decisions of the three classes of tribunal above mentioned are not subject to appeal, if I may accept what Mr. Roebuck states

---

[1] Note by Tocqueville: I think the Justices of the Peace only try serious cases in their collective capacity.

Journey to England (1835)

as a known fact in his article 'On Municipal Corporation Reform'.[1]

This same Mr. Roebuck states that more than half the cases decided in England can never come to the knowledge of the central courts sitting at Westminster.

*　*　*

Privileges of Wealth (11th May 1835)

The whole of English society is based on privileges of money. Demonstration of this:

A man must be rich to be a Minister, since the style of living

---

[1] Cf. 'Municipal Corporation Reform', *London Review*, April 1835, pp. 48 ff. In this article Roebuck writes: 'the justices at quarter-sessions practically adjudicate on every offence except such as necessarily involve the life of the party. . . . The justices of the corporations are justices of the peace, and try all offences against the police of their towns. Besides this, there are generally local Acts of Parliament, creating petty jurisdictions; and in many cases, the recorders try for petty offences.' Tocqueville had studied this article and presumably means by 'local courts' courts established as stated above. Other local courts existed which had been established by royal charter, and one of these, that in Bath, is referred to in a footnote to Roebuck's article (op. cit. p. 51). There were, however, many courts which Tocqueville in 1835 could describe as local courts. We mention some:

1. The Court of Pié Poudre (*Curia pedis pulverisati*). It was held in summer and the respective parties came there with dusty shoes. It exercised summary jurisdiction in regard to the police of markets and of trade. (It is now obsolete.)

2. The special jurisdiction of the Cinque ports. (Dover, Sandwich, Romney, Hastings and Hythe, to which Winchelsea and Rye have been added.) It was conducted by the Mayor and jurats. Its civil jurisdiction was abolished in 1856.

3. The old Knights' Court or Court of Chivalry. It judged damage to life and limb on occasion of jousts and tournaments; but decided also questions arising from the rule of chivalry, the code of honour governing the conduct of knights. It still retains jurisdiction over disputes to armorial bearings. After 1737 the last litigation took place in 1954 when the Corporation of Manchester invoked the jurisdiction of this Court to decide whether a certain theatre was entitled to display above the curtain the City's arms. Cf. P. Archer, *The Queen's Courts*, Penguin Books, 1956.

4. The Stannary Court of Devonshire and Cornwall (abolished in 1896). It was founded on ancient privilege granted to the workers in the tin mines to sue and to be sued in their own courts, so that they may not be drawn from their work by attending their law-suits in other courts.

5. The Court of Marshalsea held plea of all trespasses within verge of the Court where one of the parties was of the Royal Household and of all debts and contracts where both parties were of this establishment. The Court is now abolished.

6. The Palace Court at Westminster held plea of all actions arising within twelve miles of the Palace at Whitehall. This Court is likewise abolished.

Cf. Franqueville, Le *Système judiciaire de La Grande Bretagne*, Paris 1893, vol. I, pages 227–44. Se also Holdsworth, *A History of English Law*, vol. I, London 1922.

expected from him runs him into expenses much greater than what he receives from the State, which is obvious when one thinks of the lavish political world in which he must live.

A man must be rich to get into the House of Commons because election expenses are immense.

A man must be rich to be a Justice of the Peace, Lord Lieutenant, High Sheriff, Mayor, or Overseer of the Poor as these duties are unpaid.

A man must be rich to be a barrister or a judge because the education necessary to enter these professions costs a lot.

A man must be rich to be a clergyman again because the necessary education is expensive.

A man must be rich to be a litigant since one who cannot give bail must go to prison. There is not a country in the world where justice, that first need of peoples, is more the privilege of the rich. Apart from the Justices of the Peace there is no tribunal for the poor man.

Finally, to gain that wealth which is the key to all the rest, the rich man again has great advantages since he can easily raise capital and find opportunities to increase his own wealth or to enrich his relations.

Why should one be surprised at this people's cult of money? Money is the hallmark not of wealth alone, but of power, reputation and glory. So where the Frenchman says: 'He has 100,000 francs of income', the Englishman says, 'He is worth £5,000 a year'.

Manners go even further than the laws in this direction; or rather it is the laws that have moulded manners.

Intelligence, even virtue, seem of little account without money. Everything worthwhile is somehow tied up with money. It fills all the gaps that one finds between men, but nothing will take its place.

The English have left the poor but two rights: that of obeying the same laws as the rich, and that of standing on an equality with them if they can obtain equal wealth. But those two rights are more apparent than real, since it is the rich who make the laws and who create for their own or their children's profit, the chief means of getting wealth.

Journey to England (1835)

Without being rich one cannot obtain the fashionable education of Oxford or Cambridge; one cannot even get a degree from one of those universities, a thing which is necessary, or at least very useful, for the acquisition of great wealth. . . .[1]

The English have centralised justice in almost all the cases where great money interests are at stake; they have abandoned most criminal cases to the caprices of various sorts of petty tribunal. The Justices of the Peace decide without appeal almost all the crimes that do not carry the death penalty or that of transportation for more than fourteen years. The salutary guarantees which uniformity and the wisdom of a great central tribunal provide, are reserved for the fortunate; the uncertain application of the law by judges of doubtful competence has been left for cases that concern the life and liberty of men. There are several reasons for this,[2] but this above all that the rich bring cases of the first kind, whereas it is almost only the poor who are involved in the second.

Apparent equality, real privileges of wealth, greater perhaps than in any country of the world.

Central idea; all the facts bring my attention back to it.

(8th June 1835)

Obscurity and clumsiness of the law of contract; to be certain of the ownership of a piece of land it is absolutely necessary to engage the services of an able lawyer who can only guarantee you against expropriation or double payment by elaborate and very expensive researches. So only large properties are bought, and the buyer is already very rich. So the poor are shut out from the ownership of land.

Fresh information obtained from Mr. Sharp (14th June 1835)

Q. What is the Grand Jury?

A. The Grand Jury is an assembly of the chief landowners of the county.

[1] The dots are Tocqueville's.

[2] Note by Tocqueville: Among others that cases of the second sort, turning above all on matters of *fact*, are easier for little separate jurisdictions to try. As the determination of facts can but seldom be aided by rules of law, centralisation in such cases would often be useless and sometimes harmful.

Q. Who assembles the Grand Jury?

A. The Sheriff of the county.

Q. How does he choose them, what are the qualifications for belonging to that body?

I have forgotten all his answers.

Q. What are the functions of the Grand Jury?

A. The Grand Jury has functions of two sorts, *administrative* and *judicial*.

Q. What does it do in its administrative capacity?

A. It makes what we call *presentments*: it points out what roads are in bad repair, what bridges dangerous, what prisons defective. Altogether it has a general duty to inspect the functioning of public administration in the county. But it does not act on its own except, if occasion arises, by bringing actions against delinquent administrators in the appropriate courts.

Q. What are the judicial functions of the Grand Jury?

A. Clearly its administrative functions are to a certain extent judicial. But its really judicial functions consist in deciding in the case of all crimes or offences submitted to it, whether there is a case which should be taken to court.

Q. Are the semi-administrative functions of the Grand Jury the same in all the counties?

A. No. There are some counties where the Grand Jury hardly has a hand in anything except sending ordinary criminals for trial.

Q. Who is the High Sheriff?

A. The High Sheriff is an official who represents the King or the central government in each county.

Q. How is he nominated?

A. This is the procedure: every year the Grand Jury tenders the names of three landowners of the county to the judge from Westminster who presides over it. The judge submits these three names to the King who always chooses the first.

Q. Is one bound to accept the duties of High Sheriff?

A. Yes.

Q. Do people seek them?

A. No. People are afraid of them, though it is useful to a man's political career to have been High Sheriff at least once. The duties are not paid, lead to considerable expense and are often unpleasant to perform. So they only last for a year and the custom is to take each of the chief landowners in turn.

Q. But how can a man picked like that by chance and changed at the end of a year fulfil his duties properly?

A. To be precise, the High Sheriff only takes the responsibility. All his work is done by the Under-sheriff who is usually a lawyer chosen yearly by the new High Sheriff. This official receives quite good 'fees' for his functions and it is very easy to find someone glad to fill the post.

Q. What are the Sheriff's duties?

A. The Sheriff generally takes the chair and looks after county elections. He transmits the 'writs of convocation' to the county members. He makes the list of jurors, I think. Finally it is his duty to see to the execution of all the orders of courts. In that respect there is a close analogy between him and the *procureur du roi* in France. The Sheriff must be there and direct the proceedings when an execution takes place.

2. FROM BIRMINGHAM TO DUBLIN

Birmingham (25th–30th June)

We found as much goodwill here as in London; but there is hardly any likeness between these two societies. These folk never have a minute to themselves. They work as if they must get rich by the evening and die the next day. They are generally very intelligent people, but intelligent in the American way. The town itself has no analogy with other English provincial towns; the whole place is made up out of streets like the rue du Faubourg St-Antoine.[1] It is an immense workshop, a huge forge, a vast shop. One only sees busy people and faces brown with smoke. One hears nothing but the sound of hammers and the whistle of steam escaping from boilers. One might be down a mine in the New World. Everything is black, dirty and obscure, although every instant it is winning silver and gold.

* * *

Social, moral and political condition of the working classes in Birmingham

Birmingham, 29th June 1835. Mr. Carter, lawyer.

Q. What is the prevailing opinion in Birmingham?

[1] In Paris.

A. By far the great majority is Radical.

Q. Do you refer to both industrialists and workmen?

A. Yes, both.

Q. Do you know what happened at the time of the great political union of Birmingham?

A. Yes. That union, especially at the time when the Duke of Wellington tried to re-enter the Ministry, included almost the whole population of Birmingham. It was agreed to march on London if the Reform Bill was not passed; the arms manufacturers would have given rifles; the urge was irresistible. I am convinced that it was proof of that danger which forced the Tories to agree to the bill. Birmingham is only 111 miles from London, and public opinion was favourable.[1]

Q. Have political unions formed again after that time?

A. They began to form again during Peel's last Ministry;[2] but now they do not exist at all; and at this moment the population here is very little concerned with politics. But it has learnt to know its power. The presence of 150,000 work people crowded together so near the capital and with an immense store of arms always there is a very serious matter.

Q. Is there a class of unoccupied people at Birmingham?

A. No. Everybody works to make a fortune. The fortune made, everyone goes somewhere else to enjoy it.

* * *

Ideas concerning centralisation and the introduction of the judicial power into the administration

Birmingham, 29th June 1835. About the introduction of judicial power into the administration. About its necessity. The different means used by peoples to bring it in. The subject needs not a chapter, but a *book* to cover it, and one of the most important books one could think of. The necessity of bringing the judicial power into the administration is one of those *central* ideas to which I am brought back in all my researches to discover what allows and can allow men the enjoyment of political liberty.

[1] Cf. E. L. Woodward, *The Age of Reform*. 1815–1870, Oxford 1938, pp. 81 f.

[2] December 1834 to April 1835.

Journey to England (1835)

Deduction of ideas

How one should conceive of society's obligations to its members.

Is society obliged, as we think in France, to guarantee the individual and to create his well-being? Or is not its only duty rather to give the individual easy and sure means to guarantee it for himself and to create his own well-being?

The first notion; simpler, more general, more *uniform*, more easily grasped by half-enlightened and superficial minds.

The second; more complicated, not uniform in its application, harder to grasp; but the only one that is true, the only one compatible with the existence of political liberty, the only one that can make citizens or even men.

Application of this idea to public administration. Centralisation, division within the administrative power. That is an aspect of the matter that I do not want to deal with at the moment, but on which what I see in England and have seen in America casts a flood of light and allows one to form general ideas. The English themselves do not realise the excellence of their system. There is a mania for centralisation which has got hold of the democratic party. Why? Passions analogous to those of France in '89 and from much the same motives. Ridiculousness of medieval institutions. Hate for the aristocracy which has superstitiously preserved them, and uses them to its profit. Spirit of innovation, revolutionary tendency to see the abuses only of the present state; general tendency of democracies.

Lucky difficulties which obstruct centralisation in England; laws, habits, manners, English spirit rebellious against general or uniform ideas, but fond of peculiarities. Stay-at-home tastes introduced into political life.

These last two paragraphs are perhaps more a digression from the subject than the subject itself; here we are.

The most salutary of all the institutions which one could create to give the individual access to the means to work for his own well-being, would be the establishment of really independent justice with a much wider scope for its activity than that to which we have confined it. Many other advantages, too, reacting in a still more direct way on the existence of free institutions.

The English principle in matters of criminal justice is perhaps carried too far. We make the opposite mistake. The English, by making civil litigation very expensive, fall essentially short of the principle stated above. They have not, it is true, made the poor man depend on the support of society in this matter; but they have left everything in its primitive state.

Principles of the English[1] in questions of public administration. (Perhaps I ought not to call it a principle, for it came about on its own from the necessity to let elected bodies exist and to make them obey.) Division of the local administrative authorities. No hierarchy among them. Continual intervention of the judicial power to make them obey. Division of judicial power to make it less formidable. Almost all administrative acts end in judicial proceedings or are clothed in judicial forms. System of fines substituted for reprimands or dismissal from office. Its usefulness, its great advantages in the control of the *details* of society. Customary and conservative power which it puts in the hands of private people. System of obligatory duties; its advantages; its necessity.

Publicity. Pleading by those affected. Possibility of endless individual action either to make the administrative power act, or to protect oneself against its excesses. Immense political and moral advantages of this system, partly indicated by the general idea at the head of this note.

Why the English government is strong although the localities are independent. Special and often hierarchic administration for matters of importance ·to the whole Empire. Intervention by the judicial power, even in these matters, but by the central tribunal.

Difference between the constitution of the judicial power in England and America. Analogies. Differences.

Application of all these ideas to France. That the future of political liberty depends on the solution of the problem. Impossibility of an *elected* administrative power existing side by side with a *nominated* one without the arbitration of the judicial power. What happens in France proves it. We are working towards the independence of the provinces, or to their complete subordination and the destruction of municipal life. . . .

Practical discussion on this subject. Gradual introduction of

---

[1] Note by Tocqueville: I must *re-examine* the Americans in the light of this question. Analogous principles *perhaps* more simple and more rational.

the English and American principle which, in truth, is only the *general principle of free peoples.* Precautions that must be taken to preserve a strong central power. Perhaps that is the only way by which it can continue to be. . . .[1]

How the English have placed almost all the national power in Parliament. Advantages and vices of this system. How one could give up their principle on this point, while keeping it on many others. Advantages of their actual system applicable to a different system, such as publicity, judicial forms and guarantees.

Poor rates. Lot of the industrial population (29th June)

After the peace of 1814, great distress was felt in Birmingham. In 1818 the poor rates were raised to £61,928. This burden was borne by only 4,000 houses out of the 18,000 contained in the town. The inhabitants of 14,000 houses being too poor to pay the tax. The tax then amounted to two-thirds of the rent of those 4,000 houses.

In the year 1834 the number of houses was 31,000 and the poor rates only came to £44,312.

In 1823, 1824 and 1825 there was great prosperity.

In 1825 there occurred a panic which ruined some of the masters and forced a large proportion of the workers to ask for parish assistance.

Hutton's *History of Birmingham*[2]

Poor rates. Parochial rates of Birmingham. Unfairness of the tax. Democracy. 29th June. (Only the parish of Birmingham is in question. Presumed population of the parish in 1834: 118,981 inhabitants.)

On 1st June 1835, Mr. Clark told the Birmingham Literary and Philosophic Society that the total number of assessments to the poor rates was 30,662 and the amount of poor rates per annum was estimated at 44,000; that the first class of assessments, or those assessed at £12 and upward per annum, in

---

[1] The dots are Tocqueville's.
[2] William Hutton, *A History of Birmingham*, 6th edition in 1835.

number 4,374, contributed to the poor rates £31,900; that the second class, assessed at more than £5 and less than £12 per annum, in number 10,351, paid £8,400, and that the third class, assessed at less than £5 per annum and in number 15,937, contributed only £3,700.[1] *That is a tax that is progressive.*

He added that, as regards the highway rate, the same state of things was observable in an even more striking degree, this rate being entirely levied on the first two classes alone; the third class or those assessed at less than £5 per annum contributing nothing towards this rate; its amount is £11,000 per annum, of which the first class pay £9,500 and the second £1,500.

This is also the case with the lamp and watch levy, the whole being paid by the first two classes. Its amount is £9,000 of which the first class of assessments pay £8,000, the second £1,000.

The Town Hall rate, amounting to £3,000 per annum, is paid entirely by the first class, or those assessed at £12 and upward per annum.

He concluded with observing that if we took the whole of the parochial rates as amounting to £67,000 per annum, it will be found that the first class of assessments, in number 4,374, pay £32,400, that the second class, in number 10,351, pay £10,900, and that the third or lowest class, in number 15,937, contributed only £3,700 towards the whole of the parochial taxes. So that the first class, one-seventh only of the whole assessments, pay three-fourths of the whole amount levied, while the third class, constituting more than half of the assessment, pay only about one-sixteenth. He assumed therefore, that the assessment on the poorer classes was taken at a very low rate.[2]

Another member pointed out that from 1815 to 1831, the population of the parish had increased by 52 per cent (population of the parish; 1815: 77,812—1831: 110,914), while the increase in the amount of assessments had been, in the same period, 12½ per cent.

[1] From 'that the total number . . .' to '£3,700' in English in Tocqueville's manuscript.

[2] The last four paragraphs are likewise in English in Tocqueville's manuscript.

Journey to England (1835)

Copied from the Society's minutes, 29th June 1835.[1]

Content of surface	Estimated population	Estimated value of fixed property*	Number of assessments to poor rate
2,810 acres	118,000	£5,692,632	30,662

Annual value of fixed property as poor assessment	Number of assessments of 12 and upward	Number of assessments above 5 and under 12	Number of assessments under 5
£281,611	4,374	10,351	15,937

* This figure does not represent their real value as property is estimated at one-fifth below its real value.

The preceding table was made out in 1834 to show the value of property in the Parish of Birmingham and the poor rates charged . . .

In 1815 the population of Birmingham was 77,812 inhabitants; the poor rates came to £281,611.

Birmingham. *Wages*

Today, 29th June 1835, Mr. Smith, a manufacturer, told us that workmen's wages were continually going down, but that none-the-less the workmen were in flourishing condition because the cost of the necessities of life, bread among others, was going down even faster than wages.

Q. So landowners are in trouble?

A. Yes, the whole time.

Q. What makes you lower wages?

A. Foreign and internal competition. If wages did not go down at all, we should have little incentive to give work.

Q. But that seems to me a continuous process; the lowering of the cost of necessities seems accidental. What would happen if a bad year or general causes which one need not specify, made the cost of primary necessities go up to the level they were at before?

A. There would probably be outbreaks, the repeal of the Corn Laws, and perhaps the sale of church property.

Act of 23rd May 1828 which created the Commissioners of Streets at Birmingham; good example of a *local act*. Conception of legislation and administration in England. 29th June 1828.

[1] Tocqueville gives the following table in an appendix.

Journey to England (1835)

An act for better paving, lighting, watching, cleansing and otherwise improving the town of Birmingham and for regulating the police and market of the said town. 23rd May 1828.[1]

The law provides that all the Justices of the Peace for the county of Warwick residing less than seven miles from the town and eighty-eight other individuals, whose names are given in the act, are appointed *commissioners* for putting the act in execution.

When a vacancy occurs, they are to elect a new member.

Qualification: to be a commissioner a man must reside and be rated in the poor books at not less than £15 per annum.

The commissioners are not paid.

Before taking office the commissioners swear that they fulfil the stated conditions and anyone who swears falsely is liable to a fine of £50 imposed by one of the courts at Westminster. Any citizen can prosecute.

The commissioners will meet from time to time as arranged by themselves.

At each meeting they will elect their chairman. Their debates will be recorded in minutes signed by all the members present and these will be open to inspection by all individuals *rated* or *assessed* under this act. If the clerk refuses to show the book to someone who has the right to see it, he can be prosecuted and fined £5. The commissioners can appoint treasurers, clerks, assessors and collectors . . . and dismiss them at will.

The same individual cannot be clerk and treasurer.[2] If he accepts both positions, he can be prosecuted before the courts at Westminster and fined £100.

All the above-mentioned officials must keep accounts in specified form. If they fail to do this and money is missing, there are provisions for energetic, summary proceedings before a Justice of the Peace.

The commissioners can initiate and defend actions in the name of their clerk.

The lamps and everything to do with the lighting system belong to the commissioners who are completely free to dispose

---

[1] This paragraph is again in English in the manuscript. All dots in this note are Tocqueville's.

[2] Note by Tocqueville: We must have some rules analogous to this in France about the compatibility of officials of the Treasury. Look into that.

of them. It is their responsibility to have them put in the streets, and to establish *watch-houses* or *watch-boxes*.

If anyone damages these things, he can be tried summarily before a Justice of the Peace and ordered to pay a fine half of which goes to the prosecutor.

The commissioners have the power to have all signs, stalls . . . destroyed which might impede the circulation of traffic.

They control the placing of gutters and drains, and those disobeying their orders are to be fined.

They see to cleaning in front of houses, passages . . . with the sanction of a fine against recalcitrants.

They must see that no one roofs his house with wood or thatch; fine.

They fix the prices of cartage for the carrying and conveying of any coal, iron, ironstone, goods, wares . . . and to make orders, rules and by-laws for the better governing of such quarters under penalties.

They have power to make by-laws for licensing hackney coachmen and regulating other public carriages, under threat of fine.[1]

(The law itself here indicates a certain number of rules to be imposed on industrialists listed below.)

The by-laws must be published in the papers.

The commissioners can place horse-troughs, stop pumps being put in the public road and have those that are there taken away; stop doors from opening out on to the street.

Then the law makes provision that people must clear snow from in front of their houses. It makes rules about how public lavatories are to be emptied, but it does not seem to give the commissioners responsibility to see to the execution of these regulations; it just fixes fines. One often finds that in the law: it is as much a police code for Birmingham as a charter of incorporation for the Commissioners of Streets.

The commissioners will prosecute people who obstruct the public way, let cattle stray. . . .

They, or a surveyor appointed by them, must supervise new buildings to see that circulation in the streets does not suffer. Fine for those who will not obey.

Vehicles left in the streets at night must be lighted.

---

[1] Paragraph in English in the manuscript.

Journey to England (1835)

They must take precautions to prevent houses in ruin from endangering the life of passers-by; fine.

They will appoint watchmen or constables.

These watchmen or constables will do police duties at night, will arrest vagabonds, disorderly persons. . . .

The commissioners can order the payment of compensation to watchmen who have been wounded. . . .

They decide the lines of new streets; those who do not conform are to pay a big fine; they look after the paving.

From time to time they will fix the limits of the town.

They may widen streets and, in consequence, buy houses.

They can widen the pavements, have a *corn exchange* built, enlarge the *public office*.

One or more rates for the purpose of lighting, cleansing, watching and improving the streets shall be made, levied and assessed by the commissioners.[1] The proportion and the maximum of the tax are stipulated.

The commissioners may build a town hall, which town hall, says the law, will be used for town-meetings regularly called by the High Sheriff, and then for musical entertainments, several of which will be for the benefit of the poor; the regulations for the entertainment are more or less stated.

They can impose a tax, with stated maximum, for that object; it must only hit those who have *£15 of property*.

How these taxes are to be levied. Rules to follow.

The commissioners appoint collectors and assessors.

The commissioners may borrow to fulfil the duties imposed on them by the act, but only up to a certain sum.

All the formalities of these loans indicated.

The commissioners must publish yearly accounts.

They make by-laws for the market.

They fix market *tolls*; the act indicates many general rules to follow in this matter.

They can pave the streets and impose rates for that purpose.

In case of complaint against the rates imposed under this act: appeal to Quarter Sessions.

The last clauses state the general rules of procedure to be followed when action is taken against any defaulter under this act.

---

[1] Sentence in English in the manuscript.

Journey to England (1835)

Manchester (2nd July 1835)
Peculiar character of Manchester

The great manufacturing city for cloth, thread, cotton . . .[1] as is Birmingham for iron, copper, steel.

Favourable circumstances: ten leagues from the largest port in England, which is the best-placed port in Europe for receiving raw materials from America safely and quickly. Close by the largest coal-mines to keep the machines going cheaply. Twenty-five leagues away, the place where the best machines in the world are made. Three canals and a railway quickly carry the products all over England, and over the whole world.

The employers are helped by science, industry, the love of gain and English capital. Among the workers are men coming from a country where the needs of men are reduced almost to those of savages, and who can work for a very low wage, and so keep down the level of wages for the English workmen who wish to compete, to almost the same level. So there is the combination of the advantages of a rich and of a poor country; of an ignorant and an enlightened people; of civilisation and barbarism.

So it is not surprising that Manchester already has 300,000 inhabitants and is growing at a prodigious rate.

Other differences between Manchester and Birmingham

The police are less efficient at Manchester than at Birmingham. More complete absence of government; 60,000 Irish at Manchester (at most 5,000 at Birmingham); a crowd of small tenants huddled in the same house. At Birmingham almost all the houses are inhabited by one family only; at Manchester a part of the population lives in damp cellars, hot, stinking and unhealthy; thirteen to fifteen individuals in one. At Birmingham that is rare. At Manchester, stagnant puddles, roads paved badly or not at all. Insufficient public lavatories. All that almost unknown at Birmingham. At Manchester a few great capitalists, thousands of poor workmen and little middle class. At Birmingham, few large industries, many small industrialists. At Manchester workmen are counted by the thousand, two or three thousand in the factories. At Birmingham the workers work in their own houses or in little workshops in company with the

[1] The dots are Tocqueville's.

104

master himself. At Manchester there is above all need for women and children. At Birmingham, particularly men, few women. From the look of the inhabitants of Manchester, the working people of Birmingham seem more healthy, better off, more orderly and more moral than those of Manchester.

Exterior appearance of Manchester (*2nd July*)

An undulating plain, or rather a collection of little hills.[1] Below the hills a narrow river (the Irwell), which flows slowly to the Irish sea. Two streams (the Meddlock and the Irk) wind through the uneven ground and after a thousand bends, flow into the river. Three canals made by man[2] unite their tranquil, lazy waters at the same point. On this watery land, which nature and art have contributed to keep damp, are scattered palaces and hovels. Everything in the exterior appearance of the city attests the individual powers of man; nothing the directing power of society. At every turn human liberty shows its capricious creative force. There is no trace of the slow continuous action of government.

[1] Tocqueville has written in the margin: 60,000 Irish.
Political division: five or six townships.
Evident lack of government.
Political parties: the very rich on one side, the working classes on the other.
Poverty. Good wages *at the moment*. What must it be like at another time?
7,000 voters at the last election. A great many *ten-pounders* do not vote because they do not pay any rates. Reform candidate, majority of 1,500.
The people's fear of soldiers.
Political union: after the arrival of Lord (*sic*) Wellington, union of the rich and the poor. Impetus resulting from that.
Inability of the poor to act in isolation.
Charitable societies. *Provident Society*. Effort of the middle class to keep the direction of the lower classes and to establish links with them.
Separation of classes, much greater at Manchester than at Birmingham. Why? Large accumulations of capital, immense factories.
Three weeks' stoppage of work would bring society down in ruins. Dr. Key said that.
Report of a clergyman: a fifth of the parishioners at his church on Sunday. *According to Key:* 75,000 out of 300,000. Much higher proportion still in the lower classes than in the higher. Protestant workers stay at home on Sunday or go to the pub.
Working population absorbed in material pleasures and brutalised.
The clear lack of government one sees at Manchester. Good and bad effects resulting from this. Disorder, dirtiness, improvidence. Effort, activity, individual liberties.
Mancunian industry is growing daily.
Wages: general tendency to go down, but not now.
[2] Note by Tocqueville: Rochdale, Bridgewater, Ashton and Stockport canal.

Journey to England (1835)

Thirty or forty factories rise on the tops of the hills I have just described. Their six stories tower up; their huge enclosures give notice from afar of the centralisation of industry. The wretched dwellings of the poor are scattered haphazard around them. Round them stretches land uncultivated but without the charm of rustic nature, and still without the amenities of a town. The soil has been taken away, scratched and torn up in a thousand places, but it is not yet covered with the habitations of men. The land is given over to industry's use. The roads which connect the still-disjointed limbs of the great city, show, like the rest, every sign of hurried and unfinished work; the incidental activity of a population bent on gain, which seeks to amass gold so as to have everything else all at once, and, in the interval, mistrusts the niceties of life. Some of these roads are paved, but most of them are full of ruts and puddles into which foot or carriage wheel sinks deep. Heaps of dung, rubble from buildings, putrid, stagnant pools are found here and there among the houses and over the bumpy, pitted surfaces of the public places. No trace of surveyor's rod or spirit-level. Amid this noisome labyrinth, this great, sombre stretch of brickwork, from time to time one is astonished at the sight of fine stone buildings with Corinthian columns. It might be a medieval town with the marvels of the nineteenth century in the middle of it. But who could describe the interiors of these quarters set apart, home of vice and poverty, which surround the huge palaces of industry and clasp them in their hideous folds. On ground below the level of the river and overshadowed on every side by immense workshops, stretches marshy land which widely spaced muddy ditches can neither drain nor cleanse. Narrow, twisting roads lead down to it. They are lined with one-story houses whose ill-fitting planks and broken windows show them up, even from a distance, as the last refuge a man might find between poverty and death. None-the-less the wretched people reduced to living in them can still inspire jealousy of their fellow beings. Below some of their miserable dwellings is a row of cellars to which a sunken corridor leads. Twelve to fifteen human beings are crowded pell-mell into each of these damp, repulsive holes.[1]

[1] Note by Tocqueville in the margin: Lines of washing block the roads. A coal fire lights the hovel and fills it with a damp and stuffy heat. No chairs.

Journey to England (1835)

The fetid, muddy waters, stained with a thousand colours by the factories they pass, of one of the streams I mentioned before, wander slowly round this refuge of poverty. They are nowhere kept in place by quays; houses are built haphazard on their banks. Often from the top of their steep banks one sees an attempt at a road opening out through the debris of earth, and the foundations of some houses or the recent ruins of others. It is the Styx of this new Hades.

Look up and all around this place you will see the huge palaces of industry. You will hear the noise of furnaces, the whistle of steam. These vast structures keep air and light out of the human habitations which they dominate; they envelop them in perpetual fog; here is the slave, there the master; there the wealth of some, here the poverty of most; there the organised effort of thousands produce, to the profit of one man, what society has not yet learnt to give. Here the weakness of the individual seems more feeble and helpless even than in the middle of a wilderness; here the effects, there the causes.

A sort of black smoke covers the city. The sun seen through it is a disc without rays. Under this half daylight 300,000 human beings are ceaselessly at work. A thousand noises disturb this damp, dark labyrinth, but they are not at all the ordinary sounds one hears in great cities.

The footsteps of a *busy* crowd, the crunching wheels of machinery, the shriek of steam from boilers, the regular beat of the looms, the heavy rumble of carts, those are the noises from which you can never escape in the sombre half-light of these streets. You will never hear the clatter of hoofs as the rich man drives back home or out on expeditions of pleasure. Never the gay shouts of people amusing themselves, or music heralding a holiday. You will never see smart folk strolling at leisure in the streets, or going out on innocent pleasure parties in the surrounding country. Crowds are ever hurrying this way and that in the Manchester streets, but their footsteps are brisk, their looks preoccupied, and their appearance sombre and harsh. Day and night the city echoes with street noises. But it is heavily loaded wagons lumbering slowly. . . .[1]

From this foul drain the greatest stream of human industry flows out to fertilise the whole world. From this filthy sewer

[1] The dots are Tocqueville's.

pure gold flows. Here humanity attains its most complete development and its most brutish; here civilisation works its miracles, and civilised man is turned back almost into a savage. It is amid . . .[1]

FACTORIES (Manchester, *2nd July* 1835)

The pressures which drive men from the fields into factories seem never to have been so active as now. Commerce flourishes and agriculture is in trouble. We hear in Manchester that crowds of country folk are beginning to arrive there. Wages, low though they seem, are nevertheless an improvement on what they have been getting.

WAGES

Messrs. Connel's factory, one of the biggest Manchester spinners: 1,500 workers labouring sixty-nine hours a week.[2]

Average of wages: 11 shillings a week. These wages are enough, say Messrs. Connel, to keep an industrial worker in comfort, but, in general, the worker is improvident. On 6 shillings a week it is very difficult to live.

In this factory wages have a tendency to go down. Labour-saving devices are constantly being invented and, by increasing the competition among the workers, bring down the level of wages. Three-quarters of the workers in Messrs. Connel's factory are women or children: a system fatal for education and dangerous for the women's morals, but one which follows naturally from the fact that this work needs little physical strength, so that the work of women and children is enough and costs less than that of men.

A huge proportion of the factory's output is sent to Russia, Germany and Switzerland. A little first-quality thread goes to France since the lowering of the duty.

---

[1] Here Tocqueville's description of Manchester breaks off as his dots indicate.

[2] Note by Tocqueville: What room for the life of the spirit can a man have who works for about 12 hours a day every day except Sunday? What a need he must have for rest or lively distraction on Sunday. So in Manchester the workers stay in bed that day, or pass it at the pub. Few but the Catholics go to church. In England, Protestantism which keeps a very strong hold on the upper classes, seems to be losing its power over the lower classes. The opposite with Catholicism; easy to see the reason.

Journey to England (1835)

There is a great deal of centralisation in England; but of what sort? Legislative and not administrative; governmental rather than administrative; but as with us it sometimes extends down to very small, puerile details. The mania for *regimentation*, which is not a French mania, but one of *men* and of *power*, is found here as elsewhere. But it can only have a single, passing effect, and can only very imperfectly achieve its object.

That is because the *centralising* power is in the hands of the *legislature*, not of the *executive*.

Annoying consequences: Delays, expenses, impossibility of certain measures, impossibility of inspection.

Lucky consequences: Publicity, respect for rights, obligation to refer to local authorities for the execution of the law; natural tendency to divide administrative authority so as not to create too strong a rival power. Centralisation very incomplete since it is carried out by a legislative body; *principles* rather than *facts*; *general* in spite of a wish to be *detailed*.

Greatness and strength of England, which is explained by the power of centralisation in certain matters.

Prosperity, wealth, liberty of England, which is explained by its *weakness* in a thousand others.

Principle of *centralisation* and principle of *election of local authorities*: principles in direct opposition. *Use of fines* as administrative weapons: *agency of the tribunals*; *intervention* of *third parties*: only means of combining the two principles to some extent, since the one is essential to the power and existence of the State, the second to its prosperity and liberty. England has found no other secret. The whole future of free institutions in France depends on the application of these same ideas to the genius of our laws.

Find a means: (1) to subject the centralising power to publicity; (2) to have its *local* decisions carried out by *elected* authorities, then I see no objection to extending its power as much as you like. . . .[1]

Parliament which has a hand in everything; which has the power to waive the application of all laws: a conception which

[1] The dots are Tocqueville's.

has the utmost importance for the understanding of the political and administrative machinery of this society.

Parliament authorises individuals to break the law which makes marriage indissoluble. It authorises a company to have assessed the value of land which people do not wish to sell, a principle contrary to civil law.

Feudal powers, delegation from the central power to the boroughs, to *trustees*, to local administrations of every sort. Parliament alone having the absolute right of government, a right applicable to the whole Empire and to each part of it: only general principle. All the rest, exceptions.

Liverpool (*4th or 5th July 1835*)

Liverpool. Town destined to become the centre of English trade. A fisherman's harbour three centuries ago. A small town sixty years ago. The slave trade, basis of its commercial greatness. It carried slaves to the Spanish colonies at better prices than all the others. The foundation of the United States, the manufacturing development of Manchester and Birmingham, and the spread of English trade over the whole world, have done the rest.

Liverpool is a beautiful town. Poverty is almost as great as it is at Manchester, but it is hidden. Fifty thousand poor people live in cellars. Sixty thousand Irish Catholics.

Liverpool (*5th July 1835*)

French industry: customs-duties and prohibitions.

Conversation with M. *Laine*, French Consul at Liverpool.

Q. Is there much trade between France and Liverpool?
A. Very little to speak of. In trade one needs, above all else, exchanges. Now our tariff is so fixed that we can buy nothing from England; so they look for nothing from France.
Q. And our wines?
A. The English reduced their duties on our wines: the result was one very difficult to foresee: the consumption of wine went down rather than up. I think the reason was that the lowering of the tariff allowed horrible French wines to be introduced. The taste for French wine has always been a *fashion*. Naturally, the

Journey to England (1835)

English prefer the warm wines of the South and strong spirits. The lowering of the price and the introduction of bad French wine has almost killed that fashion.

Q. Is much of our brandy drunk?

A. Yes, quite a lot, and increasingly more.

Q. Do you think that if the English customs-duty was very substantially reduced, consumption would go up?

A. Immensely; brandy is a need of the lower classes and not a fashion of the upper ones.

Q. Do you think it would be easy to get the English to lower the duty?

A. No. I think it would be almost impossible. If brandy became commoner the consumption of beer and gin would go down in proportion. Now the making of beer and gin is closely linked to the prosperity of English agriculture, which is anyhow in difficulties. The agricultural interest still dominates national counsels, and one would never persuade them to deal themselves such a blow. If the French iron-masters, instead of arguing in favour of their monopoly, offered to give it up on condition that the English would give up the brandy duty, it is almost certain that they would not be taken at their word.

Q. What do you think the result for us would be if we lowered the duty on English iron?

A. I think it would bring great advantages. The inquiry has already done much good. It has woken French commerce up.

Many French merchants have come here to study the progress made by English industry, and to get ready to carry on the struggle. The lowering of a great number of duties would goad them on a great deal more. At present our iron-masters and manufacturers of iron are sound asleep, and let the English make such progress that soon it will be impossible for us to hope to compete with them. The French government needs steamships on the Mediterranean. It offers the French manufacturers to charge the English a duty of 33 per cent, but even with that advantage they cannot accept the order.

Probably Mr. X's yard (which we had just visited) will get the order for those ships which cost £7,000 or £8,000 each.

Q. English industry, which I had imagined to be stationary, seems to be growing fast?

A. Yes. It is undertaking ever greater developments.

111

Journey to England (1835)

Q. To what do you chiefly attribute this result? To the spirit of enterprise, to the daily improvement of processes, to the intelligence and boldness with which new outlets are found, to the advance already made? The huge capital available must make a great difference.

A. Certainly. It is recognised that the bigger the scale on which an enterprise can get started, the better its chances of success. It would be difficult to find so much capital with us, but the difficulty is made much greater by the rate of interest on our debt. What incentive is there for a man who can easily get 5 per cent on his money to go into commerce?

Q. Liverpool is growing the whole time?

A. Incredibly fast. Everything goes at a run. The railway will further speed up the rate at which London can be by-passed as a seaport. Already London deals almost only with European trade, and soon the trade of Northern Europe will pass through Liverpool, Hull and Derby. Probably in ten years Liverpool's commercial power will be greater than that of London.

Q. Is the consumption of cotton going up?

A. Immensely. It is only limited now by the production of the raw material. Almost all the cotton grown in the world comes to Europe: 200,000 bales go to France; 700,000–800,000 to England. A bad year in America would make Europe go entirely short, and suddenly send prices up. You have seen for yourself that all the South of the United States is covered with cotton-fields: it cannot be planted in America as quickly as it is consumed in Europe. Little iron ships have just been made which can go up the smallest American streams, and go to fetch the cotton everywhere where it grows.

Q. Does cotton pay customs-duties in England?

A. Very low ones, almost nothing. But it pays fairly considerable ones in France.

Q. How does the silk trade go?

A. It is decidedly increasing. Ten years ago there were only two silk factories at Manchester. Now there are twenty-two. There at least you can see that it is not free trade which has killed the industry. French competition is allowed, but in spite of it the silk industry develops rapidly.

Q. Are railways still proving profitable undertakings?

A. Yes. They go on paying 9 per cent, and you can see that

they are prospering by the great works the Company is undertaking. For instance the passenger tunnel which is going to go
under almost the whole town and arrive near the port, having
gone a mile-and-a-half underground.

Q. Have any French engineers come recently to look at the
work?

A. Not so long ago M. Navier and several others came. They
only wanted to stay three days; they visited the railway only,
and, when someone told them a fact, M. Navier, after making
some calculations, often said: 'The thing is impossible, it does
not fit at all with the theory!' Those gentlemen have not left the
English greatly impressed with their ability, at least in practical
matters.

Q. Birmingham is placed over iron- and coal-mines; Manchester in a coal-mining district and two steps from the sea;
Liverpool in the middle of all sorts of wealth. Near by is Wales
with the richest of iron-mines, so that iron, coming by sea,
reaches Liverpool, Manchester and Birmingham almost without
cost for transport. Those are immense natural advantages. Do
you not think that the unbelievable prosperity of those districts
and of England in general, should be attributed to that?

A. In my view intellectual qualities and, in general, practical
knowledge and acquired advantages play a much greater part
still.

Dublin (7th July 1835)

Administration. Administrative powers prosecuting in the
courts. Beaumont told me that he had seen in the paper yesterday
the account of proceedings against a Mr. Wood, of Manchester,
because he had employed children of under twelve years in his
factory, and had made them work more than the stipulated hours.

A few years ago Parliament passed a law forbidding the employment of children under a certain age and for more than a
certain time in factories. The same law, I believe, appointed
officers to see to its execution in the most highly industrialised
parts of the kingdom.[1] These officials prosecute those who break
the law before the ordinary courts. That gives a good example
of English administrative habits. In general, the party concerned

---

[1] Tocqueville refers here to the Factory Act of 1833.

prosecutes. But here is a question where it is unlikely that any-one would prosecute; for who is harmed by the offence? The child and his parents. But the child himself has little idea of his rights, or the use of the law, and his parents are accomplices in the offence. In that case Parliament is obliged to employ an official with the duty to prosecute. But as the central power has no officials stationed in the provinces, it has to appoint *ad hoc* agents in certain places charged with this special function. Everywhere where it has no agents a law is stillborn.

Public Administration

Administrative action by the *government* is scarcely found in any detail in England.

Almost all the public services are in the hands of small de-liberative bodies, called *trustees* or *commissioners*, created from time to time by Parliament which, at the time of their creation, appoints their members by name.[1] If after that vacancies occur, it is almost never (I think I might say *never*) the King or his agents who fill them up: it is the electoral body or, more often, the remaining members themselves. That is what is called the system of *self-elected bodies*.[2] That is the predominant system. It extends even to *corporations*.

One never hears a reference to the King in the administration.

(7th July 1835)

Why part of their commercial and manufacturing prosperity should be attributed to English political principles

Originally political power, in England as in the rest of Europe, was exclusively in the hands of the nobility properly so called. The English nobility felt in good time their need to rely on the support of the middle classes, and could not do so without giving them some political power. In this way an aristocracy of wealth was soon established and, as the world became more civilised and more opportunities of gaining wealth presented

[1] Note by Tocqueville: All this results from having administrative power in the hands of the legislature.

[2] Note by Tocqueville: This system of *self-elected bodies* seems to me a dangerous aristocratic institution.

themselves, it increased, whereas the old aristocracy, for the same reasons, continually lost ground. Fifty years ago, more or less, this was an accomplished revolution in England. Since that time birth is but an ornament of, or at most a help towards getting wealth. Money is the real power. So in England wealth has become not only an element in reputation, enjoyment and happiness; it is also an element, and one might almost say the only element, in power, a thing which, as far as I know, has never happened in any other nation, or in any other century. Wealth, with its weight immensely increased in this way, attracted every other element in man's make-up towards it and the whole spirit of humanity was, so to say, carried captive there. Wealth was given not only what is naturally due to it, but also things which are not its due. Wealth has given material enjoyment, power and also standing, esteem, intellectual pleasure. In all countries it is bad luck not to be rich. In England it is a terrible misfortune to be poor. Wealth is identified with happiness and everything that goes with happiness; poverty, or even a middling fortune, spells misfortune and all that goes with that. So all the resources of the human spirit are bent on the acquisition of wealth. In other countries men seek opulence to enjoy life; the English seek it, in some sort, to live.

Take into account the progressive force of such an urge working for several centuries on several millions of men, and you will not be surprised to find that these men have become the boldest sailors and the most skilful manufacturers in the world. For manufacture and trade are the best-known means, the quickest and the safest to become rich. Newton said that he found the world's system by thinking about it the whole time. By doing the same, the English have got hold of the trade of the whole world.

Carefully considering the greatness which the English people has now attained, I see many virtues among the causes of this greatness, but wonder if vices have not done even more.

Dublin, 7th July 1835

Liberty. Trade. Dublin (7th July)

Considering the world's history I can find some free peoples who have been neither manufacturers nor traders. But I can find no example of a manufacturing and, above all, a trading people

115

who have not been free. Take for example the Phoenicians, the Greeks, the Carthaginians, the medieval Italians, the Flemings, the Hansa towns, the Dutch, the English and the Americans of the United States. So there must be a hidden relationship between those two words: *liberty* and *trade*. People say that the spirit of trade naturally gives men the spirit of liberty. Montesquieu asserts that somewhere.[1] That is true in part. But I think it is above all the spirit and habits of liberty which inspire the spirit and habits of trade. One finds them together in the same places, just as one often sees two generations under one roof; they are not there by chance; one has produced the other and that is why we find them together.

If I had the time, I could explain why I think liberty gives birth to trade.

To be free one must have the capacity to plan and persevere in a difficult undertaking, and be accustomed to act on one's own; to live in freedom one must grow used to a life full of agitation, change and danger; to keep alert the whole time with a restless eye on everything around: that is the price of freedom. All those qualities are equally needed for success in commerce ...[2]

Looking at the turn given to the human spirit in England by political life; seeing the Englishman, certain of the support of his laws, relying on himself and unaware of any obstacle except the limit of his own powers, acting without constraint; seeing him, inspired by the sense that he can do anything, look restlessly at what now is, always in search of the best, seeing him like that, I am in no hurry to inquire whether nature has scooped out ports for him, and given him coal and iron. The reason for his commercial prosperity is not there at all: it is in himself.

Do you want to test whether a people is given to industry and commerce? Do not sound its ports, or examine the wood from its forests or the produce of its soil. The spirit of trade will get all those things and, without it, they are useless. Examine whether this people's laws give men the courage to seek prosperity, freedom to follow it up, the sense and habits to find it, and the assurance of reaping the benefit.

[1] Tocqueville refers here to Montesquieu's *Esprit des Lois*, Book XX, Chapter VII.

[2] Note by Tocqueville: Why then should one say that freedom is the mother of trade, and not trade the father of freedom? The dots are Tocqueville's.

Journey to England (1835)

Freedom is, in truth, a *sacred* thing. There is only one thing else that better deserves the name: that is virtue. But then what is virtue if not the *free* choice of what is good?

Dublin, 7th July 1835.

Freedom in the world of politics is like the air in the physical world. The earth is full of a multitude of beings differently organised; but they all live and flourish. Alter the condition of the air, and they will be in trouble. Put them where there is no air, and they will die. . . .[1]

Change your laws, vary your customs, alter your beliefs, adjust your conduct: if you bring this about so that man has full freedom to do anything that is not bad in itself, and is sure to reap in peace where he sows, you have attained your end. The end is the same, but the ways are different.

(Dublin, 7th July 1835)

[1] The dots are Tocqueville's.

IV

Journey to Ireland (1835)

Conversation between Mr. Senior and Mr. Revans[1] on 7th June 1835)[2]

Senior. To what do you chiefly attribute the poverty of Ireland?

Revans. To the system by which the landlords take advantage of the intense competition between the labourers to demand excessive rents for their farmlands. From the moment the farmer starts making a profit the landlord raises the rent. The result is that the farmer is afraid to make improvements lest the landlord should raise his rent by an amount greater than the value of the improvements, and is concerned simply to keep alive.[3]

S. Do you think that a proper Poor Law[4] would diminish this evil?

R. Yes, by diminishing the competition among the labourers, and putting the common man in a position to lay down the law to some extent to the owner of his land.

S. Is poverty here as great as it is said to be?

R. It is horrible. The people live only on potatoes and often do not have even those.

[1] Note by Tocqueville: Mr. Revans is the Secretary of the Poor Law Commission. He is a very intelligent young man who belongs to the Radical Party.

Editor's note: John Revans is the author of a pamphlet: *Advantages and Merits of a Public Provision for the Destitute in the Comparative States of England and Ireland* (London, 1836); cf. also for a review of this important publication, *The London and Westminster Review*, July 1836, pp. 332 f.

[2] This conversation took place in London, but as it is dealing with Irish problems, we have placed it here.

[3] Note by Tocqueville: This difficulty arises everywhere when the landlord and the tenant treat each other as strangers. But the situation is far worse where large landed properties are concerned.

[4] The Poor Law Amendment Act was already in force in England; since 1833 a similar law was envisaged for Ireland. To that purpose a commission of inquiry was sent to Ireland; amongst its members was William Nassau Senior, Tocqueville's friend. Cf. R. B. McDowell, *Public Opinion and Government Policy in Ireland, 1801–1846*, London 1952, pp. 191 f.

Journey to Ireland (1835)

S. Are there many children?

R. Yes, it is said that the poorest have the most children. They believe they have nothing more to fear. They marry in despair and try to forget the future.

S. What is the state of morality in Ireland?

R. That requires much explanation. . . .[1] There is not a gentler people than the Irish once the moment of anger is passed. They forget injuries easily. They are very hospitable. There is not an Irishman so poor that he would not share his last potato with someone who needed it. Crime is very rare among them except theft, which occurs almost only to keep them alive. They steal things which will immediately serve as food. This is the good side. Here is the bad one: there is no other country where it is more difficult to get the truth out of a man.[2]

S. Is party spirit very strong in Ireland?

R. To a degree almost impossible for you to imagine. It would take a foreigner ten years to understand the Parties. Party spirit pervades everything, particularly the administration of Justice in Ireland. To tell the truth, there is no justice in Ireland. Almost all the magistrates are at open war with the population. Moreover the population has no sense of public justice. In Ireland almost all justice is extra-legal. Unless Englishmen are sent to serve as judges, things will remain as they are. The jury system is almost impracticable in Ireland.

S. Why do the Irish hate us so much?

R. Mainly because we have always supported the Orangemen[3] whom they consider as their oppressors.

S. Of what is the Catholic Party composed?

R. Almost the whole nation. But there are few men of fortune or vision in this Party which has always been oppressed. That is a great misfortune.

S. Could an agriculturalist bringing substantial capital into Ireland be sure of reaping the fruits of his diligence?

R. No. The people are prey to too great wrongs, and are therefore in too great and continual a state of agitation for pro-

[1] The dots are Tocqueville's.

[2] Note by Tocqueville: This has always been the vice of the unfortunate and of slaves.

[3] The Rebellion of 1798 was put down by an alliance of government forces with protestant loyalists who in memory of William III took the name of Orangemen (Orange Lodges). The anti-Orangist traditions remain alive in Ireland to this day.

perty to be secure. This lack of security is the greatest evil in Ireland.

S. Do you not think that this inferiority in the Irish compared to the English springs from racial inferiority?

R. I do not know. But I am not inclined to believe it. In districts where the peasant's land is secure, he shows himself to be orderly and progressive.

* * *

Conversation with Mr. W. Murphy[1] (*June or July* 1835) Mr. Murphy is said to be the richest Catholic in Ireland. He is one of O'Connell's friends.

Q. At what number do you estimate those who are unemployed in Ireland although they want to work?

A. Two million.

Q. Do you think there should be a Poor Law?

A. The question seems to me so vast and so complicated that I confess I cannot make up my mind. I am afraid that a Poor Law would greatly increase the number of paupers, and the landlords would get nothing at all out of their lands.

Q. Then what do you think can be done?

A. I think, but this is only an idea of mine, that it would be a great help if some of the Irish poor could be moved on to fertile, but at present uncultivated, land.

Q. Is there much of this uncultivated but nevertheless fertile land?

A. Yes.

Q. But it is owned by somebody?

A. Yes. It forms part of vast properties acquired long ago for nothing by rich individuals. Because these people do not use this land, Parliament could take it out of their hands and pay them a certain price when the land is under cultivation.

Q. But do you think that the Irish poor could easily be uprooted and moved at will to the selected places, and that they would work profitably when they got there?

A. The majority of the Irish poor want only work and would work enthusiastically to escape from the depths of poverty in which they live. As for moving the population, nothing could be

[1] The manuscript is not dated.

easier. Such wretched people have no attachment to the place of their birth.

Q. What you have just said is the most complete proof that could possibly be given of the wretchedness of the population. It is only the last known degree of unhappiness that could force an *ignorant* and *moral* people to leave their homes. Is the lack of foresight among the Irish poor as great as it is said to be?

A. It is extreme. They marry at 16 or 18. Very often they have to borrow to pay the priest. The more intolerable their poverty becomes, the more they seem to live from hand to mouth.

Q. Do you consider that if the land were more divided up, more people could live in greater comfort in the same space?

A. It would be extremely difficult to carry out such a division, even without the existence of a law of inheritance. The farm labourers are too poor to buy land. The landowner would find no buyers if he wanted to sell in small lots; he could only hope to get a good price by selling it all.[1] At the present the land is divided between a small number of owners. The whole Irish population, so to say, consists of very small and very poor tenant-farmers, and labourers even poorer than they. It is impossible, for the present, to imagine a way of changing this state of affairs. As things are, one prefers to deal with a great landlord rather than a small one who exploits his tenants even more.

Q. So nobody cultivates a field which is his own?
A. No.

* * *

Visit to the Poorhouse and the University (*9th July 1835*)

A vast building maintained from year to year by voluntary gifts. 1,800 to 2,000 paupers are received during the day; they are given food, and, if they are capable of it, work. They go to sleep where they can.

The sight within: the most hideous and disgusting aspect of wretchedness. A very long room full of women and children whose age or infirmity prevents them from working. On the floor the poor are seated pellmell like pigs in the mud of their sty.

[1] Note by Tocqueville: This is the opposite to the situation in France. A difference that gives food for thought.

Journey to Ireland (1835)

It is difficult to avoid treading on a half-naked body. In the left wing, a smaller room full of old or disabled men. They sit on wooden benches, crowded close together and all looking in the same direction, as if in the pit of a theatre. They do not talk at all; they do not stir; they look at nothing; they do not appear to be thinking. They neither expect, fear, nor hope anything from life. I am mistaken; they are waiting for supper which is due in three hours. It is the only pleasure that remains to them; apart from that they would have nothing to do but to die.

Further on are those who are able to work. They are seated on the damp earth. They have small mallets in their hands and are breaking stones. They receive a penny at the end of the day. They are the fortunate ones.

On leaving there we came across a small covered barrow pushed by two paupers. This barrow was going to the doors of the houses of the rich. They throw the leftovers of their meals into the barrow and these debris are taken to the Poorhouse to make the soup.

From the Poorhouse they took us to the University. An immense, magnificent garden kept up like that of a nobleman. A granite palace; superb church; admirable library. Liveried lackeys; twenty-four fellows. . . .[1] Enormous revenues. Men of all religions receive education there. But only members of the Church of England can administer the establishment and benefit from its revenues.

The University was founded by Elizabeth I on land confiscated from the Catholics, the fathers of those whom we had seen sprawling in the filth of the Poorhouse. The University provides for 1,500 students. Few belong to rich Irish families. Not only does the Irish nobility live away from their homeland; not only do they spend abroad the money their country earns; they have their children educated in England, no doubt for fear that a vague instinct of patriotism and youthful memories might one day attract them to Ireland.

If you want to know what can be done by the spirit of conquest and religious hatred combined with the abuses of aristocracy, but without any of its advantages, go to Ireland.

*   *   *

[1] A blank in the manuscript.

Journey to Ireland (1835)

Mr. Kelly is a very intelligent Irish lawyer who has been appointed Director General of National Schools by the Government. Mr. Wilson, an Anglican clergyman (clearly one of the most moderate of his order) was present at this interview and what follows represents the opinions of both these men.

Q. Is it true that there are no small landowners in Ireland?

A. I do not think that there is a single one.

Q. However all real estate is not entailed, and your entails, as in England, are not perpetual.

A. It often happens that land is sold, but then it is sold in large lots. The landowner changes occasionally, but the land is never divided. The idea of buying a small piece of land never comes into anybody's head, still less the idea of selling a plot. Besides, our law of property makes the transfer of land very difficult and expensive.

Q. Is it true that the land is split into very small farms?

A. Yes, the system of small farms is universal.

Q. What are the causes of this state of things which is contrary to the interests of agriculture and the well-being of the people?

A. There are several causes. The first is the poverty of those who wish to become tenant-farmers. To exploit a large farm one needs capital, and there is no Irish peasant who has any. The second is purely political. For a long time the minimum property qualification required to become an elector had been fixed very low, and the tenant-elector has always voted according to his landlord's interests. The landowner therefore gained a great political advantage by dividing up his land into as many small farms as possible, in order to increase the number of electors voting in his interest.

Q. But the increase of the property qualification to £10,[1] by diminishing the number of electors, and the hostile spirit existing between tenants and landlords should eliminate the second cause?

[1] In April 1829 the Catholic Emancipation Act, which allowed Roman Catholics to sit in Parliament, had been passed. At the same time the forty shilling freeholders were disfranchised and the qualification for the franchise was fixed at £10 a year. Daniel O'Connell ('The Liberator') had won the County Clare election in 1828 by organising the freeholders' vote, although he could not then take his seat. O'Connell continued to secure election despite the restriction of the franchise.

Journey to Ireland (1835)

A. It has also led to the following results; since the change in the electoral laws and the Emancipation Bill, the landowners have busied themselves in destroying the excessively small farms and making larger ones out of them. With this in view they have evicted all the small farmers who were in arrears with their rent, as almost all of them were. This rapid eviction of a large proportion of small cultivators has strikingly increased poverty recently.

Q. Is it true that the Irish landlords exploit the agricultural population to the extent of almost taking away their means of livelihood?

A. Yes. Here we have all the evils of an aristocracy and none of its advantages. There is no moral tie between rich and poor; the difference of political opinion and of religious belief and the actual distance that they live apart, make them strangers one to the other, one could almost say enemies. The rich landlords extract from their land all that it can yield; they profit from the competition caused by poverty; and when they have amassed immense sums of money, they go and spend them abroad.

Q. Why is the whole working population drawn to agriculture, which increases competition to such an extreme extent?

A. Because there are so very few industrial undertakings, and that is for lack of capital and enterprise. Capital and enterprise are lacking because the wealth and superior culture of our English neighbours attract it all. Dublin once had a flourishing cotton trade. Manchester has killed this business.

A. The yields are immense. There is no country where the price of farms is higher. But none of this money remains in the hands of the people. The Irishman cultivates beautiful crops and takes his harvest to the nearest port, and puts it on an English ship; then he goes home and eats potatoes. He rears cattle, sends them to London and never eats meat.

Q. Do you think that a Poor Law would be a good thing for Ireland?

A. I think it would.

Q. But do you not think that this is a dangerous remedy?

A. Yes, but Ireland is in such an exceptional situation that one cannot apply universal theories to it. A way of making the landowners spend a part of their money inside the country must be found. Do you know any other solution?

Journey to Ireland (1835)

Q. Lately there has been talk of demanding the Repeal of the Union. Is this still in question?

A. The question is dormant; O'Connell raised it;[1] then other matters took up his attention; there the matter rests.

Q. What do you think about it?

A. I believe that the English would never consent to Repeal of the Union and that there would be no chance of obtaining it short of armed force.

Q. But, if it could be done peacefully, would you consider it desirable?

A. No. When we had an Irish Parliament, England would in a way regard us as a foreign power and a rival. Her jealousy being roused, and she being rich and powerful, she would make us feel her superiority much more harshly than now when she regards us as part of herself. When we had an Irish Parliament, the two races which divide this island were always face to face, party spirit was more active, and the tyranny of the strongest party (the Orangemen) was intolerable. The laws of that period are detestable.

Q. Do you not think that in our times things have changed? Today the Catholic Party, so long suppressed, would at once dominate Parliament?

A. That would be a complete revolution. A tyranny of another sort, but no less great.

Q. Do you consider that England could hope to remain united with Ireland, if the Irish Parliament were established anew?

A. No. I am sure that the certain consequence of such a measure would be the separation of Ireland. And, taking everything into consideration, I believe that the union of England and Ireland is necessary for the latter and will in time become very profitable, if the English Government, as all signs indicate, continues to take trouble about this country and to put itself in the position of a mediator between the two parties.

* * *

[1] In 1834 O'Connell brought the question of Repeal before the House of Commons, but he gained the vote of only one English member. His agitation at this stage failed completely.

Journey to Ireland (1835)

Mr. Kelly. Government

The Kingdom is divided into parishes and counties like England. Administration is local here, as there. In fact the administrative laws are almost the same, and if their effect is different, this would appear to arise from the state of civilisation, the temper of the population and particular political circumstances, rather than from the nature of the laws themselves.

The Lord Lieutenant represents the King. He is the head of the armed forces. He has the right to grant pardons; he holds court; but he does not take part, I believe, in the administration, except for the nomination of the Lord Lieutenants of the counties, who, I believe, nominate the Justices of the Peace. His influence is rather indirect. The political tendency, from what Mr. Kelly and Mr. Wilson have told us, is to leave the Lord Lieutenant only the appearance of authority and to concentrate the real power in the hands of the Minister in London. This tendency is natural and shows itself in many other things.

*   *   *

Schools. Education (11th July 1835)

This morning we lunched with two Anglican clergymen, Mr. Smith and Mr. Todd, who told us much in criticism of the National Schools.[1] They held that when the clergy of the Anglican Church in some sense had a monopoly of primary education, because the annual grant from Parliament was placed in their hands or in those of a lay society entirely under their influence, there were more Catholic and Protestant children in the same schools and more hope of union between the two populations, than under the aegis of the present legislation whose aim is to unite the two populations in the same schools. This is quite true, as we shall see. But I shall not draw the same conclusion as the reverend gentlemen.

The same day I went to dine with Mr. Kelly, the Inspector General of National Schools. I asked him to explain their history to me. What he said follows, and I find it probable:

Until 1824 the Irish Catholic population seemed to be in a deep slumber. It submitted to its fate. At that time a large

[1] A system of national schools had been instituted in 1831 by Lord Stanley.

126

number of Catholic children went to the schools of the Established Church. The teachers in these schools did not try at all to influence their beliefs, at least the parents did not fear this. About 1824 the Catholic population began to agitate. It claimed its political rights; animosities became violent on either side. The clergymen of the Established Church wished to make proselytes; the children's parents became frightened. As the Catholic question came to the fore, and as the rights of the Catholic population were recognised in England, the situation became worse. Everyone thought it more and more unfair that Parliament only lent its support to a type of education that could not do otherwise than arouse the suspicions of a great majority of the inhabitants of the country and particularly of the poorer classes for whom it was intended. In 1832 (I think) Parliament itself was of this opinion, and its grant was transferred to the new schools which the Minister had set up in the meanwhile.[1] The schools were founded on the following plan:

A directing body was founded in Dublin:

This body was composed from two members of the Catholic clergy, two from the Established Church and two from the *Dissenters*. For details see the official report. Mr. Kelly then gave us many practical details from which it seemed to result that:

(1) The number of schools and pupils was rapidly increasing.

(2) The English refused to lend themselves to this system of schooling.

(3) The Dissenters only took part when the number of their children was large enough to enable them to form a school all on their own.

(4) That the Catholics alone embraced the idea eagerly, zealously helped in its execution and drew great profit from it. Thus, as nearly always happens when a weak government tries to proceed impartially between factions, after taking a stand on neutral ground, it is, in spite of itself, drawn into the current of one party.

To sum up; for the present the aim of the measure has not been attained. If it had only been wished to encourage education in general, it would have been enough to have given each of the

[1] Note by Tocqueville: Thus the National Schools are not yet established by law. They only exist by virtue of the Minister's wish annually approved by Parliament.

127

sects aid in proportion to their needs. But it was wished to found schools that belonged to no sect and which brought together the members of all. But up till now it seems that the members of only one sect have attended them.

Mr. Kelly. Roads in Ireland (11th July 1835)

Mr. Kelly explained to me the present road system in Ireland in this way.

Q. Have you turnpike roads ?[1]

A. We have a certain number, but most of our roads are not toll ones at all.

Q. How are the latter maintained ?

A. Every year the Sheriff of the county chooses from the great landlords 24 who are Grand Jurors (English system); these 24 persons, or more than 12 out of their number, gather together twice a year (I think) and after deciding what roads should be opened or repaired in the county, fix the increase in tax which is to be paid by the inhabitants. This tax can only be levied when the Judge of Assizes has *ordinanced* the expenditure.

Q. Are the roads, so built and maintained, good ?

A. For a long time they were very bad. Now most of them are good.

Q. Is this change due to legislation or to accidental causes ?

A. Our roads were bad and they became good under the rule of the same laws.

Q. To what do you attribute the change ?

A. To public opinion which turned its attention to this question and gave a new impulse to the Grand Juries.

Q. You said a part of your roads are turnpikes. How can you combine the two systems ?

A. We find no difficulty in doing so. When it is found that a stretch of road is sufficiently used easily to pay for its upkeep, we ask Parliament to discharge the county of the expense by setting up a turnpike. Almost all the roads in Ireland which are very much used, are organised in this manner.

Q. Do you entrust the supervision of this work to a body of

---

[1] This fragment was certainly suggested by the Highway Bill which became law in 1835. The problem was equally urgent for Ireland.

trustees nominated by Parliament, who thereafter fill up any vacancies themselves?

A. Yes, and we have found, as I believe they have found in England, that these trustees who account to nobody for their actions, are sometimes the occasion of great abuses.

Q. Who, in general, are *trustees*?

A. Landlords of land near the road. They receive no emolument, but they very willingly undertake these functions which occupy their leisure and give them a certain importance in the district. When I spoke earlier of the abuses which result from the present system of trustees, I in no way suggest that these are accused of putting the money for the roads in their own pockets, but there are indirect misappropriations such as sinecures to oblige some individual; certain work given to one person rather than another although he will not do it as cheaply. . . .[1]

* * *

Kingstown Races (*11th July 1835*)

Entertainment given in honour of the Lord Lieutenant and Lady Mulgrave by the railway company. The Vice-Roy treated with full royal formality. A great luncheon is given in his honour at Kingstown. Clearly a large proportion of the company are Irishmen who are not Orangemen. The toast to 'the Resident Nobleman' is received with acclamation. A peculiar toast which cannot be understood until one has lived for some time in this country.

* * *

Appearance of the country between Dublin and Carlow

Pretty country. Very fertile soil. Beautiful road. Tollgates far apart. Here and there very beautiful parks, and rather beautiful Catholic churches. Most of the dwellings in the country seem very poor; a large number of them wretched to the last degree. Mud walls; thatched roofs; one room; no chimney; smoke comes out of the door. A pig lies in the middle of the room. It is Sunday, but the population looks very wretched. Most of them

---

[1] The dots are Tocqueville's.

are dressed in clothes with holes or very much patched. Most of them are bare-foot and bare-headed.

19th July 1835

* * *

Dinner with the Bishop of Carlow (*20th July 1835*)

An archbishop was there, four bishops and several priests. All these gentlemen carried themselves very well. The meal was decently but unostentatiously served. The dinner was good but not elaborate. These ecclesiastics drank very little. They all appeared to be gentlemen.

The conversation turned on the state of the country and politics. The feelings expressed were extremely democratic. Distrust and hatred of the great landlords; love of the people, and confidence in them. Bitter memories of past oppression. An air of exaltation at present or approaching victory. A profound hatred of the Protestants and above all of their clergy. Little impartiality apparent. Clearly as much the leaders of a Party as the representatives of the Church.

* * *

Conversation with Mgr. Nolan, Bishop of Carlow (*20th July 1835. Carlow*)

He is a middle-aged man who expresses himself with spirit and style.

It is above all important to consider this conversation (as all others) as indicating the state of feelings rather than the bare truth.

Q. Is the land divided up in Carlow county?

A. No, no more so than in the rest of Ireland. The county practically belongs to two families, and these two families are not among the richest in Ireland. In the neighbouring counties, the Duke of Leinster for example has a rent-roll of £70,000.

Q. Are there many 'middlemen' in county Carlow? That is to say men who take a lease of some of the land of the great landowners of whom you spoke, to sublet it to other people?

A. Yes. The two great families I mentioned have given very

130

long leases of most of their land. The original tenants who are themselves very rich people, have let the land to others, and they in their turn to yet others.[1] In the county of Carlow most of the land has to serve the needs of four classes of people. You can no doubt believe that the fourth is poverty-stricken.

Q. Is there a great rift between the people and the landlords?

A. A great rift which seems to be increasing rather than decreasing. Since the last election when the Catholic candidate won, the two families of which I spoke introduced a new system of cultivation. They have evicted all their small farmers. One alone evicted 150 families. They enlarged their farms and put in Protestant farmers. They have done so in most counties. The enlargement of farms is a great evil. It diminishes the number of hands needed on the land, and, as the great majority of the Irish population has no other outlet but the land, it causes frightful poverty.

Q. Then, according to you, poverty is increasing?

A. Without a doubt. The population is rapidly increasing, and means of employing it are diminishing. It is a terrible state of society. I, for my part, regard the enactment of Poor Laws as indispensable. The link which should unite the high and low classes is destroyed; the latter have nothing to expect from the former unless the law comes to their aid.

Q. What, in your opinion, is the morality of the poor?

A. They have many good qualities mixed with the faults which poverty brings. They are gentle, polite and hospitable. English people would not stand for a week the poverty in which they are obliged to live. But when the chance of a drunken orgy offers, they do not know how to resist it. They become turbulent and often violent and disorderly. Theft is very rare among them. Their morals, in the narrow sense of the word, are very chaste. Acts of violence are rather frequent, but they all arise from drunkenness or political passions.

Q. Have you in this county many 'whiteboys'[2] or 'whitefeet' as they generally call themselves now?

[1] Note by Tocqueville: Clear advantage here of laws which divide up property.

[2] The White-boy movement originated during the second half of the eighteenth century. It was a movement of agrarian protest against too high land rents and tithes. Several acts of Parliament were voted against the movement which, however, broke out again and again. Cf. E. Curtis, *A History of Ireland*, London 1945, pp. 306 sq.

A. Few in this county. Many two years ago in the surrounding counties. I remember that at that time Mr. X (I forgot his name), a local priest discovered a gang of whitefeet. He went to meet them and reproached them severely. Their leader, who was an educated man, replied almost word for word as follows: 'The law does nothing for us. We must save ourselves. We have a little land which we need for ourselves and our families to live on, and they drive us out of it. To whom should we address ourselves? We ask for work at eightpence a day and we are refused. To whom should we address ourselves? Emancipation has done nothing for us. Mr. O'Connell and the rich Catholics go to Parliament. We die of starvation just the same.'

Two years ago I went to a prison to visit a man who had killed the agent of a rich landowner. This agent wanted to change the method of cultivation and to this end he evicted the small farmers and destroyed their houses. One of them had a sick wife and asked for a respite. The agent had the sick woman brought out into the open air and destroyed her house before her very eyes. A few days later he was murdered by the man who was speaking to me, and who was not in any way personally interested in the action of which I told you, but did it in vengeance for that deed. These crimes are ghastly. But what a horrible state of society.

Q. Do you think that the Irish Catholic clergy should receive an allowance from the English government?

A. No. The Catholic clergy would then lose their influence over the people. I do not know what is suitable for other countries, but I do not doubt that in Ireland the clergy would lose a great deal by the change, and that religion itself might suffer. Clergy and people in this country are unbelievably united.

* * *

Carlow (*20th July 1835*)

Conversation with Mr. Fitzgerald, the President of the Catholic College at Carlow. Mr. F. is a lovable old man; democratic and Catholic fervour is shown more openly with him than with the Bishop.

Q. Are the ills suffered by the people very great?

A. Terrible. You can see it for yourself. The people is treated as a conquered one by the landowners, and in fact those later occupy lands confiscated from the same Catholics who are dying of hunger. The upper classes are to blame for all the ills of Ireland.

Q. Is it true that the rift between upper and lower classes is increasing?

A. Yes. As long as the upper classes saw the Catholics as slaves submitting with resignation to their fate, they did not treat them violently. But since political rights have been granted to the Catholic population and they wish to use them, they have persecuted them as much as they can and try to drive them out of their land to put Protestant farmers in their place.

Q. Is it true that the population has not the slightest confidence in justice?

A. Not the slightest. The poor believe themselves to be somehow outside the law.

Q. Is the clergy as united as I am told with the people?

A. Intimately so. It should be the same in all countries. When I was in France ten years ago, I saw the absurd way in which the French clergy tried to influence the people. I felt no doubt that another revolution was near. The French priests struck me as far from enlightened and far from wise. Their plantation of missionary crosses, among other things, struck me as a great folly in the interests of religion.

Q. Would you like a grant of money from the State?

A. No, certainly not. In general we are opposed to any link between Church and State.

Q. How do you choose your bishops?

A. When there is a vacancy, the parish priests of the diocese assemble. They nominate three candidates between whom the Pope chooses. Generally he chooses the first.

Q. From which class do your priests generally come?

A. From the tenant class.

Q. How much does a priest receive?

A. About £300.

Q. And the bishoprics?

A. The best paid £1,000. The worst paid, like that of Carlow, £500.

Q. How do the ecclesiastics get paid?

A. Most of their activities as ministers are paid; furthermore there is a collection for them once a year.

Q. And the bishops?

A. A Bishop's salary consists in the revenue of a parish priest and in addition a certain sum with which each priest is bound to provide him.

Q. Do the poor contribute proportionately more than the rich?

A. Yes. I think so.

Q. What was the cost of your cathedral in Carlow, which seems to me quite new?

A. £30,000. This money was raised all over Ireland.

Q. The college over which you preside, which has 180 students both lay and clerical, is entirely supported by voluntary contributions?

A. Entirely.

Q. Are there many rich Catholics?

A. Many have considerable fortunes in personal property. But nearly all land is in the hands of the Protestants.

Q. Is the rift between Catholics and Protestants so great as to harm social intercourse?

A. The Catholics and Protestants of Carlow avoid seeing and speaking to each other. The inn where you lodge is kept by Protestants. I am sure that when they saw me coming in to visit you, they were extremely surprised.

Q. Your age enables you to make comparisons. Do you think the poverty of the population is increasing or decreasing?

A. I think that it is increasing.

Q. You have lived in the times of oppression. Was it great?

A. Terrible. Would you believe, sir, that in my youth a Catholic could not become a schoolmaster? Children had either to be left untaught or sent to a Protestant school.

Q. Does the population now show enthusiasm for education?

A. Yes, great enthusiasm. There are parents who beg so that their children can go to school. But this is a recent occurrence. The rising generation will be infinitely better educated than the present one.

Q. Do the people pay tithes?[1]

[1] The obligation to pay tithes had been a grievance for a long time, for it contributed substantially towards the upkeep of the clergy of the Anglican Church

Journey to Ireland (1835)

A. No, they have stopped paying them, and will never pay them now. If responsibility for the tithe is taken off the tenant and put on the landlord, and should he, as a result of this new arrangement, try to increase the rent, I am sure that the poor will resist just the same, for their attention has been focused on this matter. Is it not revolting that the Protestant clergy, who do hardly anything for the people, should enrich itself at their expense, and employ for its own ends the tithe which was established not only to provide for the needs of the priest, but also for those of the poor and for public education?

* * *

The Irish aristocracy judged by itself and by all parties

I have met no man in Ireland, to whatever party he belonged, who did not acknowledge with a greater or less degree of bitterness that the aristocracy governed the country very badly. The English say it openly; the Orangemen do not deny it; the Catholics shout it out at the top of their voices.

I find that the language of the aristocracy proves it more than all the rest.

All the rich Protestants whom I saw in Dublin, speak of the Catholics with extraordinary hatred and scorn. The latter, they say, are savages, incapable of recognising a kindness, and fanatics led into all sorts of disorder by their priest.

Now these same people who speak thus are those who once controlled the government of the country and who still control part of it. How can people moved by such feelings and imbued with such opinions (rightly or wrongly, I do not know) treat those of whom they speak like that, with gentleness, with trust or even with justice? (*Carlow, 20th July* 1835)

* * *

to which the greater number of people did not belong. During the agrarian agitation of the 1830's, payment of tithe was refused in a great number of places. Peel proposed to change the tithes into rent and to reduce the sum. These proposals were finally adopted in 1838. Cf. R. B. McDowell, *Public Opinion and Government Policy in Ireland, 1801–1846,* London 1952.

Journey to Ireland (1835)

Carlow. Irish Clergy (20th July 1835)

There is an unbelievable unity between the Irish clergy and the Catholic population. The reason for that is not only that the clergy are paid by the people, but also because all the upper classes are Protestants and enemies.

The clergy, rebuffed by high society, has turned all its attention to the lower classes; it has the same instincts, the same interests and the same passions as the people; state of affairs altogether peculiar to Ireland, a point which one should keep well in mind in speaking of the advantages of voluntary remuneration.

In the streets of Carlow I noticed that the people saluted all the priests who passed, very respectfully. . . .[1]

I dined today with an archbishop, four bishops and several Irish parish priests. They unanimously agreed that it was important at all costs to avoid being paid by the Government. They admitted however that there were some individual priests who would like nothing better.

Schools (Carlow, 20th July 1835)

The national school for girls at Carlow is in a convent and is conducted by nuns. The Catholic priests seem very pleased with these schools, a further proof that it is only the Catholic party which takes advantage of them.

Carlow (21st July 1835)

The enthusiasm of the Catholic population for learning. This is a new development attested by the Archbishop of Munster and the President of the College.

* * *

Journey from Carlow to Waterford. General appearance of the country (21st July 1835)

We went on to county Kilkenny. From Carlow to Thomastown the look of things seemed a little less wretched. Almost all the houses had got chimneys. Some seemed new and built to a

[1] The dots are Tocqueville's.

slightly better plan. Sometimes the pig had a sty to itself.
Fewer bare-headed and bare-foot people than in the neighbourhood of Dublin. From Thomastown to Waterford the look of
the country again became very wretched; many houses in ruins.

From Carlow to Waterford, undulating country, quite high
hills and extensive views. No woods and hardly any hedges.
Fields surrounded by stone walls which give them a sad appearance. Few villages but many scattered huts. No churches. Near
to Thomastown, the ruins of a convent. The ground remains
consecrated in the eyes of the inhabitants, for round these ruined
walls they bury their dead: a touching illustration of the attachment of this poor population to their beliefs. No manufacture.
No passable dwellings. We travelled along the sides of two or
three very well-kept and magnificent parks. All the rest merely
tells of the life of the poor. In the villages, no small tradesmen—
but such as there were, were almost as poor as the peasants themselves. No sign of work except on the land. Farm labourers in
rags. There is an upper class and a lower class. The middle
class evidently does not exist, or else is confined to the towns as
in the middle ages. In Thomastown I asked my host what is the
average price of leases in the neighbourhood. He replied £4
per acre. He complained of the poverty of the inhabitants and
the harshness of the landlords who strip the people to extract
immense profits. I ask him if there are still any whiteboys or
whitefeet. He replies that there are not and that the country is
very tranquil now. In a village between Thomastown and
Waterford, I ask a peasant what is the usual rent of farmland;
he answers £2. I remarked on the poverty of the inhabitants
and the repulsive appearance of the houses. Smiling, he replied
that it is the same everywhere in Ireland. I ask him if there are
big landlords in the district. He answers that there are several,
but like all the others they live in England where they spend
their country's money. I ask him if there is not a way of forcing
them to stay in the country. Answer: by taxing the *absentees*.

Q. Is there a Catholic church?
A. Yes. A mile away. The parish is very large; one parish
priest and two curates.
Q. How many Protestants are there in the parish?
A. Three.
Q. Where is the Protestant clergyman?

Journey to Ireland (1835)

A. He lives in Waterford.

Q. Do they still pay tithes?

A. No. They stopped paying it three years ago.

Q. What did the tithe amount to?

A. Ten shillings for an acre of wheat or potatoes; eight shillings for an acre of barley. Meadows exempt.

* * *

Persecutions

Mr. Plunkett,[1] a Dublin lawyer, said to me today (22nd July 1835): 'It is only since 1792 that Catholics could own land. Before that time the law prevented it. One should not therefore be the least surprised that the Irish population is excluded from the land and that the land is so little divided.'

Waterford

* * *

Waterford County Assizes (22nd and 23rd July 1835)

Sixteen murder cases. All these affairs turned out to be manslaughter or homicide by negligence. But in all of them, I believe, men had been killed. These Assizes gave us the strong impression that the lower classes in this county are very prone to quarrels and fights, and that almost every village forms a kind of faction with a code name. Factions which started nobody knows when, and which continue nobody knows why, and which take on no political colour. When men of different factions meet, at a fair, a wedding or elsewhere, it is exceptional if they do not come to blows just for the love of fighting. These quarrels very often end in someone getting killed; generally speaking, human life seems of little value here. I base myself on what we have seen ourselves and also on all we hear.

In a civil case heard by the same court, a 'gentleman' was accused of striking another with a cane. The latter cited him before the court and, to excuse this *legal* way of acting against accepted prejudices, his lawyer said, 'What would happen, gentlemen, if *the state of barbarism and violence in which the lower*

[1] Spelling uncertain.

138

classes in this country unfortunately live, were to spread to the higher classes? If men of the upper classes resorted to physical force at every turn like the people, would not civilisation soon disappear from this country?' This was clearly everybody's opinion.[1] Most of the accused and the . . .[2]

[The jurors are called and take the oath. The first witness is called at once. (The others remain present in court.) The Prosecutor for the Crown examines the witness. Counsel for the defence undertakes the 'cross examination'. If the Judge thinks that a question being asked by one or the other is 'improper', he stops it being asked. After the witnesses have been heard, the Judge, who has taken notes, makes his summing-up in which he often openly shows the jury what he thinks. Then the jury retire. They give their verdict. If the accused is found guilty, the Judge immediately pronounces sentence, or acquits if innocent. Throughout the entire hearing the accused looks like a spectator. He says nothing; he is asked nothing. He speaks if he wishes to, but nobody asks him to speak.

My general impression is that English procedure is much more expeditious than ours; that it often excludes incriminating evidence; that the system of 'examination and cross examination' is better than ours for petty cases; that the position of the accused would be infinitely better than in France, if there were not under the Judge's robes an English Protestant, and if religious and political fervour did not often do violence to the impartiality of the Judge. . . .]

At Waterford Assizes the Crown counsel was a Dublin lawyer who followed the circuit. Although momentarily fulfilling the functions of a public attorney, he had not lost his character as a barrister. Having conducted a criminal case against the accused, he changed places and argued a civil case before the same judge. He even went so far, drawn on by an advocate's zeal, as to be surprised that his client's adversary did not have recourse to arms rather than appeal to a court of law. What made this even more surprising in his mouth was that five minutes before he had been prosecuting five or six peasants

[1] Note by Tocqueville: This disposition of the Irish to quarrels and violence is so widespread that the law regards these failings in a more unfavourable light than in England, and shows far less tolerance to unintentional homicide.

[2] A page of Tocqueville's manuscript is missing. So here we print, between square brackets, the text from Beaumont's edition.

for behaving in the way he now seemed to think it right to behave. This 'inconsistency' was noted by the judge and counsel for the other side . . .[1]

The jury did not change except when jurors were challenged. Otherwise the first jurors chosen handled the whole day's cases, which saved much time. . . .[1]

All the functions of the two courts of justice comprising the circuit were carried out with a rapidity unknown in France. Administrative arrangements and civil and criminal cases were interspersed so as not to lose a moment. The grand jury is in session at the same time as the courts and *functions* as quickly as they do. The same man is often accused by the grand jury, found guilty by the petty, and condemned by the judge in the space of an hour. . . .[1]

The Prosecutor for the Crown told us: 'A multitude of criminal cases in the south of Ireland spring from the desire to possess land. In this part of Ireland there is no manufacturing, no industry; the people have only the land to live off and, since they are ever accustomed to live on the minimum from which a man can subsist, when a man comes to have no land he really faces death. That is why evictions give rise to these implacable hatreds and numberless acts of violence.'

* * *

Political Condition. Conversation with Mgr. Kinsley, Bishop of Kilkenny (24th July 1835)

Mgr. Kinsley is a likeable man, very witty and perspicacious, and has enough sense to be impartial (as far as an Irishman can be) and finds pleasure in showing it. In everything he says there is a note of triumph, which shows that he is the leader of a party which has attained power after long oppression. I think him very sincere in his belief that the Church should not be part of the State, but wonder whether he does not think, at bottom, that the State would do well enough as part of the Church. These are nuances, perhaps I am mistaken.

Q. I have often heard it said in England and even in Ireland that the Catholic population is half-savage. That is probably false?

---

[1] The dots are Tocqueville's.

Journey to Ireland (1835)

A. I must admit that it is in part true. But whose fault is it,
if not theirs who have reduced them to this state by bad government? What became of the Greeks under the Turks? Before
1792 we could have no schools, we could not be called to the
bar, the magistracy was closed to us, we could not possess
land. . . . [1]Examine the laws of that time; you will be startled.
Now I confess that the people has some of the characteristics
and, unfortunately, some of the defects of savage people. This
people has all the virtues dear to God; it has faith; there is no
better Christian than the Irishman. Their morals are pure;
premeditated crime is very rare. But they basically lack the civil
virtues. They have no foresight or prudence. Their courage is
instinctive; they throw themselves at an obstacle with extraordinary violence and, if they do not succeed at the first attempt,
give it up. The Irishman is unstable and loves excitement and
fighting. The Englishman, on the contrary, coldly calculates
chances, approaches danger slowly, but does not withdraw
until he succeeds. I knew an English General who had long
commanded an Irish brigade. He said to me: 'I could train my
soldiers to do anything, except be masters of themselves.'

Q. Is the memory of the confiscations still alive?

A. Yes, as a vague instinct of hate against the conquerors.
There are many places where families are known to have been
dispossessed. The family of Mr. Fitzgerald whom you saw in
Carlow, possessed the great estates through which you passed
this morning, and which are now in the hands of Mr. X. There
is a family of labourers in this county who owned the immense
properties of the Ormonde family. But the direct line has been
broken and nobody any longer dreams of establishing their rights.

Q. What, in your opinion, is the chief cause of this country's
poverty?

A. A too numerous population. It is certain that the land
divided up, or rather undivided, as it now is in Ireland, cannot
provide a constant source of employment for our population. I
think that the effects of absenteeism have been exaggerated. It
does harm, but I see it chiefly as a vexatious sign of the aliena-
tion between the classes.

Q. Do you think that a Poor Law is necessary?

A. Yes, I believe so without any hesitation. It would have

[1] The dots are Tocqueville's.

this result among other things: today not only is there a shortage of land, but much arable has been turned into grassland. So where there were once 150 labourers, ten shepherds are enough. If there were a land tax, the owner of this grassland would find that he would make very little by using it like this. For if the land makes a better return that way, and if the owner were compelled by the Poor Law to give all or part of his surplus to those whom he prevents from earning a living, he would put his grassland back into wheat, or at least he would not turn the land growing wheat into grassland.

Q. It is said that in Ireland there are large tracts of land which are not at present cultivated, but which could be cultivated.

A. Yes. But up to the present farmers have been little disposed to work on a clearing, for hardly would the land be under cultivation before the tithe collector and the State tax collector would appear.

Q. You have told me that morals were chaste?

A. Yes, extremely chaste. Twenty years of confession have taught me that for a girl to fall is very rare, and for a married woman practically unknown. Public opinion, one might almost say, has gone too far in this direction. A woman *suspected* is lost for her whole life. I am sure that there are not twenty illegitimate children a year among the Catholic population of Kilkenny which numbers 26,000. Suicide is most rare. Hardly ever in town, still less in the country, does a Catholic fail to make his Easter communion. I say again that they have the virtues dear to God, but they are ignorant, violent, intemperate and as incapable of resisting the first impulse as savages.

Q. Do the Catholics of the upper classes have the same beliefs as the people?

A. Yes. Real unbelief is only to be found among some Protestants.

Q. Is it true that the Protestant aristocracy is very much in debt?

A. Yes. Nothing is more true. Most of them give way under the burden of their commitments. Every day we see the rich Catholics of the towns lend money to Protestants, and the latter finally are obliged to break the 'entail' and to sell their land. In this way much land gradually falls into the hands of the Catholics. Recently in this county two Catholics, Mr. X and

Mr. Y, bought land, the one for £20,000 and the other for £30,000.

Q. If the Catholics have a certain number of rich men among them, why do they not send more distinguished people to Parliament?

A. The Catholic aristocracy has only just come into existence. Furthermore it must be confessed that the unstable spirit of our people shows itself in elections as elsewhere. In the first place they chose the most capable men; afterwards they were replaced by less capable ones. Perhaps, just because of his great talents, Mr. O'Connell is an obstacle. He himself alone represents the whole Party.

Q. Is it true that there are village and family vendettas which often lead to violence?

A. Formerly there were infinitely more than at present. But they still often occur. The Government has long noted these differences without distress, for it feared our union against itself.

Q. Was the Government more tyrannical under the Irish Parliament than since the Union?

A. Infinitely more so. All the persecuting laws date from that period.

Q. Is it true that in the past the peasants loved their landlords?

A. No, the peasants never loved their landlords, and very few of the latter deserved to be loved. But they submitted with a patience they no longer possess.

Q. But is their hatred not more envenomed than it was in the past?

A. Yes. I must admit it. Because the fight is now begun, and both sides seek to injure the other. Many of the great landlords no longer give leases so as to prevent the farmers becoming electors. Others only give their farms to Protestants.

Q. When did the agitation which led to emancipation begin?

A. For thirty years since voting rights were granted to the Catholics, they have always claimed the right of sending members to Parliament. This claim became more and more threatening. In 1825 Mr. O'Connell finally decided to attempt to turn out a Protestant enemy of the Catholics by putting another Protestant in his place. The county of Waterford and the Beresford family, who owned almost the whole of the county and had represented it in Parliament for two centuries, were chosen. Everyone, even the Beresfords' own servants, voted against them. The election was a landslide. The next year we made an attempt against a member of the Ormonde family. We succeeded. In the end O'Connell decided to run for county Clare himself. We know the result.[1]

Q. What are the proportions of Catholics and Protestants in Ireland?

A. In the South we are twenty to one, in the North only three to one.

Q. These facts have not been known long?

A. No. The Protestants made out that the number of Protestants in Ireland was much greater than others thought and were opposed to a census. But the present government has had a census taken. (At this stage the Bishop showed us the census tables for his diocese. In general the contrasts were most striking. In one parish there were five or six thousand Catholics and only forty Protestants: there was a church, two parsons, and the value of the tithes reached 60,000 francs a year.)

Q. But as the Catholic population learns its rights and exploits them, one must begin to *reckon* with it?

A. Yes, certainly. In the South care is taken not to offend the Catholics. Most of the members of the Protestant aristocracy of my diocese visited me when I came here. This was not because these gentlemen had ever heard tell of me, but they intended a mark of respect to the head of the Catholics in the county.

Lord X, who is entertaining the Lord Lieutenant when he passes here next Tuesday, took care to press an invitation to this meal on me. We often correspond unofficially with agents of the Government or the Administration who accept our advice.

Q. How many Catholic priests do you estimate are in Ireland?

A. About 3,000. I only count parish priests and their curates in this number.

Q. Have you got priests for all your parishes?

---

[1] In 1826 and not in 1825 O'Connell and the Catholics beat Sir George Beresford at the Waterford election. Their successful candidate was Villiers Stuart, a Protestant, who favoured Catholic emancipation. Two years later O'Connell stood for County Clare and was elected. His election led to Peel's Emancipation Act.

Journey to Ireland (1835)

A. We had been short for a long time. But now we can choose.

Q. What is the revenue of your bishopric?

A. £500. But I have to do the duty for one parish, which takes up a lot of my time.

*   *   *

Grand Jury

The Grand Jury in Ireland forms a kind of representative body for the county; it is chosen by the Sheriff. But the Sheriff is obliged to take at least two jurors from each barony; this results in an almost complete representation of the county.

The sittings of the Grand Jury are public, a recent innovation which makes the behaviour of the Grand Jury more liberal and greatly reduces the number of *jobs*. The Grand Jury takes much more part in administration in Ireland than in England.

Information from the Bishop of Kilkenny; 24th July 1835

*   *   *

Religion. Dr. Kinsley, Bishop of Kilkenny (*24th July 1835*)

Today we went to see Dr. Kinsley, Bishop of Kilkenny. We found him very simply lodged. He said: 'My income is not large, still less fixed. I have only what comes to me from the free gifts of the faithful, but sometimes I can give friends dinner. I have a gig and a horse. I find I'm rich enough, and would be very upset if the State wanted to pay me. Last spring I went to London for the sole object of preventing the proposal of such a scheme. It would break the union now existing between clergy and people. Now the people regard us as their own handiwork, and are attached to us because of what they give us. If we received money from the State they would regard us as officials of the State, and when we advised them to respect law and order they would say, "That is what they are paid for." '

Dr. Kinsley added: 'In 1828 I was in France. Arriving at Rouen, I saw two sentries at the gate of the Archbishop's palace. "What's that?", I asked a French ecclesiastic who was with me. "It is a guard of honour for the Archbishop." "I don't like that

K   145

sort of guard of honour," said I. "They make people think of your Archbishop as the representative of the King much more than that of Jesus Christ." After that I saw the Fête-Dieu procession. It went between two lines of soldiers. "What's that?" said I again. "What are those soldiers for? Who wants a military show as part of a religious fête?" I was at the seminary and said to the priest who came to see me that I thought they were using the wrong means to make religion flourish. They only laughed and said I was a revolutionary. I answered: "I live in a country which is very like yours. The mass of the people has beliefs, but part of the upper classes professes a religion different from yours, or has no religion at all. Far from trying to offend the people, we identify ourselves as much as possible with their interests and views. We try and show our adversaries the substance of our religion without rasping their prejudices by external details. We avoid contact with the State. We behave as missionaries in a non-Christian country. If since the revolution you had acted as we have, religion would again be flourishing in France. Avoid contact with the State. Never use force. If a man is not married in church, you go and tell him that his children are bastards; it is not by hurting people's sensibilities that you bring them back into the fold." '

Dr. Kinsley went on to say: 'When I got to Paris, I met an Irishman who had been my pupil at the seminary. I had refused to let him enter orders because I knew he was completely incompetent; he had gone to France and been admitted to the priesthood. I told a *grand vicaire* of the Archbishop of Paris about this, and he said: "What would you have? We are short of applicants." I answered: "It would be a hundred times better to leave a parish without a priest than to give it a bad one." I watched some classes in your seminaries and noted that the pupils were very imperfectly taught and roughly brought up. No clergy so composed can lift religion up. But yet religion seems to have deep roots in France. It still has a hold on the people.'

I told Dr. Kinsley that there were also good friends of religion in the upper classes. 'I do not know.' he answered, 'whether such friends may not be more dangerous than useful. I remember a priest in Paris taking me to the house of the Marquis de —— whose almoner he was. The Marquis de —— was a Peer of

146

Journey to Ireland (1835)

France and his son was a deputy. I spoke of the Charter,[1] and he told me that the Charter only helped to make rebels, that freedom of the press was a great scourge . . .[2] all opinions and maxims which could not fail to make the people hate him, and which are flatly opposed to the spirit of the times in which we live. They told me that many others of his class felt as he did. If that is so, an alliance between religion and the upper classes can only be against the interests of religion, for, after all, the clergy must not get separated from the masses. A religion is not a government, it cannot be imposed.'

* * *

Kilkenny Assizes. Session of the Jury (25th July 1835)

Light on manners. Criminal Procedure

The first case threw much light on the criminal investigation police, and on the state of the country.

A man was accused of being a member of a gang which raided houses to steal arms with which he could afterwards exercise those acts of public justice which are called 'whiteboyism'.

The Crown had pardoned the accomplice of the accused on condition that he told what he knew to the Court, and that he would agree to leave England [sic] for ever.

We pointed out to the lawyers that such a procedure is wrong on several counts. Firstly because it saves a guilty man who is even worse than the man he causes to be condemned. Secondly because it rewards that kind of false evidence most to be feared, that which tends to condemn an innocent person.

They answered that it was an old custom; that the accused did not suffer as much as we thought, because it was a rule not to believe an accessory except when he is supported by the statements of other witnesses. Nevertheless I am still of my first opinion: the moral impression on the jury being the greatest risk the accused has to run, and that impression not being capable of control by the rules of jurisprudence.

In the same case a policeman was heard giving evidence of the

[1] This refers to the Charter of June 1814. Cf. J. P. Mayer, *Political Thought in France. From the Revolution to the Fourth Republic*, London 1949, p. 8 f.

[2] The dots are Tocqueville's.

admissions which the accused had made to him. This is even more dangerous for the prisoner than our system of examination.

The accused was condemned to deportation for life under the 'Whiteboys Acts'.

The Judge in his summing-up pointed out to the Jurors the frequent occurrence of these crimes which consist in stealing arms from no motive of greed, but merely in a desire to upset the country.

The second case was also characteristic of the state of Ireland; a farmer dismissed his servant who appeared the next day with a Bible in one hand and a pistol in the other to force him to swear to take him back into his service. If he who has thus sworn, breaks his oath, the other believes himself authorised to kill him.

These crimes are very common. There is nothing which better shows the imperfect state of civilisation in Ireland. What a peculiar mixture of religion and villainy; of respect for the sanctity of an oath, which forms the foundation of every society, and of distrust for all the laws of society!

Three witnesses came to prove the alibi of the accused. The general belief was that they foreswore themselves; but a false oath to save a man and to trick a justice which oppresses you and which you detest, is hardly blameworthy any more in the eyes of the population.

The third case was equally characteristic of Ireland. A farmer had been evicted from his land. The wife of his successor had been maltreated in revenge. Almost all these crimes in Ireland arise from quarrels about the possession of land.

While the jury deliberated in this case, the Judge formed another jury, before which he began the next case without any loss of time. This was interrupted for a moment to hear the verdict and to pass sentence.

General remark: in all the cases which we had seen the jury fulfilled its function infinitely more quickly than a French jury, in spite of the necessity for unanimity.

Officials analogous to those of the Office of Public Prosecutor

For each Assize district there is an official called the Clerk for the Crown. There are six such officials in Ireland. They usually reside in Dublin. But they correspond with the Magistrates and police in their district. It is they who prepare criminal cases and who name the witnesses to be called. This state of affairs is incomplete, but nevertheless very useful.

Information gathered in Kilkenny, 25th July 1835

* * *

Political condition of the country. Conversation with Mr. Point-dergast[1] [sic. *Presumably Prendergast*]. *Kilkenny* (*25th July 1835*)

Mr. P. is a Dublin barrister. He seems very intelligent. He is a Protestant and full of fanaticism against the Catholics, which makes what he says particularly interesting.

Q. It seems that crime in Ireland shows a tendency to diminish?

A. For eight or ten months that has been so, but I see no lasting reason for such a tendency.

Q. When did the sort of popular justice known as 'Whiteboyism' begin?

A. About 1760. It started as a form of resistance to the payment of tithe. Afterwards whiteboyism spread to include relations between tenants and their masters. When a tenant is turned off his land, it very often happens that his successor personally suffers for it, or his harvest or his cattle are damaged, or, most frequently of all, the landlord's agent is attacked. The crime is never committed by the person chiefly concerned, but always by a stranger to those parts, who had never seen the victim he strikes.

Q. Don't you think that if this country separated from England, you would have a violent revolution at once?

A. I don't doubt it. I even think we will have one whatever happens. The time is past when gentle remedies could cure the ills of Ireland.

We came to this country as conquerors. By 'we' I mean we English Protestants. The country's aristocracy has always regarded the Catholic population as a crowd of savages and treated them as such. The latter is accustomed to regard the upper classes as their natural enemies. Now they have become strong by numbers and through political rights. The time for

---

[1] Tocqueville spells English or Irish names on occasions phonetically.

concessions by the aristocracy has passed. No one takes it into account any more, and kindnesses now would be used against it. On the other hand how is one to govern the country without the aristocracy? For the Catholic population has really turned savage, and has no enlightened ideas. Its only aristocracy is the clergy. For the Irish, religion is not only a question of faith; it is also a question of patriotism. All Ireland is under Catholic influence. We know what the tyranny of the priests would be; again recently the meeting at Exeter Hall[1] has shown how abominable their principles are, lest we should ever want to put the government of the country in their hands. So then Ireland can neither be governed nor govern herself.

Q. Don't you think that temporary English dictatorship would be a blessing?

A. Yes, but no one in Ireland would submit to it. The English are regarded as foreigners.

Q. What are the commonest crimes?

A. Violence due to drunkenness or village quarrels; premeditated acts of violence committed to resist authority or to fight against the aristocracy; theft is rare. You cannot imagine the hatred existing between landlords and people. The landlords fear and distrust the people without hiding the fact. The people loathe the landlords and it would take very little to rouse them against them.

Q. Don't you think that the best means to loosen the close tie between people and clergy would be for the State to pay the latter?

A. I don't think so. The Catholic clergy everywhere and especially in Ireland is eminently a dominating body. It has conceived the hope of chasing the Protestants out and reigning without control over Irish society. It will never forget that hope; whatever is done it will not sacrifice it to money interests and is more likely to use the money it receives to forward its object.

[1] Exeter Hall was built in 1831 in Clapham at the outskirts of London. It became the centre of the Evangelical movement; it was there that Evangelists from all parts of England met in enthusiastic meetings. Exeter Hall became a household word. While it is generally remembered for the part it played in the anti-slavery movement, Exeter Hall was also a centre of anti-catholic activities. Cf. G. R. Balleine, *A History of the Evangelical Party in the Church of England*, London, 1909; see also *The Clapham Sect* in James Stephen, *Essays in Ecclesiastical Biography*, vol. ii, London 1853.

Journey to Ireland (1835)

Q. Do you know Bishop Kinsley?

A. No. We Protestants know very few of those gentlemen. You cannot conceive the distance that holds these two groups apart, especially at the moment. Believe me, I have only *once* in my life dined in the house of a Catholic and that was by accident. We hardly ever meet each other in society. Among the barristers here now there are about as many Catholics as Protestants. They see each other, but there is no social contact.

Q. But is there not a natural tendency for a Catholic who becomes rich to mix with the aristocracy?

A. They would often like to, but cannot do it. I am sorry to say that people close their ranks against them. The Protestants cannot get used to seeing them on a footing of equality with themselves. They mistrust them.

Q. But are you not afraid that those whom you rebuff, will behave as the middle classes did in France, who finished by making themselves the leaders of the people in a revolution which ended in the complete ruin of the aristocracy?

A. I am afraid that that will happen. But what would you have? Things have come to such a pitch that passions, not reason, rule. Left to their natural inclinations the rich Catholics are more aristocratic than ourselves. They have more mistrust than we for the people in general; we Protestants do indeed distrust the Irish, but, as a general principle, we have confidence in the intelligence of the masses.

Q. Is the administration still in the hands of Protestants?

A. Yes. Almost all the grand juries are Protestant. The Sheriffs are Protestants. There isn't one Catholic among the judges.

Q. In such a state of the country, with a government so composed, how do you expect the Catholics not to become a nation apart?

*   *   *

Forceful and exceptional measures still in force

The county of Kilkenny is still at this moment (25th July 1835) subject to very rigorous exceptional measures.

At a fixed hour every evening all the inhabitants must be back in their homes, and the police have the right to enter and see if this is so.

The 'Coercion Bill'[1] was much more severe before it was toned down a year ago, for then, in certain conditions it allowed the government to set up courts martial. . . .[2]

The Irish population cannot possess arms. An Irishman must have a judge's permission to carry arms, and, should he do so without that, the penalty is a very big fine, and, if that is not paid, imprisonment. . . .[2]

Numerous police force hated by the people.

*　*　*

Dinner with the Bishop of Kilkenny (26th July 1835)

At this dinner there were two or three priests and eight or ten laymen. They were Catholic landlords and Catholic lawyers from Dublin; among others Mr. Lawler,[3] a member of the Catholic Association.

Dinner passed very quietly, but from the moment the servants left and the wine was on the table, conversation turned towards politics and took on a general and animated character. They spoke of the Poor Law for which all but one individual seemed to wish.

'The circumstances in which this country finds itself,' said the Bishop raising his voice, 'make such a law indispensable. Who in Ireland today supports the poor? The poor. The rich man looks at the poor from over the top of the walls of his splendid park, or if he meets him on the road, he answers his entreaties saying, "I make it a duty not to give anything to those who do not work." And he gives them no work. He has big fat dogs and his like die at his door. Who feeds the poor? The poor. The wretch who has only 100 bushels of potatoes for himself and his family, gives 50 of them to the even more wretched men who present themselves hungry at the door of his cottage. Is it right

---

[1] The Coercion Bill was a legislative measure for the suppression of the insurrectional movement of the *Whiteboys*. It established in fact partial martial law and partially suspended *Habeas Corpus*; it was voted in August 1833 and renewed under Melbourne's Ministry in 1834.

[2] The dots are Tocqueville's.

[3] No doubt John Lawless (1773–1837); one of the most active members of the Catholic Association.

that this man wears torn clothes, does not send his son to school and suffers the hardest privations to relieve miseries to which the rich landowner remains insensible?

'Go to Mayo. You see thousands of men literally on the point of dying of hunger. In the same county the Marquis of Sligo has 70,000 acres of land whose revenue he consumes in England. Should not the law force this man to give to his like some of his superfluities? Why are so many people dying of hunger in Mayo? Because the landlords serve their own interests by making grassland so that they can get a little more money. At the present time, gentlemen, the landlords of Ireland wish to make the people as wretched as possible, for the more threatened the cultivator is by starvation, the more ready he will be to submit to any conditions they wish to impose on him. Let us give the landowners reason to make the poor comfortable.' This long democratic tirade was heard with enthusiasm, and was interrupted several times by cries of 'Hear' from the guests.

'Where can we see,' cried Mr. Lawler, 'a greater proof of what my Lord has said than what is going on in Dublin? Who supports the Poorhouse in Dublin? The shops and the small merchants. Who remains indifferent to the miseries of the people? The rich. This state of things is intolerable.'

The conversation followed its course in this way for two hours. It was impassioned, superficial, light, often interrupted by jokes and witty remarks. I might have been in France. Nothing resembled England. The guests had a cordiality unknown in that country.

I should also say that they were generally less distinguished and less careful in their manners, in one word less 'gentlemen' than Englishmen of the same class or Irish Protestants.

* * *

Kilkenny. Political condition. Conversation with Mr. George (26th July 1835)

Mr. George is a young Dublin barrister. A well-brought-up and very likeable man.

Q. How do you interpret the 'Coercion Bill'.

A. It is a law authorising the government, in appropriate

cases, to subject Ireland, or parts of the country, to certain exceptional regulations. Under the Coercion Bill, for example, the government has the right to order people to be in their homes by a stated time, and to authorise policemen to go into houses at night to make sure that everyone is there. It can have certain offenders tried by Courts Martial. . . .

Q. Has the Coercion Bill been applied recently to several parts of the country?

A. The police regulations of which I just spoke apply now still to county Kilkenny. Anyhow you know that the Coercion Bill expires this year and the ministers have said that they will not ask for it to be renewed.

Q. For what reason was the Coercion Bill applied to county Kilkenny?

A. In general the prevalence of the 'whitefeet' and in particular a terrible event which took place two leagues from here (Ballymackey, I believe) two years ago; it was a question of selling up the goods of someone who refused to pay tithe. As resistance was feared, fifty policemen were going to the place. But the population ambushed them behind walls in the village. Eighteen policemen and one officer fell on the spot; the others were put to flight. At the moment the county is very quiet. It is about the same as in Tipperary. At the winter assizes at Clonmel (county town of Tipperary) I remember seeing about 200 people for trial, fifty of them murder cases.

Q. Yesterday at the assizes I saw a man condemned for using force to make another swear to a promise. Is that a common crime?

A. It is one of the commonest crimes in this country. You know that in this county there have long been gangs whose object or pretext was to resist the oppression of the aristocracy, and to set up a sort of popular justice. Those gangs call themselves 'whiteboys, whitefeet' . . .[1] those elements always exist, but at the moment they show no sign of action. In general their mode of action is as follows: some of them traverse the country at night armed. They enter some individual's house and force him to swear on the Bible to help their plans. If the latter breaks his oath it is at the risk of his life.[2] At other times they enter the

---

[1] The dots are Tocqueville's.

[2] Note by Tocqueville: one can see that the oath was just a means by which these rough men sought to justify in their own eyes the murder they intended to commit.

house of a tenant who has taken the place of some unfortunate whom the landlord has driven out of his farm. The whitefeet make him swear that he will leave the farm, and if he does not, he is killed.

Q. Do you see a remedy for the ills of this country?

A. I confess that I do not. The Catholic population has long been oppressed; now it is so no longer, and I truly believe that at the time of the emancipation the Protestants were quite prepared to allow the Catholics to share all their political advantages. But the latter are not prepared to forget their old injuries; they want not equality only, but domination. They want to put us in the position of a conquered people, the position in which we long held them. That is what we cannot allow. Never has a country been in a worse state. On one side a small minority which has almost all the wealth and enlightenment in the country. On the other an immense preponderance of material force. In England and in all the countries of the world, I think, people are more or less divided into two great parties; the rich and the poor; those who want to get, and those who want to keep. Here it happens that those who want to get are of one religion, and those who want to keep of another. That makes for a violence of opposition between the two great parties unknown elsewhere.

Q. Don't you think that a temporary dictatorship under firm and enlightened guidance, like that of Bonaparte after the 18th Brumaire, would be the only way of saving Ireland?

A. I think so. But England herself wavers. No Party has a majority in England. How can you expect a firm political line? At this actual moment we think that the English Government is prepared to let us be oppressed, and to leave us entirely at the mercy of the Catholics. How could you expect it to be otherwise? The life of the Ministry depends entirely on the will of O'Connell and the sixty Irishmen who make up his Party.

*   *   *

How aristocracy can be one of the best or one of the worst forms of government that exist in the world. Kilkenny (26th July 1835)

Imagine an aristocracy which was born on the very soil it dominates, or whose origin is lost in the obscurity of past centuries. Assume that, not being different from the people, they could easily assimilate with them. Give this aristocracy an interest in uniting with the people to resist a power greater than that of the aristocracy or of the people alone, but weaker than that of the people and the aristocracy united together, so that the more rich and enlightened the people are, the more the aristocracy is assured of its preservation, and the more the rights of the aristocracy are respected, the more the people are certain of retaining the enjoyment of theirs. Imagine an aristocracy having the same language, the same manners, the same religion as the people; an aristocracy which would be ahead, but beyond the ken, of the people's understanding; an aristocracy which surpasses the people a little in all respects, but immensely in none. Imagine a middle class gradually increasing in importance in the context of this state of affairs, and by degrees coming to share the power and soon afterwards the privileges of the ancient aristocracy, in such way that money which everybody can hope to obtain, gradually takes the place of birth which depends on God alone. Thus inequality itself will work to forward the wealth of all, for, everybody hoping to come to share the privileges of the few, there would be a universal effort, an eagerness of all minds directed to the acquisition of well-being and wealth. Make of this nation a huge centre of commerce, so that the chances of attaining the wealth with which all the rest can be obtained, multiply infinitely, and ever give the poor a thousand hopes, and so a thousand reasons for remaining satisfied with their lot.

Imagine all these things, and you will have a people among whom the upper classes are more brilliant, more enlightened and wiser, the middle classes richer, the poor classes better off than anywhere else; where the State would be as firm in its plans as if it were governed by one man, as strong and as powerful as if it relied on the free will of all its citizens; where the people would submit to the law as if they had made it themselves, and where order would reign as if it were only the question of carrying out the will of a despot: in fine, where everyone being content with his lot would be proud of his country and would wish to be proud of himself.

Now imagine an aristocracy that was established by a conquest at a time so recent that the memory and the traces of the event were present in all minds. Place the conquest in a century

when the conqueror already had almost all the lights of civilisation and the vanquished was still in a state of half savagery, so
that both in moral power and in intelligence the conqueror was
as far as possible superior to the conquered. Give to these two,
who are already so dissimilar and unequal, a different religion,
so that the nobility not only distrusts the people, but also hates
them, and the people not only hates the nobles but damns them.
Far from giving the aristocracy so constituted any particular
reason to unite itself with the people, give it a particular reason
not to unite with the people in order to remain similar to the
nation whence it came, from which it still draws all its strength,
and to resemble which is its pride. Instead of giving it a reason
to take care of the people, give it a special motive to oppress
them, by placing its trust in this foreign support which provides
that it should have nothing to fear from the consequences of its
tyranny. Give to this aristocracy the exclusive power of government and of self-enrichment. Forbid the people to join its ranks,
or, if you do allow that, impose conditions for that benefit which
they cannot accept. So that the people, estranged from the upper
classes and the object of their enmity, without a hope of better-
ing their lot, end up by abandoning themselves and thinking
themselves satisfied when by the greatest efforts they can extract from their land enough to prevent themselves from dying;
and meanwhile the noble, stripped of all that stimulates man
to great and generous actions, slumbers in unenlightened
egoism.

You would certainly have a terrible state of society, in which
the aristocracy would have all the faults and maxims of oppressors; the people all the vices and faint-heartedness of slaves. The
law would serve to destroy what it should protect, and violence
would protect what elsewhere it seeks to destroy. Religion
would seem only to lend its strength to the passions which it
should fight, and to exist only to prevent hatreds from being
forgotten and men from establishing among them the fraternity
it preaches every day.

The two societies I have just described were however both
founded on the principle of aristocracy. The two aristocracies of
which I have been speaking, have the same origin and manners
and almost the same laws. But the one has for centuries given
the English one of the best governments that exist in the world;

the other has given the Irish one of the most detestable that could ever be imagined.

Aristocracy then can be subjected to particular conditions which modify its nature and its results, so that in judging it one must bear circumstances in mind. The truth is that the aristocratic principle was conditioned in England by particularly happy circumstances, and in Ireland by particularly baneful ones. It would not be fair to make a theoretical judgment about aristocracy on the strength of either of these examples. The rule lies elsewhere.[1]

*   *   *

Journey from Kilkenny to Cork (*27th July 1835*)

From Kilkenny to Mitchelstown the country looks the same as before. Little hills despoiled of trees, cut up into a huge number of small fields. Occasionally broad moors. Few villages; no belfries. One finds churches without parishioners, and sees none with them. The inhabitants scattered along the roads. The same type of house, perhaps even more wretched than in Kilkenny. Mud houses, thatched roofs, often broken down. No chimney, or such an inadequate one that almost all the smoke comes out of the door. No windows. A little dunghill by the door; a pig in the house. Labourers in rags. Almost all the way relays of children importuning passers-by. I imagined that these were the wretched dwellings of beggars, but my companions assured me that they were the homes of small tenant farmers who had twenty or thirty acres of land to cultivate.

At Mitchelstown there is a splendid mansion belonging to Lord Kingston. He has 75,000 acres round the house. He lives there. I was shown a huge clearing which he has had made, and which is covered with fine crops; and a row of clean and convenient cottages which he has had built for his tenants. It is said that he has made money out of doing this. The town of Mitchelstown does not look as wretched as the rest of the country.

I ask where the 'lord' is. I am told that he went off his head two years ago. Why? I am told that it is because he found him-

---

[1] Note by Tocqueville: Here, to complete this passage, one must search out what are the vices and virtues most natural to aristocracy.

self burdened with £400,000 of debts without hope of ever being able to pay them off. The money had been lent him by Catholic merchants in Cork on mortgage of the huge estates which I had seen, and absorbed almost all his income. It is like that almost everywhere in Ireland. Witness the finger of God. The Irish aristocracy wanted to remain separated from the people and be still English. It has driven itself into imitating the English aristocracy without possessing either its skill or its resources, and its own sin is proving its ruin. The Irish were turned out of their lands by force of arms. Hard work is bringing them back again into these estates.

In a village I saw about thirty peasants sitting in a circle by the door of a little house. I was told that that was the parish priest's house and that they were waiting their turn to confess.

We arrived at Fermoy, rather a pretty town on the banks of Black Water river. The town seems comparatively prosperous. The source of this prosperity is two infantry regiments whose huge barracks cover the neighbouring height. A nasty source for a country's prosperity.

The entry into Cork is very fine. The tradesmen's quarter is beautiful. In the suburbs are filthy houses and inhabitants who are even more frightful still and such as one could find nowhere but in Ireland. The Catholic Archbishop lives in the middle of that quarter of the town. The shepherd in the midst of his flock . . .[1]

In our open diligence there were two young men both very uproariously drunk. They talked to and made jokes at almost every passer-by. All, men and women, answered with laughter and other pleasantries. I thought I was in France.

* * *

Cork (*28th July 1835*)

Straits of almost all Irish landowners, which prevents them from helping the population at all even when they want to, and from improving anything for fear of risking capital and squeezing the poor to increase their revenues, which makes the poor even more incapable of doing without them.

A new complication, peculiar to this unhappy land, one which

[1] The dots are Tocqueville's.

one must keep in view when speaking about it. That is one of the chief reasons for the present state of affairs. But this cause itself is only the effect of a more general underlying cause which has made the Irish aristocracy a stranger in the country, and has led it to ruin itself by imitating the English aristocracy, without having the virile spirit of the latter or understanding its way of exploiting the freedom and comfort of the lower classes as yet more sources of revenue.

The Duke of Bridgewater doubled his fortune by opening a canal, the Duke of Newcastle by opening up coal-mines. What would be the use of opening a canal in Ireland where no one has goods to transport? Or mining coal which no one could buy?

* * *

A Catholic priest and a Protestant clergyman[1] in Ireland. Begun at Cork (28th July 1835)

I had taken the trouble before leaving Dublin to provide myself with a large number of letters of introduction. I got them to men of all parties and especially to the priests of both religions which divide Ireland. On arriving at Tuam, in county Connaught, I looked at my letters and found that two of them were addressed to the same village. On reading the contents of both letters, one turned out to be addressed to the Catholic priest of the parish and the other to the Protestant clergyman. I eagerly seized this opportunity of seeing on a very small scale the interaction of elements already observed, and so I set out. I left the diligence at the nearest township and set off on foot for the village X.[2]

First I followed a beautiful short-cut which led to a mansion. As it turned to the right, I took a path to the left down a valley. Soon I found myself at the beginning of the village which was built at the bottom of a valley, or rather a ravine, shut in by two highish hills covered with pasture. At the bottom of the ravine there flowed a stream which no doubt swells in winter, but then exposed an almost dry, rocky bed. Not a tree grew on its banks which were as bare as almost all other Irish river banks. This

---

[1] Note by Tocqueville: All this should be told very simply, but better and with more detail.

[2] X in the manuscript.

stream's bed, dry or full, was apparently the only road in the
village. The houses seemed to be flattened to find room between
the stream and the two neighbouring hills. I quickened my pace
to hurry through this unhappy village whose look repelled me.
But in passing through I could not help noticing what I had so
often seen in Ireland. All the houses in line to my right and my
left were made of sun-dried mud and built with walls the height
of a man. The roofs of these dwellings were made of thatch so
old that the grass which covered it could be confused with the
meadows on the neighbouring hills. In more than one place I
saw that the flimsy timbers supporting these fragile roofs had
yielded to the effects of time, giving the whole thing the look of
a molehill on which a passer-by has trod. The houses mostly had
neither windows nor chimneys; the daylight came in and smoke
came out by the door. If one could see into the houses, it was
rare to notice more than bare walls, a ricketty stool and a small
peat fire burning slowly and dimly between four flat stones. A
stranger's footsteps kicking up the stones of the stream soon
attracted the villagers' attention. Young and old pressed to the
doorways and cast surprised looks at me.

The pig in the house. The dunghill. The bare heads and feet.
Describe and paint that . . .[1]

Further on I saw five or six men full of strength and health
nonchalantly lying by the banks of the brook. If I had known less
of Ireland, this laziness in the midst of so great poverty would
have excited my indignation. But already I understood enough
of this unhappy country to realise that there was a ceaseless lack
of employment. They cannot earn their bread by the sweat of
their brow as God commanded.

At last I stopped to look for a villager whom I could ask the
way to the priest's house. Just here the bed of the brook was
narrow and one could see a tiny streamlet of deep and clear
water flowing fast between the stones which hemmed it in. Near
this sort of natural reservoir, a little girl of seven or eight was
collecting water in a clay jug. I went to her and, while she was
still leaning over the water, I asked her: 'My child, do you
know where the village priest lives?' At the sound of my voice
the child quickly looked up, and pushing back her fair hair from
her forehead with her little hands, fixed her intelligent, sensitive

---

[1] The dots are Tocqueville's.

blue eyes on me. I repeated my question whose naïvety had brought a smile to the child's lips. 'Come along with me, sir,' she said in reply, and leaving her jug half-full, she began to walk or rather to run in front of me without seeming to feel the sharp stones on her little bare feet, though thick shoes did not save mine from them. Thus we came to a part of the valley which opens out a little and allows the village to spread. There we left the bed of the brook and, after passing two or three miserable hovels, we found ourselves before a house whose exterior promised at least some comfort. It was a little house, built of stone, with four windows in front and two stories. This building was covered with thatch like the others, but the thatch was new and the rafters in good repair. There was a small vegetable garden all round the house with a fence which protected it from domestic animals. It was closed by a small gate which you could open any time you wished. The child, acting as my guide, pushed the gate open, crossed the garden, and without hesitation opened the door of the priest's house. I then noticed very clean wooden stairs inside the house leading to the upper floor. My guide nimbly climbed up to the top of the stairs and, without troubling to turn round to see if I were following, knocked lightly on the half-open door. A strong voice inside replied, 'Come in.' The door opened and we found ourselves in the presence of the man I came to see. On seeing him the little girl curtseyed low and said, 'Here is a gentleman wishing to speak to your honour.' 'Good, my child,' said the priest smiling to the child, and my little guide disappeared in the twinkling of an eye. I gave my host the letter of recommendation which I had been charged to give him, and while he read it, I looked with curiosity at the man and at his dwelling. A square room, simple, but very clean and light. A few engravings of religious subjects hung on the walls and a small ebony crucifix on the mantelpiece. On the table a breviary and newspapers; by the side a wooden chair against which leaned a thick knotted stick with a wide-brimmed black felt hat balanced on top. Such was the appearance of the interior of the room. The priest seemed to be a man in his prime; his muscular limbs and sunburnt skin testified to an active, healthy life. He was dressed and wore his hair like a layman.

After glancing through the letter which I handed to him, he cordially gave me his hand and fixing a firm and frank look on me, said: 'Welcome to you, Sir. I do not know if you are Catholic or Protestant, but in either case you will have to fast today (it was a Saturday). I did not in the least expect you, and you must content yourself with my supper. As for sleeping, my assistant left for Galway yesterday to visit his family, and you can have his bed.' I assured him that I would be wonderfully comfortable in his home and, having led me into my new bedroom which was on the other side of the landing, he left me to go and give orders for supper.

After a quarter of an hour he came back to tell me it was ready, and we both went down to a room on the ground floor where the table was laid. The linen was white, the cover simple and the meal very modest; it consisted of a large piece of salmon, potatoes and a sort of a cake made in a hurry, the only extra that my presence had occasioned. An old man, half sacristan, half valet, watched us with a benign and tranquil air, and provided for our needs with great care.

The dinner, as may be believed, was short and my host noticing that I did not care for the English custom of remaining drinking at table, said to me: 'I have a few visits to make to some of my parishioners, Sir. If you wish to accompany me, perhaps we will have a chance for a talk along the way, which we would not have here.' I eagerly accepted this proposition, and my host having put his boots on and his stick under his arm, we left together and came into the village. On seeing him the women curtseyed and crossed themselves devoutly, the men respectfully took off their hats. He saluted nobody and did not seem to notice the respect with which he was received, but, walking on without stopping spoke a word to each: 'How is your old father today, Mr. X?' he said to one. 'When will your wife be churched, John?' he said to another. 'What name will you give to your child?' he said to a poor woman who was taking a breath of air outside her hovel. 'If your honour would care to choose himself,' said the woman, 'it would be a great joy to us.' 'Let us leave it to Providence,' said the priest smiling, 'let us give him the name of the Saint on whose feast day he was born.' 'Why have you not sent your son to school these last few days?' he asked a peasant better dressed than the others, in a serious and almost severe tone. 'It is up to you to set an example.' Going along like that we reached the end of the village where I had already seen those young people idly lying by the brook. I saw them from far off in the same place, but they got up at our approach. 'Then you were not able to find work today,' the priest said to them. 'No,' they replied. 'We went to farmer O'Croly as your honour suggested. But farmer O'Croly himself has just been evicted from his farm by the Lord's agent.' The priest hunched his shoulders as if he felt a heavy burden placed on them. 'What do you expect, my children,' he said, 'perhaps the day will come when there will be nothing in Ireland but lazy people left to die of hunger. But that time has not yet come. Have confidence in God.'

We left the village street here and took another sunken path on the left which led to another valley. When we had taken a few steps along it, my companion suddenly stopped, struck the ground with his stick, turned round, and said to me, 'Is such a state of things to be borne, Sir? God said to man after his fall that he must earn his bread by the sweat of his brow, but here they go even further than the divine malediction. For you have just seen men who ask for nothing but to work for their living, but cannot succeed in doing so; and when you think that in Ireland more than a million of our fellows are reduced to this extremity, do you not say, as I do, that such a state of things cannot be tolerated much longer?'

'I have heard,' said I in reply, 'that the Marquis of Sligo who, I believe owns large properties in this parish, has come to live in his castle. Do you think that, if he knew what was happening, he would not seek to lessen the extreme distress which at present prevails on his domain?'

'You must be very ill informed about the state of Ireland,' the priest replied, 'to put such a question. Do you not know that the aristocracy is the cause of all our miseries and that it does not soften any of the ills it has created? Sir, do you know what it is that prevents the poor from starving to death in Ireland? It is the poor.[1] A farmer who has only thirty acres and who harvests only a hundred bushels of potatoes, puts aside a fifth of his harvest annually to be distributed among those unfortunates who are the most terribly in need. In Ireland, Sir, it is the poor who provide for the needs of the poor. It is the poor who raise and

[1] Note by Tocqueville. Generalities about equality and liberty. At the end of the conversation, faith, piety of the people.

maintain the schools where the children of the poor are educated. Finally it is the poor who furnish the poor with the means of obtaining the comforts of religion. The starving man presents himself at the door of the cottage without fear; he is sure to receive something to appease his present hunger. But at the doors of the mansions he will only meet liveried lackeys, or dogs better nourished than he, who will drive him roughly away. In order to give alms the farmer will stint his land of manure and wear rags, and his wife will sleep on straw and his children not go to school. What will the lord do all this time? He will take walks in immense grounds surrounded by high walls. Within his park everything breathes splendour; outside misery groans, but he does not notice it. His doormen take care to keep the poor from his sight, and if by accident he meets one he answers his entreaties by saying, 'I make it a duty not to encourage begging.' He has big, fat dogs, and his fellows die at his door. Not only do they not help the poor in any way, but they profit from their needs to charge enormous rents which they spend in France or Italy. If for a short time one returns among us, it is only to evict a farmer who is behind with the rent and chase him from his home, as happened to poor O'Croly. Does it seem fair to you, Sir, that this man with 80,000 acres and an income of £40,000 escapes from all the duties of society, and does not alleviate directly by gifts, or indirectly by giving work, the misery which he has caused, while the poor man gives something from his own necessities to relieve miseries which are not of his causing? Our aristocracy, Sir, has a definite, permanent interest in making the people poverty-stricken. For the more wretched the people are, the easier it is to impose hard conditions of rent for farms. Daily we see great landlords, for a trifling pecuniary advantage, change the system of farming and put half the farm-labourers in a district out of work from one moment to the next.'

'I can just understand,' I said, 'that a Protestant nobleman living amid a hostile population is not much given to relieving public distress. But you have some Catholic landowners in Ireland. Should not they give the others an example?'

'Not at all,' said the priest. 'Catholics and Protestants oppress the people in about the same way. The moment a Catholic becomes a great landowner he conceives the same egotistical dislike which seems natural to the aristocracy, for the interest of the

people. Like the others he eagerly seizes on all means of en-
riching himself at the expense of the poor.'[1]

* * *

Talking like this we came to a house which though larger than
those of the village seemed almost as wretched. What most distinguished it was a certain number of windows, or rather holes
in the mud walls into which the remains of window-panes had
been put. A few peasants were sitting at the door, and inside I
noticed the heads of several children. 'This is our school,' said
the priest. 'It is not at all magnificent, but the desire the people
have to learn makes up both for the lack of means of instruction
and of skill in the teacher.' We entered the house, or rather the
room, for the whole house consisted of one room, containing
about thirty children. The space was too crowded to sit down,
and in any case there was only one seat in the school. At one end
stood the teacher, a middle-aged, barefoot man teaching children in rags. This was certainly a very wretched school, but there
was, as the priest had said, an eagerness to learn which is not
always found in the rich English universities.

We continued our walk and the priest took up the conversation again: 'Forty years ago, Sir, a Catholic who dared to give
these poor children instruction, would have been severely punished. And they complained that the Catholic population was
still half savage. You cannot imagine, Sir, the eagerness which
these unfortunates show for education now that the means have
been put at their disposal. The rising generation will not be like
the present one. There lies the hope for the future.'

'Do you think,' I said, 'that if civilisation gains, faith may
perhaps lose by the change?'

'We refuse to take any account of such a possibility, Sir,'
replied the priest vigorously, 'our religion rests on proofs too
strong to fear the light. Furthermore, Sir, how can one expect
this poor people ever to resist the oppression which weighs them
down, if knowledge is only to be found where riches and power
are too? Education, Sir, is today a vital necessity for Ireland.
The Protestants say that the Catholic population is half savage

[1] Note by Tocqueville: Church. Separation of Church and State. School teaching.
Newspapers. Dying. Generalities in speaking again of equality and liberty.

and that it is ignorant and lazy. This is partly true. But whose fault is it, Sir, if not of those who by three hundred years of tyranny have reduced the most active and intelligent people in the world to this state? This people will one day govern itself; the moment is approaching; it cannot be far off. What would become of society if the poor, while becoming strong, remained plunged in ignorance?'

'The English Government itself,' I said, 'is beginning to realise the danger. It is at present endeavouring to set up schools which are neither Catholic nor Protestant and which consequently both Catholics and Protestants can attend. Do you approve of this new plan?'

'Yes,' said the priest. 'But up to now our parish has found itself too poor to meet the initial expenses required for a school established by the State.'

'And you do not fear,' I added, 'that education thus separated from religion might prove more dangerous than useful?'

'No, Sir,' said the priest. 'On leaving school the children come into our hands, and it is for us to direct their religious education. The school would teach them the elements of human knowledge; the Church would teach them the Catechism. All means of instructing the public are good. Education is a vital necessity for Ireland.'

'I forgot to ask, Sir,' I said to my guide, 'with what object were the group of peasants sitting together at the door of the school?'

'I was going to tell you,' replied the priest, 'to show to what extent our people are beginning to be seized with the desire to learn. The men whom you saw are poor labourers who have finished their day's work, and they are gathered together at the door of the school so that the teacher, when he has finished his lessons, can read them the newspaper aloud.

'And who gives them this newspaper?' I asked.

'I get it,' said the priest.

'And do you not find these readings in any way inconvenient?'

'What inconvenience?' asked the priest. 'Is not publicity a great element in public morality? Do not those who wish to do wrong, take care to hide themselves? Is not the best way of keeping everybody to their duty, to let them see that they cannot leave the right path except in the light of day? Freedom of the press, Sir, is the first and perhaps the only efficient weapon which the oppressed has against the oppressor; the weak against the strong; the people against the government and the great. Freedom of the press has nominally existed in Ireland for over a century, but only today has it become a real power.'

We had come to the beginning of a small path which twisted through a meadow and ended in a clump of elms rising at the foot of the hill round which we had come.

The priest took out his watch and said: 'Time presses; the sun is setting. But I cannot resist the desire to take you to those trees which you see there. Let us quicken our pace, and we will make up for the time lost.' He walked ahead and I followed.

Thus we soon reached the place which the priest had pointed out to me. Three large walnut trees, covered with nuts and bent with age, shaded a small country cemetery. Fifty paces further on were the ruins of an old church, an ivy-covered Gothic arch still standing and surmounted by a moss-covered wooden cross. By the side of these venerable ruins stood a small and quite new Catholic chapel surmounted by a stone cross. The priest stopped an instant at this place and leaning against the trunk of one of the walnut trees, he threw a melancholy glance on the ruins and a look of satisfaction on the small chapel which had been erected in the middle of them. 'The ruins you see, Sir,' he said to me, 'are the only remains of one of the most beautiful churches built by the piety of our fathers; the Protestants destroyed it. But it is easier to knock down stones than to drive out a religion from the hearts of men. The heretics have devastated the sanctuary; they let their flocks graze over the ruins of the altar; but they could not stop the veneration of the people being attached to these insensible stones. We could not come to pray where our fathers had prayed, but we have continued to bury our dead in the place which had been blessed long ago and which holds their ashes. Since we have had freedom of conscience, we have not tried to rebuild this broken monument. We have been too poor for that, but we have at least put a wooden cross on top of these ruins.'

The priest having said this, picked up the stick which he had for a moment leant against the tree, and went up to the newly built church. The church was a small building roughly built in stone and with a slate roof, whose mode of construction could be studied from the inside as it had neither vault nor ceiling; the floor was of beaten earth; the altar was of wood; the walls had neither paint nor pictures but remained as the mason had left them. The nave of this small church was cut in two by a wooden platform supported at intervals on pillars: this was a way of accommodating a large number of people without increasing the size of the building and the expense of construction. The chapel had a very few benches and no chair. When we came in five or six peasants, some telling their beads and others kneeling on the bare earth, seemed so deeply absorbed in religious meditation that the noise of our footsteps did not attract their attention.

The priest said a short prayer and left. When he came back to the walnut trees, looking back with happy satisfaction, he said: 'In a quarter of an hour you will see a man who still remembers the time when we held mass in a ditch with sentries from the congregation posted for fear of being seized by the agents of justice. Ten years ago, when I came to this parish, we held divine service in a barn. God be praised that we are now able to come together in a place dedicated to the glory of our holy mysteries; and this church,' he added with an air of triumph, 'this church was built from contributions freely given.'

'This church,' I said to my host, 'is built as simply as possible. But I find it hard to conceive how your parishioners could pay for its construction.'

'The whole diocese came to our aid,' replied the priest. 'We sought among our brethren; the eagerness and goodwill of the people did the rest. But we are forgetting that time presses,' exclaimed the priest, looking at the sun which was rapidly descending to the horizon.

This said, we took long strides towards the hill behind the ruins of the abbey, and instead of following the path he had taken before, he crossed the meadow which ran along the flank of the hill, and began to climb at such a pace that I had difficulty in keeping up with him. In five minutes we had reached the top, and I noticed close ahead a poor hut which was, as I was soon to find out, the destination of my host's journey.

It was one of those miserable habitations which cover almost the whole surface of Ireland; a mud house without windows. The fire was lit inside, and smoke escaping through all the holes in its thatch gave the whole house the appearance of a lime kiln.

Journey to Ireland (1835)

The door was open and, as soon as they saw us, a man, a woman and several children came out to meet us.

'Well, Mr. O'Sullivan,' the priest anxiously inquired, 'how is your father today?'

'He is getting hourly weaker,' replied the peasant, 'and if your honour does not save him, I doubt his living even through the night.'

The priest said nothing and hurried on. We soon arrived at the door of the shack; nothing could be more desolate than the sight within. A wooden bench fixed against one of the walls and a worm-eaten chest with several farm implements on it, were the only objects which attracted attention. The fireplace was made of four flat stones between which a little peat fire burned dimly and slowly, sending out much more smoke than light into the room. In one corner there was an old man lying, who seemed at the very end of life. They had put a little hay and rags of clothing under him to prevent his suffering from the damp ground. On seeing us the old man made an effort to raise himself on his hands. The priest entered and said, 'God be with you, my old friend.' 'Amen,' answered the dying man in a faint voice.

The priest came up to him, knelt on the ground and leant over to hear the dying man's confession. All the rest of the family remained outside with me and knelt on the threshold. The sun was setting. Through the door its last rays spread unaccustomed light into the little shack and for once painted the clouds of smoke that filled the room with brilliant colours. As he spoke physical pain and hope alike were written on the face of the old man, care and anxiety on the face of the priest.

'Have confidence in God, my son,' said the priest finally raising himself. 'When one has had as little happiness as you have had in this world, and when one has known how to profit by its miseries, one has nothing to fear in the next. I will come back tomorrow morning,' he added and left.

'O'Sullivan,' he said to the peasant who was anxiously studying his expression, 'your father is very ill, but his greatest danger seems to rise from his extreme weakness. Send Jane tonight,' he said, pointing to a little girl of eight or ten, who curtseyed respectfully on hearing her name, 'send Jane round to my house tonight. I will give her some fresh provisions, a little

sugar and a small bottle of wine which should be given to the
patient little by little.'

We continued on our way and going down the hill, he said to
me: 'I have before now seen many dying people, and my experience makes me fear that this poor man has not more than
twenty-four hours to live. I expected, Sir, to pass the time before mass tomorrow morning with you. But I hope that you will
excuse me. I want to pay a second visit to that poor man. After
all,' added the priest, shaking his head sadly, 'this man is not so
much to be pitied. I know that he is in arrears with his rent.
Tomorrow perhaps he will be evicted from his home, and although it is a very miserable one, he holds to it, Sir, as the only
place on earth that gives him sanctuary. His son has more
strength than he to support the sorrow that threatens the
family.'

We took the same path which we had left when we went up.
It was a small track which ran like a long ribbon of sand, down
to the bottom of the hill.

We walked in silence. The priest seemed preoccupied by sad
thoughts. We passed by the small white church surrounded by
the ivy-covered ruins of the abbey and the simple village tombs.
I stopped for a moment to consider these and, renewing the conversation, said to the priest: 'I see all the efforts which this poor
population has made to raise up its altars again, and I cannot
but feel indignant when I think that you are forced to rely solely
on your own resources.' 'What must be deplored,' replied the
priest, 'is that the tyranny of the Government, the exactions of
the aristocracy and the greed of the Protestant clergy have reduced this unfortunate people to such a state that it should be so
difficult and burdensome for it to provide even imperfectly for
the expenses of religious ceremonies.'

'And,' I replied, 'do you not think it should be regretted that
the Government does not take upon itself the task of building
the churches and of endowing the clergy. If that were so, would
not the church be more honoured and the ministers more respected and more independent?'

'It is only the enemies of our holy religion.' replied the
priest, 'who can speak thus; only they who wish to break the
bonds which unite priest and people. You have seen, Sir, how
the village looks on me. Sir, the people love me, and they have

reason to love me, for I love them too. They have confidence in
me and I in them. Every man in a way regards me as one of his
brothers, as the eldest of the family. How does this arise, Sir?
Because the people and I have need of each other all the time.
The people gives the fruit of its labours liberally to me, and I
give them my time, my care and my entire soul. I can do nothing
without them, and without me they would succumb under the
weight of their sorrows. Between us there is a ceaseless exchange of feelings of affection. The day I received government
money, the people would no longer regard me as their own. I
for my part might be tempted to believe that I did not depend
on them, and one day perhaps we would regard each other as
enemies. Then, Sir, I would become useless even to the government that paid me. If today I preach peace and patience, 1 am
believed because I am not suspected of gaining anything by
speaking thus, but if they could see in me an agent of the
government, of what moment would my opinion be?'[1]

'Do you not think,' I said to the priest, 'that if you lost something on the side of the people, you would make up for it on the
side of the upper classes, to whom you would find yourself much
closer?'

'We would lose by the change,' said the priest, 'and religion
would too. It is among the people that the roots of belief are to
be found. It is they who believe in another world because they
are unhappy in this one. It is they whose simple and naïve
imaginations lead them without reserve to faith. Any religion
which broke away from the people, Sir, would move away from
its source and lose its main support. It is necessary to go with
the people, Sir. There lies strength, and in order to remain
united with the people, there is no sacrifice which one should
regret imposing on oneself.'

[2] Inequality of the land. Resistance to the law permitted.
Discussion. Generalities about politics. Sovereignty of the
people. Its capacity. Its understanding and its true interests.
Praise of the Irish. We come to the presbytery. 'Don't say those
things in France or you will be taken for a Protestant minister.'

The next day, the priest being away, I wanted to go to the

[1] Note by Tocqueville: No connection between Church and State!
[2] The end of this part of Tocqueville's journal is more sketchy.

Journey to Ireland (1835)

Protestant minister's house. Answer of a woman from whom I asked the way. Met the priest all drenched. Tell him where I am going. Tells me that he had never been down the hill though he had often been on top. I go up. From the top, description of the mansion. Gothic style. Conservatories. Grounds. Deer. Wall all round. I do not see the church. At last I see it standing out clearly, a little Gothic church with open stonework. Pretty house at its side in the middle of garden of flowers. The church shut, but they go to open it. Sunday. The clergyman has just come back from a journey to Italy for his health. Inside the church; stove, carpet, pews. Two or three rich landlords; many servants. Frail appearance of the clergyman. Very well composed sermon about moral obligations. Allusion to the St. Bartholomew massacre on 29th August. I hand him my letter as I go out of church. I find an agreeable man with very good manners. He takes me to his house. Introduces me to his wife and to his daughter; apologises that she cannot play the piano as it is Sunday; regrets that his officer son is away as he could have shown me the park to which he has always the *entrée*. Conversation turns on the same subjects as with the priest. Education must be directed in a certain way to be good. Press which can lead astray. Kildare Place Society.[1] Need for an aristocracy, for a national church, for a clergy well endowed by the State. Incapacity of people in general and of the Irish in particular to govern themselves. Savages!

'Don't say all that in France or they will take you for a Catholic priest.'

Could not offer me dinner because he was dining with the lord. Return. At the top of the hill, on one side the hovels of the village and the priest's little house: on the other the mansion, the grounds, and the smoke rising through the trees around the parsonage.

Reflections: there wealth, knowledge, power. Here strength: difference of language according to position. Where to find the absolute truth.

*   *   *

[1] Society which founded Protestant confessional schools which received poor children.

Journey to Ireland (1835)

Catholic clergy

Today (1st August 1835) I was next to a young Catholic on the top of the diligence, who seemed very trustworthy.

I asked him for some information about the Catholic clergy and he told me the following:

'The charge of a parish in general carries £300, but that sum is generally divided as follows: the parish priest draws about £120; his two assistants have the rest.'

'This income is not much. Besides it depends on the goodwill of the people, and it is not pleasant to live like that on charity. So a wealthy father seldom intends his son to go into the Church, and the latter rarely does so of his own accord. Such things do happen, but they are exceptional. So the majority of priests are sons of large tenant farmers. We call a man a large farmer if he cultivates 150 acres. One cannot rank such men as gentlemen and that is a real misfortune. However our clergy is in general much to be respected. . . .'[1]

I have quoted this conversation because my experience of Ireland now makes me think it is a fair summary of the true position.

*   *   *

Memories of the persecutions

This morning (1st August 1835) I found myself on the top of the diligence sitting next to an old Catholic.

He told me, passing through Ennis, the county town of county Clare: 'All the surrounding country used formerly to belong to the O'Connells. They raised a regiment for King James, and, being defeated with the rest at the Boyne, were dispossessed. It is the heir to this family who, after two centuries, has reopened the doors of Parliament to Catholics, coming as the member for this same county Clare of which his ancestors once possessed the greater part.'

That set my companion going. He went on to tell me what had been the fate of a great many families and a great deal of land, passing through the times of Cromwell and of William III, with a terrifying exactitude of local memory. Whatever one does

[1] The dots are Tocqueville's.

the memory of the great persecutions is not forgotten and who sows injustice must sooner or later reap the fruits.

* * *

(*1st August 1835*)

Today I dined with all the lawyers who follow the circuit. Half of them, I had been told, were Catholics, but I had nothing but Protestants at my side and most of them seemed to me to be wild Orangemen. There was one among others who told me that it was a mistake to blame the evils of Ireland on bad government. I then spoke to him of the time of the penal laws, believing that he would withdraw. But not at all. He said that at that time the penal laws were necessary; that it was necessary to restrain by force men whom one could neither govern, nor let govern themselves.

* * *

Mr. West. Galway (*1st August 1835*)

Mr. West is a Dublin lawyer, the Tory candidate of the town which O'Connell captured from him by only a few votes.

Q. Do you think that a Poor Law will be of benefit to Ireland?

A. On this point I am in agreement with Mr. O'Connell that it would be a bad thing. In England where there are eight rich to one poor man, where comfort and wealth are incredibly great; even in England they have difficulty in bearing the burden of the Poor Law. What would happen in Ireland?

Q. I have heard it said at three assizes which I have just seen that the number of crimes was decidedly less great this year than in the previous ones. What is the cause of this change?

A. It is due to the wish of Mr. O'Connell and of the clergy to support the present ministry. They keep the population calm, but can stir it up at will.

Q. Is the power of Mr. O'Connell as great in this country as is supposed?

A. It is immense, and unfortunately Mr. O'Connell has a permanent interest in using his power to disturb the country. Before he entered politics Mr. O'Connell was a very distinguished and busy lawyer. He earned £5,000 a year. He gave up his

175

profession to enter Parliament, and since then the Catholics have given him a voluntary indemnity which often reaches £10,000 to £12,000. It is known that the sum is more or less according to whether the agitation is greater or less. You see that it is thus in his interest to create a new cause of trouble as soon as the present one weakens.

Q. Is it true that the Irish aristocracy is in debt?

A. Yes, to a certain extent.

Q. What is the cause of it?

A. During the war, the value of land increased immensely. The rent on an acre (on average) is £1. At that time it was £3. All landowners acquired certain habits and took on certain obligations which they could not drop. That is the cause of their present distress.

Q. Do you not think that the Bill of Sir R. Peel has contributed to it?[1]

A. No; that is a great mistake.

Q. Is it true that there are a certain number of Catholic families which have recently become rich?

A. Yes. We have begun to refuse Catholics the right to become landowners. But then, in granting them this right, we have excluded them from public functions, from which it results that all the intelligent men among them are naturally attracted to the acquisition of wealth, and, not having the same opportunities of spending their money as the rich Protestants, they rapidly acquire fortunes. In spite of this, what the Catholics still most lack, and what even in their interest prevents them from governing themselves, is the absence of an aristocracy. It is an immense body without a head. Unfortunately in this country one can say that society is clearly divided into two camps; those who have the soil and the wealth and those who have neither. Slight differences apart, all the landowners are conservatives. You can count on that.

Q. Has the new law about grand juries abolished 'jobbing'?[2]

[1] Tocqueville refers here probably to Peel's Emancipation Bill of 1829.

[2] From 1817 to 1836 a series of acts was passed to regulate local government, including the administrative powers of the grand juries. R. B. McDowell (*Public Opinion and Government Policy in Ireland 1801–1846*, London 1952, p. 80) says: 'The grand juries were shockingly careless when dealing with road contracts, and the excellent Irish communications system resulted largely from the facilities afforded by road-buildings for using public money primarily for private purposes.' This explains the term 'jobbing.'

176

A. I think that everybody agrees that it has rather increased it. (This is the first time that I have heard such a statement.)

Q. Do you not think that it is very disadvantageous to have the grand jury chosen by the sheriff and to compose it solely of great landowners? Would it not be better to have it elected?

A. I do not like elections applied to this sort of thing. They maintain society in a perpetual state of excitement and do not destroy intrigues nor jobbing. (Argument of a minority.)

Q. From when does the strength of Mr. O'Connell date?

A. He has worked for twenty years to acquire it.

Mr. O'Connell is certainly a man gifted with immense talents, of an extreme perseverance and of an indefatigable ardour. But he has a profound distrust of moderation and, among other things, of the truth. His reputation began by meetings. There is no man who knows how to handle a crowd as does Mr. O'Connell. He began by persuading the people that they were very unhappy; he spoke to them of the injustices of which they were the object. He inflamed their passions and finally advised them to offer illegal resistance by not paying the tithe. In fact a few individuals began to trample on the law in this way, then others, and finally this evil became so general, that the majority of the recipients of the tithe have been forced to renounce the exercise of their rights.

Q. But where do you think that he intends to stop?

A. When he is the absolute master of Ireland. I have heard him say himself that he would impose three conditions on the ministers for his support, to break the Orangist party, destroy the Church of Ireland (I have forgotten the third). '

Q. You have, I believe, a great number of corporations in Ireland.

A. Yes. A bill has been introduced in Parliament to ask for a reform of them. But we hope that the Lords will at least retain the right of the existing freemen, who are Protestants and Conservatives. In Dublin, for example, where the chances of the two candidates are almost equal, the two thousand freemen vote for me. You can see that if the new law took away their electoral right the balance would be reversed. It would be the same in most of the towns of Ireland.

Q. Is it true that the Tories and the Radicals are now face to face and that the middle party or the Whigs, is almost destroyed?

Journey to Ireland (1835)

A. Yes. The less advanced Whigs have become Tories, the more advanced ones Radicals. Now it could be said that Ireland is only divided into two parties.

Q. I have often heard talk of the frauds committed by Catholics to become electors. What does this signify?

A. To become a voter it suffices to swear that one has the revenue prescribed by the law. It is true that anyone can contradict the oath. But at the time of the Reform Bill, when the Registration took place, the Orangemen were so disheartened that they let things go without looking into it. A multitude of voters swore falsely. Others eluded the oath in this manner: A farmer had ten acres of land, but nine of them were on bogs and were almost unproductive. He swore that he had ten acres without subtracting anything, and he became a voter. In this way the majority of the electoral body is composed of false voters.

Q. But is this wrong not reparable?

A. Hardly. The registration was made for eight years, and at the end of these eight years it will be enough, if the voter shows his patent for him to get his new one. This absurd law does not exist, as you know, in England. Once an Irish elector is put down on the list, he cannot be removed from it except after an inquiry in the House of Commons, an inquiry which can only be instituted at great expense.

Q. Is it true that the Irish landlords squeeze their tenants as much as possible?

A. Yes. But they are in great trouble themselves. Furthermore we have never behaved as generously towards tenants in Ireland as in England. In England few farms are rented at their value. The practice in England is to divide the revenue of the land in three; one-third for the expenses of farming, one-third for the owner and one-third for the farmer. A farmer who cannot obtain these conditions seeks his fortune elsewhere. Here things are not so. Furthermore our great landowners, by dividing their land excessively to increase the number of voters, have greatly increased the wretchedness of the population.

*　　*　　*

178

Journey to Ireland (1835)

Conversation with Mr. X, judge of the Assizes Court in Galway (1st August 1835)

Mr. X is an old man much respected for his experience and knowledge.

Q. Are acts of violence very common in this part of Ireland; quarrels between different villages; fights at fairs?

A. Yes.

Q. Does your experience make you think they are getting more or less frequent?

A. Less frequent, I am convinced.

Q. What is the usual reason for these quarrels?

A. That the people are only partly civilised and so enjoy all the pleasures of rough excitement, such as the thrill of a fight and physical violence. The second reason, and perhaps the chief, is the love of strong drink; one drinks first and fights afterwards.

Q. Are the crimes committed in this part of Ireland of an especially odious character?

A. In general, no. Killings are hardly ever premeditated. They result from a fight, not from an ambush. Theft is very rare, and highway robbery almost unknown. There is no country in the world where the stranger has less to fear than in Ireland.

Q. I have seen in various crime lists many cases of rape. I have heard it said that morals are very chaste. How can those two facts be reconciled?

A. Morals actually are very chaste. Almost all accusations of rape are made by girls who hope in that way to force a man to marry them. If the marriage takes place, the case is stopped as our laws provide. This behaviour of the girls proves very rough manners, but not their inchastity.

Q. Have you as many whitefeet here as in the South?

A. No. There have always been many fewer. Acts of violence seldom have a political character.

Q. Is perjury frequent?

A. Yes.

Q. The illegal forcing of a promise on oath under threat of revenge, is that frequent?

A. Yes.

* * *

Journey to Ireland (1835)

A SERMON IN GALWAY

(*2nd August 1835*)

The Protestant congregation has the ancient Gothic cathedral, a beautiful Gothic building which is used by a hundredth part of the population (the ninety-nine others are Catholics, and only received permission sixty years ago to build themselves a place of worship elsewhere at their own expense). The church is badly maintained. The paving is badly jointed, and one would say that they have difficulty in preventing the grass growing in the joints. The walls are dirty and seem half-dilapidated. In the middle of the transept there are some very clean and comfortable pews. In the middle of the choir a large stove. All the rest of the church is deserted. The pews can seat two to three hundred people. The presence of the Court of Assizes has almost filled them. All the rest is empty. The entire congregation seems to be composed of the rich or perhaps their servants as well. An hour before we had seen an immense crowd of the poor press together on the bare stones of a Catholic church too small to accommodate them.

The preacher, who is a man who speaks well, takes trouble about his delivery, and has white gloves and a large notebook in his hand, gets up into the pulpit. He said some commonplaces about charity, then suddenly turning to politics, he reveals that God had Himself given the principle of alms-giving to the Jews, but that He had never made it a *legal* obligation. That the principle of Charity is sacred, but that its performance, as those of all the principal moral obligations, should be left to the conscience (allusion to the Poor Law against which the Orangemen were fighting in Ireland). Passing from there to the advantages of charity, he discovers that it constitutes the strongest link in society and that he knew of no others. There are, it is true, senseless and perverse men who believe that it is possible to make men equal and to eliminate the link which good actions and gratitude make between the rich and the poor. But such doctrines are manifestly contrary to the will of God, who made men weak and strong, skilful and clumsy, capable and incapable. Society should form a similar social ladder, and its happiness will depend on the respect that each one has for the rank of his neighbour, and on the satisfaction with which he occupies his own. Opposite doctrines can only be preached by the enemies of order, agitators, who having deprived the people of their celestial lights (the Bible) will push them into actions which destroy civilisation.

The preacher ended by assuring his audience that the collection was not in the least destined to relieve the wretchedness of the Catholics; without doubt all misery should concern the Christian, but does not the scripture say that you must relieve your own before thinking of strangers? And is not the moral of this especially applicable to a small community, such as the Protestants of Galway, who must remain united as a living witness of the true religion, without the support of numbers?

I left thinking that charity so restricted would hardly ruin the congregation. For in Galway almost all the Protestants are rich, and all the poor with very few exceptions are Catholics.

* * *

Consequences of a bad Government

Sometimes one learns important truths even from the men most possessed by the Party spirit.

Mr. French, an Orangist lawyer, said to us today (2nd August 1835) that people complain that the Irish are lazy and liars; but it must be remembered that for a very long time they have been able to acquire nothing, which gave them no motive for industry, and that they were obliged to hide and often to lie in order to be able to fulfil the duties of their religion. When the law worked in such a way that lying was linked with a moral duty, one should not be surprised that men lost their general respect for truth.

Galway

* * *

That if the forms of liberty are allowed to subsist, sooner or later it would kill tyranny (Galway, 2nd August 1835)

Nowhere is this general truth brought more into relief than in Ireland. The Protestants while conquering Ireland left the people with electoral rights. But they (the Protestants) owned

181

the land and as masters of the fortunes of the electors they controlled their votes at will. They left the freedom of the press but masters of the government and all its accessories, they knew that they would not dare to write against them. They left them the right to hold meetings, strongly doubting that anyone would dare to gather to speak against them. They left *habeas corpus* and the jury, for being themselves the magistrates and in a great measure the jurors, they did not in the least fear that the guilty would escape from them. Things went marvellously like that for two centuries. The Protestants had in the eyes of the world the honour of liberal principles and they enjoyed all the actual consequences of tyranny. They had a legal tyranny which would be the worst of all, if it did not leave open roads towards a future of liberty. The time has at last come when the Catholics, having become more numerous and rich, have begun to claim their place among the magistrates and on the bench of the jury; when the electors are advised to vote against their landlords; when the freedom of the press has served to prove the despotism of the aristocracy; the right to assemble at a meeting has allowed them to become kindled at the sight of their slavery; since then tyranny has been beaten by the same forces under whose shadow it thought that it would always live and which served it as instruments for two hundred years.

*   *   *

Remains of the Protestant domination

In Cork they told us that all the officials of the Corporation are Protestants (there are 80,000 Catholics in a population of 107,000). This Corporation nominates the sheriff who is a Protestant and who appoints the grand jury in which there were only two Catholics at the time we passed by there.

Now the Catholics make up four-fifths of the population of the town, as I said just now, and nineteen-twentieths of that of the county, and the Protestants cry out about oppression.

Galway, 2nd August 1835

*   *   *

Journey to Ireland (1835)

Galway Assizes. Trial of a Protestant minister accused of having seduced a girl[1] (*3rd August 1935*)

In Galway I saw a very characteristic trial which throws a strong light on the social and political condition of this country; about sixty years ago a Catholic priest named O'Rourke became a Protestant and got married.

His son was brought up in the Anglican religion, became a minister and, thanks to the good example set by his father, was given the living of Moylough, a large parish in the neighbourhood of Galway.

Soon afterwards he became a Justice of the Peace and finally the Court of Chancery charged him with the management of a considerable estate. The parish of Moylough is composed of 10,000 Catholics and about a hundred Protestants. The revenues of the rector were considerable; his duties few; as minister he levied the tithe, as Justice of the Peace he saw to it that it was paid without resistance. To occupy his leisure he bought or rented land and set out to cultivate 1,200 acres of land (it was his lawyer who said this). For thirty years Mr. O'Rourke's affairs prospered. He married three times; had a large family; established his daughters and placed his sons and lived in the hope of a happy old age.

By the sole fact of his birth, as may be imagined, Mr. O'Rourke was especially abhorred by the Catholics who formed the great mass of the surrounding population. He became far more hated still when the question of tithes was raised. He persisted in levying the tithe, while his neighbours submitted to its not being paid, and exacted it with the utmost rigour. As a magistrate he showed himself to be an inflexible and violent persecutor of the poor. Further, he even had the misfortune of attracting the animosity of a group of local Protestants. Twice there were attempts to assassinate him. But he faced the storm and hoped to intimidate his enemies.

In the parish of Moylough there lived a Catholic attorney. He embraced the cause of his co-religionists with fervour, and by legal means began that battle against the Reverend Mr. O'Rourke of which we saw the last act.

This attorney who was called Kilkelly began to watch Mr.

---

[1] Cf. *The Freeman's Journal*, Dublin, 7th August 1835.

O'Rourke, and each time he broke from the letter of the law Kilkelly took him to court or got others to do so. Seven cases followed each other in this way in a short time. Mr. O'Rourke lost all of them and was ordered to pay his adversaries considerable damages. Kilkelly declared that his intention was not in the least to apply this money to his own use. He bought some ground facing the house of Mr. O'Rourke and with the money extracted from him, began to build a pretty little Catholic chapel under his very eyes.

Mr. O'Rourke, it seems, was known in the district as having irregular morals. Two years ago there was in his service the daughter of a Catholic peasant called Molly X. Molly became pregnant. Her father drove her out of the house; her friends refused to receive her. But Kilkelly's shepherd was more sympathetic and took her into his hovel, kept her for six weeks until the child came into the world. Molly took the child to a local priest and told him that Mr. O'Rourke had seduced her, that he had taken her honour actually inside the Protestant church and that he was the father of the child. The priest gave the little girl the name of Mary O'Rourke and the news soon spread through the country. Kilkelly, knowing these facts, took the father of the girl into his service, and the father at the instigation of and with the aid of his master (as Kilkelly declared openly during the hearing) instituted the case which we witnessed.

The jury is what is termed a 'special jury' (the two parties agree on forty names from which the twelve jurors are drawn by lot). These jurors are respectable local landowners. The draw yielded nine Catholics and three Protestants. But unanimity is necessary to reach a verdict. The room is packed. The two populations, the two religions are face to face. The case is followed with the most lively interest. Mr. Kilkelly's counsel speaks. He is a Protestant; he knows, says he, that most of his hearers have come to hear the Church of England humiliated. But that is not his intention. He believes that the Church of England should expel unworthy members from its bosom and that Mr. O'Rourke is of that number. In this way he preserved his personal position and only dealt surer blows at the minister.

The witnesses are heard. Their animosity against the Protestant priest appears clearly. However, they are formal and unanimous. The audience is in suspense. The judge (a Protestant

184

and a Tory) makes his summing-up in favour of the accused. The jury retire and after an hour come back and pronounce a verdict of Guilty. Everybody knew that such a verdict was an order of banishment against the Reverend O'Rourke and many people think that this has influenced the jury more than the proofs of the accusation. What is certain is that to us as outsiders they did not seem sufficient.

The next day we left Galway to go to Tuam. The diligence going in the opposite direction stopped us. Well, What's the news? What did the jury decide in the O'Rourke case?'

'The verdict went against him, he is ruined, and this time at least he will be forced to leave the country.'

'What a blow for the Church of England!'

And they separated with mutual satisfaction. . . .[1]

At the same assizes two men were condemned to death and immediately executed for murdering and mutilating a policeman. It was thought that the murderers' only motive was that he was a policeman.

High Expense of Justice (*3rd August 1835*)

In Galway a peasant pleaded that a minister had dishonoured his daughter and claimed damages.

To prove that the peasant was merely lending his name, counsel pointed out that it was absurd to suppose that a peasant could afford the expense of such an action. The peasant giving way under the load of such reasoning was reduced to admitting that the money was in fact furnished by an enemy of the accused.

* * *

Newport-Pratt (*6th August 1835*)

In the newspapers we had seen an article by a Mr. Hughes, parish priest of Newport-Pratt, revealing that the population of his parish was dying of hunger and needed aid. We thought that we should go there to see Ireland in all its misery. We left Castlebar at 10 o'clock in the morning and went to Newport-Pratt. The intervening country was the same as almost all that we had seen in Ireland; hills stripped of trees, valleys with peat-bogs at their bottoms, with miserable huts scattered here and

---

[1] The dots are Tocqueville's.

there. A harsh and desolate sight, even with the good crops at our feet. Newport is a village built on the banks of a little river which empties into the ocean half a league further on. The vale is pretty. Two country houses surrounded by trees. In the village there are several clean two-storied houses. The parish has a population of 11,000, and 100 hamlets. There are about 400 Protestants.

We are surprised to see the main street and the river banks crowded with men and children, some sitting on the bare earth, the rest in a group. Our arrival has caused a great sensation. We are surrounded, they look at us with an avidity we cannot understand. We leave our carriage and walk awhile in the street. More than a hundred people follow us without any demonstration whatever, but with a singular tenacity. Two or three of them spoke to us. We thought that they took us to be government agents sent to relieve their distress. We asked where was the priest's house? They showed us to a white one-storied house covered with large white slates, and with three windows in the front, and a small stone peristyle, by the side of a little meadow.

The priest is not at home and about fifty people are sitting around his door and seem to be waiting for him. We left our cards and went for a walk. We came back after an hour. The priest saw us and asked us to come in. He was a man of about fifty with an open and energetic face, rather stout, a strong accent, he seemed a little common, and was dressed in black and wore riding-boots. He brought us through quite a large entrance hall into a ground-floor room where two priests from the neighbourhood were sitting. The walls are covered with coloured prints of Jesus, the Virgin Mary, the Pope, and one or two religious scenes. And between these pictures are pinned political caricatures. The furniture is old but comfortable; there are newspapers on the table.[1] We told the priest that we had seen his letters in the papers and that we could not believe the extent of the misery of which he spoke and that we had come to assure ourselves of the reality. He seemed pleased with our plan, and said that he would not let us leave until we were convinced that

---

[1] Marginal note by Tocqueville: Odd furniture. A walnut table covered with an old cloth. An old couch covered with a . . . material, mahogany chairs with horsehair cushions.*

* The dots are Tocqueville's, apparently he did not know what material it was.

what he says is true, and invited us to supper. During this time the whole crowd we had seen in the street, knowing that the priest had returned, grouped itself round the door. We asked the priest what this crowd signified; he replied that he had collected about three hundred pounds by the letters we had seen. 'I have just received a further forty,' he added, drawing them out of his pocket with an air of triumph and of evident satisfaction. 'I have just formed a committee of three Protestants and three Catholics who will use the funds under my supervision. We have bought oatmeal with this money, it arrived two days ago, and I have sent it to the shop which you see over there. The problem now is how we will distribute it. All those people whom you see,' he says, pointing to the crowd, 'are there in the hope of having a share of the oatmeal.'

We: 'But do these people really need aid?'

The Priest: 'Most of them have not eaten since yesterday. They have been sitting here hungry since this morning. All of them are small tenant farmers. Last year's crop of potatoes being poor, a dearth has been felt since March. Those who had cows, pigs and sheep have sold them in order to live. All those you see here have nothing left, for we only give relief to those who have nothing left to sell to help themselves. For several months these unfortunates whom you see here have been on the point of dying of hunger. They never eat their fill. Most of them have had to dig up the new crop and to eat potatoes the size of nuts, which have made them ill.'

Then the priest opened the window facing the crowd, which immediately became quite silent. The cry 'Hear! Hear!' passed from mouth to mouth; the priest, placed as if in a pulpit, spoke (partly in English and partly in Gaelic) roughly in these terms.

'I am to let you know that your flour has at last arrived, but some of the members of the committee think that it would be better to sell part of it. I also think that it should be so. Therefore see if you have any resources left; bring us your money, the flour will be sold at half-price and with what we get we will buy more. This effort which we ask, is thus in your interest, if it is possible. You see that we will not let those who absolutely cannot do what we suggest die of hunger. I also have some bad news to tell you; the absence of some of the committee members and the lack of time to make a list of the most needy among you,

187

prevents us distributing the grain tonight. Arm yourselves with patience and those of you who still have some provisions I tell in the name of God to share them with your friends and neighbours. Tomorrow aid will come. He who lets his neighbour die for the lack of a potato is a murderer. Disperse, go home, may God bless you. I have a final recommendation to make,' he added, 'do not eat half-ripe potatoes as you have been doing these last days. We have several sick people due to this. Nothing is more unhealthy than eating unripe vegetables.'

This speech was made in a loud and animated voice; the speaker's face showed the passionate interest that he had for the populace, and at the same time an air of firmness and command. There was more kindness than softness in his voice. The crowd listened in silence. All eyes were fixed upon him, all mouths hung open; the pale cheeks and fatigued appearance of these unhappy people showed their suffering. From time to time one of the crowd shouted a comment and the priest argued with him for a moment and then continued with his address. When he had finished part of the crowd withdrew in silence and resignation. The rest sat down again seemingly in the hope that, in spite of his words, the priest might give them some aid that night.

After dinner we wanted to leave. The door was still surrounded; from the top of the steps in front of the house the priest spoke to the people again. He said that he could not help them all and that he did not wish to choose between them. 'Your misery,' he said, 'will only be short because it will become known. Look here,' he said, pointing to us, 'these gentlemen have only come to this country to know the extent of your woe and to make it known in their country.' 'God bless them,' shouted the crowd. 'They are our brothers,' says the priest, 'they are Catholics like us. I hope,' he added, fixing his eyes on a few Protestants in the crowd, 'that there is nothing in this which hurts you. You know that where charity is concerned I make no difference between Catholics and Protestants. Jesus Christ gave His blood for us all. We are all made in the image of God.'

We passed through the crowd, which respectfully opened a path for us. In spite of all his efforts, the priest, who seemed very troubled, could not help being struck by some more wretched than the others. I saw that he dropped a few small coins into some hands. After a walk we came back. The priest showed us some very interesting statistics which I examined later; conversation became more general.

The priest: 'As I have just shown you by my accounts, you will have judged, and especially you will judge tomorrow, the extent of our misery. My confrères will tell you that it is about the same in their parishes.'

'Yes,' said the two priests, 'all the time we have before our eyes the same sight as you have just seen. This state of society is intolerable and cannot last.'

We: 'But all these parishes belong to a small number of great landowners, the Marquis of Sligo, Sir O'Donnel . . .[1] Undoubtedly these men contribute to charity during these times of distress.'

The three priests (hotly and bitterly): 'Sirs, this is an error. These great landlords contribute nothing and do nothing to prevent the unfortunate population from starving to death. It is the poor who supports the poor.'

We: 'But what is the cause of this?'

The priest: 'There are several causes; almost all the big landowners are in difficulties themselves; moreover there is a profound hatred between them and the people. All the great families of this country are Catholics who have become Protestants to save their property, or else Protestants who have seized the possessions of Catholics. The people regard them as apostates or invaders and detest them. In return they have not the least sympathy for them. They let their farmers die under their eyes; they chase them out of their miserable dwellings on the slightest pretext.'

We: 'The resignation of the people seems very great.'[2]

[1] The dots are Tocqueville's.

[2] On the margin of Tocqueville's manuscript: . . . sheep. Harvests respected by the starving. Gentleness and resignation of the people which is not due to Christian virtue alone, but also to the demoralisation caused by tyranny, and by fear of the gibbet and transportation. Said in a way to make one think that a little more impatience and energy would not displease him. Without religious duty, I could not support such a tyranny. Education the only remedy. Efforts made in that direction. Quarrel with the Rector (£350 income). His house in view, a pretty one covered with blue tiles, surrounded by tall trees in a charming landscape. Quarrel with the local aristocracy. The Christian virtue of the people. Only one adult does not go to confession. Confession twice a year at a stated time in each village. Religious fervour of the people. Financial efforts made in vain to convert them. Priests who go off twenty miles into the mountains.

189

The priest: 'It really is. You have seen two hundred unfortunate people who are in constant danger of starving to death and who hardly keep alive at all. On the nearby meadows the Marquis of Sligo has a thousand sheep and several of his granaries are full. The people have no idea of making use of these means of subsistence. They would rather die than touch them.'

We: 'That shows admirable virtue.'

The priest: 'You must have no illusions, gentlemen. Religion no doubt counts for much in this patience, but fear plays an even greater role. The unfortunate populace has been at strife with such cruel tyranny, and the gibbet and transportation have carried off so many, that finally all energy has deserted them. They submit themselves to death rather than resist. There is no continental population which, in face of similar misery, would not have its "Three Days". I confess that if I were in their position, and if I were not restrained by the strongest religious feelings, it would be very hard for me not to rebel against this tyrannical and cold-hearted aristocracy.'

These last words were spoken with peculiar bitterness and were heartily echoed by the two other priests present. It was clear that these men, even if they did not encourage the people to rebel, would not be at all angry if they did so, and that their indignation against the upper classes was vigorous and deep.

The priest added: 'The only way to revive the demoralised spirits of this miserable people is to give them education with open hands. So that is what we have undertaken, and what we are doing with all our might. Tomorrow you will see the schools. The Protestants hold that we love the dark. They will soon see that we do not fear the light.'

The priest's small house looked out on the river bank. Three hundred paces from there the river divided into two branches. The promontory between the two streams formed a little hill with a pretty meadow in the centre and trees along the banks. In the middle of the meadow was a large and beautiful square house. We had admired it as we were arriving. One of us asked the priest to whom it belonged. He answered: 'To the Protestant rector of the parish.'

Conversation turned on this subject, and we found that the priest and the clergyman were at open war, and fought for souls with great heat. They attacked each other in the newspapers and from the pulpit in very bitter style. I saw some samples of the controversy. I remember that the Protestant minister called the Catholic 'a bloodthirsty priest'. I do not remember what epithets the priest used, but they were scarcely more complimentary.[1] The priest did not hide from us the fact that he was at least on cold terms, if not actually quarrelling, with the local landowners. He himself was the son of a big local farmer. All his emotions and all his conceptions clearly tended to democracy.

We questioned him about the religious beliefs of the people. He answered: 'The people have a strong and living enthusiasm for religion. In this parish, with more than ten thousand Catholics, I know only one adult who does not confess. General confession takes place twice a year. I announce from the pulpit that I shall be making my next tour at such and such a time, and fix a day for each village. All penitents must present themselves at the appointed time and place, and I hear their confession one after another.'

*　　*　　*

The distinction which must sometimes be made between good morals and decency

In Ireland where there are hardly any illegitimate children, and where, therefore, morals are very chaste, women take less trouble to hide themselves than in any other country in the world, and men seem to have no repugnance to showing themselves almost naked. I have seen young girls bathing in the sea at a short distance from young men.

In England where one birth in eighteen is, I believe, illegitimate, and where the morals of the lower classes are decidedly lax, decency is carried to the length of a ridiculous affectation.

Does not what we call 'decency' derive rather from the state of civilisation than from that of morals? Or rather is not ex-

[1] Marginal note by Tocqueville: All the policemen Protestants; all the Justices of the Peace, except one, Protestants. Good reception of the priest in a Protestant house.

ternal decency the combination of two things? Does not extreme decency come from extreme civilisation linked with rather restrained and well-regulated manners?

It is worth looking into that.

8th August 1835. Castlebar

* * *

Castlebar (8th August 1835)

Today I saw the chief constable of Castlebar. He is the man who commands all the policemen of the county. He told me that he has 250 men under him scattered in different parishes.

I asked him if crimes are frequent in the county. He replied that they are, but that they are less frequent than in the south, and that they are of a less 'insurrectional' nature. The system of whitefeet is less evident. For the rest he thinks that the number of crimes in Ireland is gradually diminishing. For twenty years he occupied a similar position at Clonmel. During that time the 'Insurrection Act' was in force. Every man who was found away from his home after sunset without leave was transported. In spite of this the number of crimes was fruightening. The police could only move in a group.

Asked if he thought this country was threatened with civil war. Replied that the peasants are quite ready for a civil war, but the difficulty is to find chiefs to lead them. Everybody who has any property dreads civil war to an equal extent, because they know that once the torrent burst through, all property would run the same risk.

'Unfortunately,' he added, 'in this country politics and religion are one. If politics were separated we could easily manage the people. Speak to the man of the people in Ireland; you can make him joke about his wretchedness, and about the oppression to which he is subject. Speak to him one word about his religion and he becomes sullen and turns his back on you. "Take our goods, but do not touch our beliefs", this is the cry which echoes a thousand times among the agricultural population of Ireland. . . .'[1]

Our interlocutor, although an agent of the Government, is evidently half an Orangeman, if he is not one entirely.

[1] The dots are Tocqueville's.

V

A Postscript:
Tocqueville and his British Friends[1]

THE ANALYST OF DEMOCRACY

Tocqueville, who was born on 29th July 1805, made three journeys to the British Isles. (He already knew an English lady, Mary Mottley, who was to become his wife.) In 1833 he knocked at Nassau Senior's chambers announcing himself: 'Je suis Alexis de Tocqueville et je viens faire votre connaissance.' He was then 28 years old and was about to write the first two volumes of the work which brought him world fame, his *De la Démocratie en Amérique*. They appeared in 1835. No doubt Tocqueville felt in 1833 that he had to observe the British political animal in the flesh before he could formulate the political philosophy which this first instalment of the *Democracy* was to teach.

'In England (Tocqueville wrote in the *Democracy*) the centralisation of the Government is carried to great perfection; the State has the compact vigour of one man, and its will puts immense masses in motion and turns its whole power where it pleases. But England, which has done such great things for the last fifty years, has never centralised its administration. Indeed, I cannot conceive that a nation can live and prosper without a powerful centralisation of government. But I am of the opinion that a centralised administration is fit only to enervate the nations in which it exists, by incessantly diminishing their local spirit.'

This central problem remains the vigilant concern of British politics.

His great book was reviewed by John Stuart Mill in *The London Review* (July-January number, 1835-36, pp. 85-129).

[1] Cf. *The Times*, 29th July 1955.

'M. de Tocqueville', [writes Mill] has set the example of analysing democracy; of distinguishing one of its features, of its tendencies, from another; of showing which of these tendencies is good, and which bad, in itself; how far each is necessarily connected with the rest, and to what extent any of them may be counteracted or modified, either by accident or foresight. . . . The author's mind, except that it is of a soberer character, seems to us to resemble Montesquieu most among the great French writers. . . .'

Mill confirmed what the greatest of Tocqueville's French critics, among them Royer-Collard and Sainte-Beuve, had already maintained; they saw in the young author the Montesquieu of the nineteenth century.

Mill's review was based on the translation of the book by Henry Reeve, who, like Senior, remained Tocqueville's intimate friend until the end of his life.[1]

In 1835 Tocqueville returned to Great Britain, now with his fame firmly established. He was already brooding over the continuation of the *Democracy*. There is a characteristic unpublished note of 11th May 1835, jotted down after a conversation with Reeve:

'Prouquoi la centralisation est-elle plutôt dans les habitudes de la démocratie? Grande question *à creuser* dans le troisième volume de mon ouvrage, si je puis l'y intercaler—Question *capitale*. Centralisation, instinct démocratique, instinct d'une société qui achève de se tirer du système individuel du Moyen Age. Préparation au despotisme.'

Here we have already in a nutshell the last two volumes of the *Democracy*. They were published in 1840. Again Mill reviewed them, this time in *The Edinburgh Review*; he reprinted the article with slight alterations later on in the second volume of his *Dissertations and Discussions*. In a sentence of this remarkable essay, which remains among the best things written on Tocqueville, Mill recognises that with the *Democracy* 'begins a new era in the scientific study of politics'.

It was during this visit that Tocqueville was invited by a Select Committee of the House of Commons to give his views

---

[1] The complete correspondence of Tocqueville with Reeve and Mill has been published as volume vi, 1, of my edition of Tocqueville's Complete Works, Gallimard, Paris, 1955.

on the question of bribery at elections. In his evidence he warned the members of the Committee of the dangers from 'the tyranny of the majority', which he considered 'the greatest evil and the most formidable danger that can attend a purely democratic government'. The warning has lost nothing of its validity.

In 1857, two years before his death, Tocqueville returned to London to study State papers relating to his work on the French Revolution. The first volume of this study had appeared in 1856 under the title: *L'Ancien Régime et la Révolution*. This work, too, was a study of State centralisation. Tocqueville showed from the example of French history how centralisation and democratisation go together. In the beginning of the democratic revolution men fought for their freedom in order to make themselves equal, but the more equality was achieved, the more freedom was threatened by democratisation. Following his master Montesquieu, Tocqueville differentiated two democracies: a free and an unfree one. It was in England that he found the methods and norms of the former. The French Revolution was to him the prototype of any social revolution, including, one might add, the social revolution of our time. It is here where Tocqueville's great achievement as sociologist must be sought.

The work was again translated by his old friend, Henry Reeve, and it received in England the same enthusiastic welcome as Tocqueville's previous book. Greg reviewed it in *The Times* (3rd and 7th September 1856). Cornewall Lewis, with whom he was in intimate personal contact for years, wrote him a deeply appreciative letter. Lord Clarendon, the Foreign Secretary, arranged an interview with Prince Albert, who was already familiar with the *Ancien Régime*.

Tocqueville was highly impressed by his interview with the Prince, for he added in a postscript to a letter to Lady Theresa Lewis, Lord Clarendon's sister:

'I re-open my letter to tell you that I have just seen Prince Albert and that I am enchanted by this visit. I could not tell you (and especially not in a postscript), how impressed and charmed I was by the justness of his mind. I have rarely met so distinguished a man and never a Prince, who seemed to me, taking it all in all, so remarkable; on leaving him, I could tell him, without flattering, that amongst all the things worthy to remember which I had seen in England, what impressed me most was the conversation which we just had. You are fortunate to have such a man so near the Throne.'[1]

The Prince Consort's reaction to the interview with the famous Frenchman was pertinent and witty:

'My dear Lord Clarendon, I return with my best thanks M. de Tocqueville's letter, which has made me blush although it could not but please me to have gained the esteem of so distinguished a man. I apprehend his feelings are the same as those expressed by the King towards his Prime Minister in Blanche's "White Cat": "He is the cleverest man in our dominion For he is always of our opinion." Ever, Yours truly, Albert.'[2]

When Tocqueville returned to his beloved Cherbourg the Admiralty honoured him by putting a warship at his disposal. So it was recognised that he had vigorously and persistently maintained the principles of an ordered freedom in spite of the régime of Louis Napoleon. Had he not on 11th December 1851, published in *The Times* a long anonymous account of Napoleon's *coup d'etat* which Mrs. Grote, wife of the historian of Greece, had smuggled from Paris to *The Times* office where Henry Reeve worked as leader-writer. It was probably Reeve himself who translated this unforgettable appeal to the British nation as guardian of the cause of freedom.

Tocqueville's impact on the next generation of British political thinkers was equally fertile. His thought nourished Matthew Arnold, Bagehot, Henry Sumner Maine, John Morley, Leslie Stephen, Henry Sidgwick, James Bryce, and, above all, Lord Acton, Maitland, and A. V. Dicey. Nor should we forget in this series of great names Harold Laski, who transmitted Tocqueville's spiritual heritage to not a few of his pupils. Thus Tocqueville's insight and political wisdom reach our present age. It is only fitting that his contribution to British political thought should be, all too briefly, marked on the day when we commemorate the 150th anniversary of his birth.

---

[1] I quote by gracious permission of her Majesty the Queen from a copy of this postscript in French in the hand of Queen Victoria at the Royal Archives in Windsor.

[2] The late Lord Clarendon kindly allowed me to copy this note from his family papers.

Appendices[1]

1. CORPORATIONS

Extracts from the Report on Corporations.[2] Number of Corporations in England and Wales: 246. (Number of parishes: 15,535; almost anything larger than a mere village has a special form of government.)

HISTORICAL

'We have not discovered that there was any general principle in the mode of forming the constituency of the boroughs, nor can we assume that any one system of policy or common law right prevailed at any period throughout the realm' (p. 16). This point is disputed by antiquarians who maintain that going back to Saxon times one finds that all the inhabitants formed the electoral bodies of the Boroughs. But I do not think there is any positive proof of this, and it seems against the medieval *spirit of locality*. Nothing, in that period, gives an impression of uniformity.

Charters of Incorporation do not seem to go back beyond the reign of Richard II: most of them were granted between the reign of Henry VIII and the Revolution.

It is between the reigns of Richard II and Henry VI that one begins to find the '*system of a municipal body politic and corporate which takes by succession, admitting members upon a mere personal*

---

[1] The appendices 1–4 are not dated; but written during Tocqueville's second journey to England. All dots are Tocqueville's.

[2] The full title is: *First Report of the Commissioners appointed to inquire into the Municipal Corporations in England and Wales*, 30 March 1835. Much of Tocqueville's quotations or summaries of this report is in English in his manuscript.

197

right, *without any qualifications either of residence or of property'*
(p. 17).

ORGANISATION: GENERAL IDEA

The *Corporation*, in the legal sense of the word, is the assembly
of men having the direct or indirect right to govern the borough.

The members of the Corporation are divided into two categories:

(1) Those called 'freemen Burghesses' . . . who have only
certain limited rights.

(2) Those who belong to the 'Ruling Body'. Often the name
Corporation is applied to them only.

According to French ideas and the customs of the nineteenth
century from the above one might have supposed that:

(1) The *freemen* form the electoral body of the Borough.

(2) That there would be some conditions prerequisite for becoming a *freeman*, representative of the Borough; residence,
payment of taxes, or personal qualifications.

(3) That these *freemen* appoint the *Ruling Body* which acts
in the name of the Borough and represents its will.

I do not know if it was like that in England in Saxon times,
but it is not so now any more.

(1) Generally one could not say that it is the Borough that
the *freemen* represent. In some places this right is acquired by
birth, in others by marriage, in others by belonging to a craft
guild; hardly anywhere is residence a necessary qualification,
and almost everywhere a greater or smaller payment to the
Ruling Body will buy the right. So to be a *freeman* is nearer to
a personal right belonging to an individual, than to a right of
representation. 'In most places all identity of interest between
the Corporation and the inhabitants has disappeared. [. . .'[1]]
In *Plymouth*, where the population [. . .] is more than 75,000
the number of freemen is only 437, and 145 of these are non-
resident. In *Norwich* the great majority of the householders and
ratepayers are excluded from the corporate body, while paupers,
lodgers, and others, paying neither rates nor taxes are admitted

[1] Cf. *First Report of the Commissioners etc.*, p. 32.

in the corporation.[1] In Ipswich, a town of 20,000 inhabitants, the resident *freemen* amount to 1 in 55 of the population and one-third of them pay no taxes; 1 in 9 are *paupers*, and eleven-twelfths of the taxable property belongs to people with no part in the corporation (p. 33).[2]

In most of the Boroughs the number of *freemen* is limited, and often it has been the policy of the *Ruling Body* to reduce the numbers to very few by refusing to sell the right.

(2) The right of *freemen* seldom consists in taking part, even indirectly, in the government of the Borough.

Seldom do they appoint all the officers of the *Ruling Body*, and still more seldom do they have a completely free choice or one applicable equally to all the officers. Their rights are of quite a different sort and fall more or less into the category of personal rights. For instance they usually nominate the members of Parliament. In many Boroughs that right counts as the only privilege of the *freemen* and that is the worst abuse of the system; many new *freemen* have been appointed to carry elections. Just one example: at Maldon in 1826, 1,870 *freemen* were admitted; the average is seventeen. See p. 34.[3]

They enjoy certain privileges such as exemption from certain local taxes, and a share in part of the communal revenue. Often *Commons* belong to the *freemen* of a Corporation and there are provisions for sharing the benefit from them. Often, as at Lancaster and Bath, they are let and the rent divided between the *freemen*. More often they exploit them themselves. At Berwick-upon-Tweed the freemen get as much as £6,000 from rent of land. See p. 31.[4]

RULING BODY

I have mentioned that the second part of the Corporation consists of the *Ruling Body*. That usually consists of an assembly called the *Common Council* presided over by a chairman generally called *the Mayor*.

The Common Council is usually divided into two branches.

[1] Tocqueville's quotation is not quite exact; the Report itself reads: 'admitted to the exercise of the functions of freemen, and form a considerable portion of the corporation.'
[2] Ibid.   [3] Ibid.   [4] Ibid.

The more important are usually called *aldermen* and the rest *councilmen*.

How is the Common Council Formed?

It hardly ever happens that the Common Council comes up for re-election at fixed times. In most Boroughs the members of the Common Council are permanent. When there is a vacancy, in some Boroughs the *freemen* are called on to fill it, but more often the remaining members fill the gap made by death in their ranks.

So not only do the *freemen* not represent the inhabitants, but the *Ruling Body* does not represent the *freemen*. One can say that the second have a personal privilege to rule, just as the first have a personal privilege to appoint the members of Parliament and to be exempt from certain local taxes.

In this then, as in many other matters, the English have only an *appearance* of popular government. Democracy on the surface, aristocracy below.

Functions of the Common Council

Usually the charters give the *Ruling Body* the right to make ordinances and regulations. They often nominate all the freemen; they appoint and settle the salaries of the corporate officers; they manage the corporate property; in many cases they elect the borough magistrates,[1] they dispense the patronage belonging to the Corporation, ane distribute the charities for which the Corporations are Trustees (p. 22).[2] They are responsible for local tribunals. We will go into that further down.

One must not forget that part of the government, properly so called, is already out of their hands. Most of the charters are very ancient and made in times of a very imperfect civilisation. The duties of the corporations are limited to matters specified in the charters. Since then Parliament has enacted many local acts to improve the social condition of one Borough and another, and usually has entrusted the carrying into effect of these acts to persons other than the corporation. It has become customary not to rely on the municipal Corporations for exercising the

[1] Tocqueville omits: and used to choose the members of Parliament for the borough Men.

[2] Ibid.

powers incident to good municipal government. The powers granted by Local Acts of Parliament for various purposes, have been from time to time conferred, not upon the municipal officers, but upon trustees or commissioners, distinct from them: so that often the Corporations have hardly any duty to perform. They have the nominal government . . .;[1] but the efficient duties, and the responsibility have been transferred to other hands (p. 17).[2] The paving, lighting and watching of the town are usually regulated by local acts.

What is meant by corporate officers; by whom appointed; what functions?

The *corporate officers* are the officials whose duty it is to act in the name of the corporation. They are its executive power, while the Common Council is its legislative power.

The principal corporate officers are:

(1) The Mayor,
(2) The Recorder,
(3) The Town Clerk,
(4) The Coroner,
(5) The Chamberlain or Treasurer.

Apart from the principal officers, there are a great many subordinate officers with whom the report does not deal.

How appointed?

Generally these officers are elected by the Common Council.

What functions have they?

That is not a very important question for the subject I am studying, and the answer would make me go into too many details.

LOCAL JUSTICE

In most Boroughs the Corporation has the right to administer justice:

(1) By Justices of the Peace.
(2) By courts of justice.

[1] Tocqueville omits: of the town.   [2] Ibid.

Appendices

(1) The Justices of the Peace are often chosen by the Common Council and are almost always taken from its members.

(2) In most Boroughs the Corporation has the right to judge criminal matters. In most cases local courts have not the right to pronounce the death penalty; sometimes they can.

I *believe I understand* that these courts are formed either by an assembly of the Justices of the Peace, or, in serious cases, by a magistrate and a jury. Sometimes the jury is exclusively chosen from the freemen.

The great majority of Boroughs have also the right to try civil cases. Often their jurisdiction is limited by the amount in dispute and their decision is always subject to appeal. Most of these courts have customs of their own. The Mayor generally presides over these courts. Juries are sometimes used.

Prisons

Most Boroughs have a prison under the authority of the Corporation.

The Poor

In some Boroughs only the Corporation is responsible for the administration of the poor.

Properties

Many Corporations have considerable sources of revenue. They consist in land, rent of glebe, fair and market dues, and customs on the import or export of certain types of merchandise.

In many Corporations the revenues are sufficient for the maintenance of all necessary municipal institutions. In others, although sufficient, they are partly applied to other objects. In most Boroughs those revenues are not sufficient and have to be supplemented by local taxes.

Expenses

The revenues of the Corporations are variously employed: a great part is usually absorbed in the salaries of their officers and entertainments of the Common Council and their friends. The cost of prosecutions at the borough sessions and of supporting the gaols, form part of the expenditures in some places. It is not often that much of the corporate property is expended on police or public improvements (p. 32).[1]

DEBTS

The debt of many Corporations is very heavy.[2] In some, payment of the interest absorbs a very large proportion of the revenue; others are absolutely insolvent.

PATRONAGE

Frequently the Corporations own patronage; that is to say that they have the right of presentment to livings, to appoint lecturers, masters of schools and hospitals, and have the power of selecting the objects of various charities.

Another capital defect of the present system of Corporations: confusion of powers. The *Common Council* exercises not only legislative and advisory functions, its members are sometimes given active, administrative duties, and, even more often, judicial functions. All three capacities are united in the Mayor.

2. JUSTICES OF THE PEACE

I take these notes from Dr. Rees's *New Cyclopaedia*:[3] Justices shall not be regularly punished for anything done by them in sessions as judges . . . if they are guilty of any misdemeanor in office, information lies against them in the King's Bench where they shall be punished by fine and imprisonment: and all persons who recover a verdict against a Justice for any wilful or malicious injury are entitled to double costs. No writ shall be sent out against any Justice of the Peace for anything done by him in the execution of his office, until notice in writing shall be delivered to him one month before the issuing out of the same,

[1] Ibid.

[2] The Report reads: extremely, *op. cit.*, p. 32.

[3] The *Cyclopaedia: or Universal Dictionary of Arts, Sciences, and Literature* by Abraham Rees, vol. xix (London, 1819), article 'Justice'. The whole summary of the article is in English in Tocqueville's manuscript.

containing the cause of action . . . nor shall any action be brought against a Justice for anything done in the execution of his office, unless commenced within six months of the act committed. . . .

'The power and office of Justices terminate in six months after the demise of the crown, by an express writ of discharge under the great seal, by writ of *supersedeas*, by a new commission, by accession to the office of Sheriff or Coroner.

'The origin of Justices of the Peace is referred to the fourth year of Edward III. They were first called *Conservators* or *Wardens of the Peace*, elected by the county upon a writ directed to the Sheriff; but the power of appointing them was transferred by statutes from the people to the king; and under this appellation appointed by 1 Edward III, Cap. 16. Afterwards, the statute of 34 Edward III, Cap. 1, gave them the power of trying felonies, and then they acquired the appellation of *Justices*. They are appointed by the King's special commission under the great seal, the form of which was settled by all the judges in 1590; this appoints them all, jointly and severally, to keep the peace, and any two or more of them to inquire and determine any felonies or other misdemeanors; and the King may appoint as many as he shall think fit in every county in England and Wales, though they are generally made at the discretion of the Lord Chancellor, by the King's leave. At first the number of Justices were not above two or three in a county . . . the number which gradually increased through the ambition of private persons, was (afterwards) restrained first to six, and then to eight, in every county by Richard II,[1] but their number has greatly increased since their first institution.

'As to their qualifications, the Statutes of Richard II[2] direct them to be of the best reputation and the most worthy men in the county, . . .[3] orders them to be of the most sufficient knights, esquires and gentlemen of the Law. By the Statutes of Henry V,[4] they must be resident in their several counties. By the Statutes of Henry VI, no Justice was to be put in commission, if he had not lands to the value of £20 per annum. It is

---

[1] Here the quotation is abbreviated.
[2] The reference is inaccurate.
[3] Tocqueville does not specify the Statutes.
[4] Reference inexact.

now enacted by 5 George II, Cap. II that every Justice, with
some exceptions, shall have £100 per annum clear of all deduc-
tions; of which he must make oath . . .[1] and if he acts without
such qualifications, he shall forfeit £100. It is also provided
that no practising attorney, solicitor or proctor shall be capable
of acting as a Justice of the Peace.'

3. THE POOR. EXAMINATION OF THE LAW OF 14TH AUGUST 1834

POOR LAW OF 14TH AUGUST 1834[2]

In this law the English have kept to the principle of the Eliza-
bethan law: anyone who lacked the necessities of life had the
right to ask for the help of society.

But they have tried to make it less onerous for society. They
have introduced great changes in the *administration* of relief and
in the *nature* of the relief.

Administration

Before the law of 14th August 1834, the law imposed on the
parishes the duty of caring for their poor but left them pretty
free to do it how they liked; thence innumerable abuses. One can
imagine what would happen in little parochial administrations
left to themselves in a matter of such importance. Thence, also,
an incredible inequality in the burden between one parish and
another. (No. 106 of the *Quarterly Review*[3] gives a well-drawn
sketch of the abuses to be found in the parishes of the county of
Kent.)

The law of 14th August 1834 has *centralised* the administration of relief to the poor in the hands of three functionaries called

[1] Reference again abbreviated by Tocqueville.

[2] Tocqueville refers here to *An Act for the Amendment and better Administration
of the Laws relating to the Poor in England and Wales*, London 1834. The small
volume is to be found among Tocqueville's working library at the Château de
Tocqueville and bears the following inscription: 'M. de Tocqueville from W. N.
Senior.' Senior was practically the author of this Act. Cf. the admirable study by
Marian Bowley: *Nassau Senior and Classical Economics*, London 1937, pp. 328 ff.
See also *Correspondence and Conversations of Alexis de Tocqueville with Nassau
William Senior. From 1834 to 1859*, vol. i, p. 12 f, London 1872.

[3] Tocqueville refers to an anonymous article in the *Quarterly Review* (Number
106, vol. liii, London 1835) which is entitled *English Charity* (pp. 473–539).

Poor Law Commissioners (for England and Wales). They are appointed by the King.

The *Commissioners* inspect the parishes, make regulations and join up several parishes into *unions*, when that will make it easier to find work for the poor or the elements of a good local administration. They are bound to make a yearly report to Parliament.

One can appeal against their decision, or complain against their regulations to the Court of King's Bench only.

Besides these chief officials, in each parish or union of parishes there are to be a certain number of officials who, under different names, are required to look into the demands of the poor. These officials are not appointed by the commissioners, but every year by the vote of all the *ratepayers*, that is to say all those who will have to contribute to the poor rate (Law of 1834, number 38). The Commissioners have the right to give them orders, but not to dismiss them or even have them punished (Law of 1834, number 38). This latter right vests in the first instance in *any* two Justices of the Peace of the county, and by appeal to all the Justices of the Peace assembled in Quarter Sessions (Law of 1834, numbers 43–54).

Let us stop a moment to look at this organisation which is characteristic of the English race, and which can be seen again in almost all the institutions created by it in the New World.

Three elements come into play:

(1) Choice of the executive power.
(2) Election.
(3) Control by the judicial power.

These three elements are combined in a way that ensures an active, but not a tyrannical administration.

Three men chosen by the King and working from the centre of the kingdom, direct the immense machine of the Poor Laws. But there is an appeal from their mistakes to one of the great Courts of the land, functioning, like them, at the centre.

They have an absolute right to give orders to the municipal officials, but they can neither appoint them nor dismiss them, since that is the duty of the parishes themselves, for the Constitution requires that no tax be *levied* without consent (the rate-payers' votes are weighted proportionately to the burden they bare, so one individual may have three votes) (Law of 1834, number 40).

Finally if the municipal officials fail in the duties imposed on them by the Commissioners, a disinterested, independent power calls them back to duty.

Changes introduced by the new law in the nature of aid

This seems to me the most important change introduced by the new law:

Under the old law relief was regarded as a *gift* to an individual; under the new it is considered as a *loan* and all relief given to a man for his wife and children under sixteen counts as being loaned to himself (numbers 58–9), so that when a poor man who has asked for public assistance in a time of distress, finds work, the poor-law officer is entitled to demand, through the agency of the Justice of the Peace, that the new master should pay his wages over to the parish, or at least such part of his wages as is above a minimum subsistence level. (Note: it is clear that here the legislator is involved in a vicious circle. If he does not insist on the labourer giving the product of his toil, it is not a *loan*, but remains as it used to be a gift; if he does so insist, the labourer reduced to poverty again becomes a charge on society.)

The second important change refers to illegitimate children.

Under the old law, when a woman had an illegitimate child, her evidence on oath naming the father was accepted, and he was made to support the child, failing which it became a charge on the parish. I have pointed out before how such legislation encourages bad morals.

Under the new law the unmarried mother is no longer believed on oath. Her oath is only an element of proof which has to be corroborated by others. If the child falls as a burden on the parish, the relief given to it, or, following the language of the law, the loan made to it, is counted as due from the mother (see Law of 1834, numbers 70–7).

Such are the principal changes introduced by the new law in poor law legislation. Looking at it closely, one can easily see that the most important change is by no means in the letter of this law, but in the spirit which caused it to be enacted.

The real, not the ostensible, object of the legislature in amending the old poor law legislation is to discourage the indigent from asking for public charity by making it distasteful for him.

The English felt that such an idea could not be expressed in the law, and that its execution depended much more on who was to carry the law into effect than on who made it. So they went no further than to establish a central authority and give it the right to make regulations. It is by the regulations that they count on making legal charity so distasteful to the poor that they will not have recourse to it except in the last extremity. To understand the object of the legislature, see the article in the *Quarterly Review* mentioned above.

Reeve told me that the object of the legislature was to succeed in abolishing *outdoor relief.* The poor who did not wish to enter the workhouse and submit to its annoying *régime*, would then have no right to anything. But before that final object of the law could be reached, it was necessary to build new *poor houses* or to enlarge those that now exist. The alternative of which I spoke above could not yet be offered.

* * *

New Poor Law, promulgated on 14th August 1834[1]

Two Justices of the Peace can order the employer to pay part of the wages to the overseer (59).

Rules for settlements simplified (64–9).

All the old laws about bastards repealed (69).

New system (71–7).

So, three orders of powers:

(1) Commissioners appointed by the King.

(2) Officers elected.

(3) Justices of the Peace . . .

Guardian of the poor elected by the ratepayers (38).

The Commissioners determine the number and prescribe the duties of guardians and also fix a qualification without which no person shall be eligible as guardian (id.).

In the unions at least one guardian for each parish. Elected

[1] Here Tocqueville's text is partly in French, partly in English.

every year. A ratepayer's vote counts for two or three according to the amount of the rate he pays (40).

It is the Commissioners who make rules, orders and by-laws. The Justices of the Peace punish infringements of these laws (43–54).

Father, mother, grandfather and grandmother are bound to maintain their children under sixteen years.

Husband too responsible for children born before the marriage (56–7).

Relief considered as a loan (58).

The loan is not returned by the poor . . . (*sic*)

Central Courts of Justice:

The Court of Chancery. The Courts.

Possessiveness is the predominant characteristic of the English race.

4. JUDICIAL POWER

Action of justice in the government.

Mr. Roebuck in his article on the Corporations (*London Review*, 1st April 1835)[1] suggests dividing the whole country into administrative districts subject to certain *legal obligations*, and to compel them to remain within the limits of their functions, he suggests putting them under the central jurisdiction of the Court of King's Bench.[2]

This idea which he does not seem to present as an innovation, shows how in the minds of the English the action of the administrative power is subject to the Courts of Justice.

In France the legal obligations of the administrative districts would be under the supervision of a central *official*, not of a Court.

[1] Cf. *Municipal Corporation Reform, London Review*, April 1835, p. 72; the article is signed J. A. R.

[2] Tocqueville adds the following quotation in a footnote: 'And as they exercise their powers under the sanction of a general law and of the general Courts of Law, the limits of their powers would in all cases in England be determined by the Court of King's Bench.'

Appendices

5. ON BRIBERY AT ELECTIONS

Tocqueville gave evidence before the Select Committee on Bribery at Elections on 22nd June 1835. The Committee had been appointed by the House of Commons on 11th March of the same year. If one examines the list of the Committee members, it is to be presumed that George Grote, the historian of Greece, had suggested Tocqueville as witness.

We must remember that the first two volumes of his *Democracy in America* had just been published which had established his authority in the science of government, and Electoral Corruption is an old theme of English parliamentary history. Already in 1696 electoral corruption was defined by law. Other acts were passed in 1729 and 1809. The Reform Bill of 1832, though it had enlarged the electorate, had by no means removed electoral bribery and corruption. 'In many constituencies, to increase the number of electors', writes Lowes Dickinson, 'was only to increase the opportunities for bribery. . . .'[1] Consequently, it is not surprising that further action had to be taken to check and control this evil. From 1842 to 1883 eight Acts of Parliament were passed against parliamentary corruption. In this context Tocqueville's exposition must be read. Though it is evidently focused on French Parliamentary conditions, it is nevertheless an essential product of his sojourn amongst us which we re-publish here for the first time, since it was printed in *Reports from Committees*.[2]

Lunae 22° die Junii 1835

MONSIEUR ALEXIS DE TOCQUEVILLE, EXAMINED, BY THE INTERPRETATION OF A MEMBER OF THE HOUSE

4012. Are you acquainted with the provisions of the laws and ordinances of France relating to the mode of taking votes at elections?—The first law which it is necessary to notice is that

[1] Cf. L. Dickinson, *The Development of Parliament in the Nineteenth Century*, London 1895, p. 43 f.

[2] Sixteen volumes. *Bribery at Elections*, vol. viii, 1835. Cf. also: Charles Seymour, *Electoral Reform in England and Wales. The Development and Operation of the Parliamentary Franchise*, 1832–1885. New Haven, 1915. G. D. Weil, *Les Elections Législatives depuis* 1789. *Histoire de la Législation et des Moeurs*, Paris 1895.

of February 1817; the law of 1817 has no particular reference to secret voting, it states that the vote shall be given in writing, but the law provides no guarantee for the secrecy of the vote. I think that the first enactment relative to secret voting is to be found in the law of 29 June 1820. That law says, in express and positive terms, that the vote is to be secret, and provides, so far as I recollect, that the elector himself, after having written his vote, or having caused it to be written by an elector chosen by himself, shall deliver to the president the paper folded; and the same law declares that immediately after the examination of those papers they shall be burnt in presence of the electors.

4013. Will you describe the mode in which, under this law, the vote is deposited in the urn?—In the first place, our law requires that nobody shall be admitted into the Electoral College but the electors. In the Electoral College, according to the law to which I have referred, there was a table at which the president and the different members forming the bureau are seated; and I think this is the proper place to inform the Committee who are the individuals whom I call the president and the members of the bureau. According to the law of 1820, the president was nominated by the King; the members of the bureau, who consisted, according to my belief, of three scrutineers and a secretary, were nominated by the electoral body itself. The functions of the president, as the name implies, were to direct the operations of the electoral body, and at the same time to direct the police of the Electoral College. Thus the law declares that without the authority of the president, no armed body can remain stationary in the neighbourhood of the Electoral College, and of course not introduce itself into it, and for a long time past, I believe there is not a single example of a president having authorized the approach of an armed body near any Electoral College.

4014. Do you mean to say, that troops are sent out of the town in which the college is altogether?—No.

4015. You only mean to say, that they must not be within the precincts of the Electoral College?—Yes, in the neighbourhood of the Electoral College, for example, no body of troops could be collected round the building of the Electoral College. With respect to the scrutineers and the secretary, their functions, according to my belief, consist in counting the number of the

voters and the number of the votes, and in general to take care
that the laws respecting elections are executed. When any
doubtful question arises, the president in general has not the
power of determining without consulting the bureau.

4016. Will you state the progress of the different operations
which the elector has to perform from his arrival in the town
where he is about to give his vote, up to the moment when the
election is declared?—The electors' right is generally established by the amount of their taxes paid. The number of the
electors, under the enactments of the law of 1820, was settled by
a list. At the approach of an election, the duty of the functionary,
representing in every 'département' the Government, was to
send to every member on the elector's list, what we call an
Electoral Chart or Ticket. Furnished with this ticket, the elector
went to the town where the Electoral College was sitting, and
on showing this ticket, he obtained the right of entering the
college itself. As soon as he entered the Electoral College,
according to the law of 1820, he presented himself to the president, and there he took an oath; after which he wrote secretly
the name of the candidate whom he had chosen, and he delivered
this paper folded up to the president. The secretary, who is a
member of the bureau, has before him a list of the electors, and
as the electors vote, the secretary writes his own name against
the name of the elector who votes, which is an attestation that
the elector has voted in his presence; the object of which is to
prevent double voting. When the elector had delivered his vote
to the president, he could remain in the Electoral College till
the end of the election.

4017. What does the president do with the voting papers?—
The moment when the president received the folded paper from
the elector, he dropped it into what is called the Electoral Urn,
in the presence of the electoral body. When the deposition of the
votes was ended, the electoral urn was emptied in the presence
of the electors. The scrutineers counted the number of the
voting papers, and observed whether the number of the papers
exactly correspond with the number of the signatures made upon
the electoral list by the secretary; that being done, every voting
paper was delivered by one of the scrutineers to the president.
The president opened it in the presence of the electoral body,
and read it aloud, and then passed the voting paper to another

scrutineer, who placed it in some open place. When all the names have been read in this manner, the voting papers having been placed one upon another by the second scrutineer, were burnt in the presence of the electoral body. Almost all these details of procedure were preserved in the enactments of the law of the 19th of April 1831.

4018. Whilst the president reads aloud the names which appear upon the voting papers, does any person at the same time take an account of the number of votes for each candidate?—Yes, that is exactly what I call the scrutineers, and the principal function of the scrutineers, as the name implies, is to follow the president as he reads the votes aloud, and to write the name of the candidate for whom they vote, by which means they can easily and correctly ascertain the number of voters for each candidate. When the result of the examination has given a majority in favour of one of the candidates, if on the first examination of the votes any one of the candidates has obtained an absolute majority of the electors, the president announces that that candidate is the deputy of the arrondissement, or of the department. When this majority is not obtained, there is then on the following day a ballotage, and it is then a question between the two candidates who have the greatest number of votes.

4019. This is the mode which prevailed under the law of 1820?—Yes.

4020. You have said that all which the law provided with regard to secret voting, was to declare that the vote should be secret, and that the voter should deliver his paper folded to the president; under the law, where did he write his vote?—The law of 1820 may be considered in a certain sense as an advantage, but two very important securities were still wanting; the first had reference to the existence of the electoral lists, the second to the secrecy of the vote. The Government were exclusively charged with the preparation of the electoral lists; they put upon those lists the individuals they wished, and when the elector, who was alone interested, and who alone had the right of objecting, he was obliged to make his claim before the public functionaries themselves; and added to which, if the electoral body did not appear to the Government disposed to follow its views, the Government had the means, to a certain extent, of increasing the electoral body by granting false tickets, therefore a great security was wanting in the law of 1820; but on the 2d July 1828, a new law appeared; by this law, which was one of the reactions against the government of Monsieur Villèle, it was established first, that where a man had been once inscribed on the electoral list, he should remain permanently there till he was removed, which prevented the Government from taking the electors by surprise; and in addition, every elector had the right of demanding the exclusion of a non-qualified elector from the permanent list; and added to which, those discussions were brought before the immovable courts. This law of 1828 is the best security we have in electoral matters; but this only corrected one of the defects of the law of 1820, it did not provide for the secrecy of votes; but custom has obtained for the nation this second security. The law of 1820 had declared that the votes should be secret; the electors thought that, from the moment when the law imposed this obligation, that law ought, by implication, to contain the means of carrying it into effect. The great disadvantage to which the elector was exposed under the law of 1820, was the obligation of writing the name of the candidate on the table, and in the presence of the president, who was an agent of the central government; but in the period which elapsed between 1820 and 1828, commenced the use of what we call cartoons in France; it is a kind of screen, 18 inches high, and which was placed between the president and the voter, so that the president, however much he might be desirous to know for whom they voted, could not possibly accomplish it. This custom has not, as far as I know, been positively recognized by law; at all the elections, even those of 1830, a certain number of the presidents refused absolutely to allow the use of those screens, but the greatest number of them, after a long resistance, have submitted to it. Such was the state of our electoral law in 1831, when the last law of elections passed.

4021–2. Will you state the nature of the last law of elections? —The object of the law of 1831 was first to increase the number of the electors, and with respect to the manner of the election, to give more efficacy to the secrecy of voting. According to the law of 1831 the use of the screens is not recognized, but matters are so arranged that there is no need of them. Thus the law of 1831 declares that a separate table shall be placed at a certain distance from the president's table, and upon this second table the elector writes the name of the candidate for whom he votes; this second table is to be sufficiently distant from the table of the bureau, that the electors can easily move round it, and at the same time the president's table must be equally isolated, so that the electors may move round it, and observe in themselves whether every thing done by the president and the bureau is legally done.

4023. Does this arrangement practically provide that the table at which the elector writes is so far from the president's table that he cannot see what he writes?—That is the object of the law; I should add that, according to the law of 1831, the president being nominated by the electoral body, the same distrust does not attach to him as did before.

4024. Do you consider it to have been the principal object of the legislature which passed the law of 1831, and the object of the electors who forced upon the presidents the use of the pasteboard screens, to protect themselves against the influence of the Government, or to protect themselves against the influence of individuals?—The principal, and I may say the almost sole object of the law of 1820, was to protect the electors against the influence of that almost omnipotent individual whom we call the Government.

4025. Was that also the object of the law of 1831?—Equally so; this result grows out of our peculiar political and social position.

4026. Are the Committee to understand that from your social and political state, any apprehension which is felt on the part of the voters is an apprehension arising out of the influence of the Government, and not out of the influence of particular individuals?—In using the words 'social position,' I mean to speak of the almost complete equality which exists between different ranks; in consequence of which there exists in France a very small number of individuals who can possibly exercise any very great influence over any great number of electors; with respect to our political condition, there are two circumstances which explain why the French electors entertain little apprehension of the influence of individuals, and do fear the power of the Government; the first is, that the number of electors being very small, and every one of them being in easy circumstances, it is very seldom that any individual is in a situation to exercise any influence over their welfare; if the electoral body was extended, and the poorer classes became a portion of it, perhaps individual influence would become more generally felt; the second is, that in France the Government has collected into its hands not only the power of directing the whole organization of society, but also of directing in a certain degree of all the local administrations, by which I mean the communes, the cantons, the arrondissements and the departments. Hence results first, that the Government has in its pay a prodigious number of public functionaries, not less than 180,000; and secondly, by the means of those individual functionaries it exerts also an immense influence over the happiness and the fortunes of those not immediately depending upon it.

4027. Were the precautions thus taken in the first instance by means of the cartoons, and in the second instance by the law of 1831, sufficient practically to secure the secrecy of the votes? —It is difficult and perhaps impossible to give a perfectly conclusive answer to that question. It is admitted in France, and I think that the attempts that have been constantly made to accomplish the secrecy of voting, proved that they were in the right; it is generally believed in France that by means of the precautions which both custom and law have introduced, any one who wishes to vote secretly can succeed in doing so; but I believe that experience has proved that in spite of those precautions, any one who wishes to make his vote public can always do it.

4028. By what means?—There are many means of doing it, but the most efficacious are to take advantage of the permission which the law gives to obtain another elector to write his name for him; I believe the law has expressed in these words, that the elector shall secretly write the name of the candidate, or shall choose another elector to do so.

4029. Was that permission given to provide for those that could not write themselves?—Yes, I think that was the object of the law; and up to the present time no objection has been made to this part of the law. The method I have just described is the easiest means of giving publicity to a vote, but there are a great many indirect methods of arriving at the same result. The vote being written upon a table, and the table being supposed to be surrounded by electors, any one who wishes to give publicity to his vote has only to write in an almost ostensible manner, keeping up the appearance of secrecy which the law requires, and five or six of the surrounding electors, being in the neighbourhood, may discover what he has done; but if his intention was decidedly not to have his vote known, he might very easily write in so as not to be seen.

4030. Do you think it was as easy for him to show his vote to the other electors around, when the vote was written at the president's table with a screen interposed between the voter and the president?—That is a difficult question to answer satisfactorily; I doubt whether it was so.

4031. Do not you think that if it had been as much the object in France to guard the voter against the influence of other electors, as it has been to guard him against the influence of the president and the Government, precautions might easily have been taken to render it impossible for the other electors to know his vote?—In France, as I have already said, the only party whose influence causes any alarm is the Government; it is particularly from the eye of the agents of Government that they have been desirous to hide themselves; and as soon as that point is accomplished, the object of the law has been effected.

4032. Do you think that the elections which took place between 1820 and the revolution of July 1830, indicated that that object in the majority of cases was successfully obtained by the use of the cartoons?—With respect to that question, I must inform the Committee, that what I have said is founded rather upon experience growing out of my observation of facts, than upon particular facts themselves; and therefore in this part of my evidence I have no right to expect from the Committee the same degree of confidence as in the former part of my evidence. I think that the election at the end of 1827 was the most complete proof that the secrecy of votes had been obtained in a very great proportion by means of the precautions I have stated. In 1827, that is to say, at the close of M. Villèle's administration, on the one side liberal opinions had made immense progress, and on the other side the substantial power of the Government had greatly increased, and the custom of bringing that power to bear had become very familiar; and the necessary consequence was that the Government, at the end of 1827, on one side made immense efforts to influence the vote of the electors, and on the other side the electors themselves, among whom were very many functionaries of the Government, conceived a very great desire not to obey that influence. The consequence was a result which, in my opinion, may be considered as an unfortunate result of secret voting, which is that a great many electors, particularly those who depended entirely upon the Government for their existence, promised their support to Government and did not give it; and the proof of that is this—M. Villèle's Government, up to the last moment of the elections, thought that they might reckon upon a great majority; almost all the prefects had stated to the Government, according to the accounts they had collected in the departments, that the majority would be in favour of Government; and it was with extreme surprise that some days afterwards, the elections having taken place, it was discovered that there was a very considerable majority against the ministry. That result was evidently obtained at that period in a manner perhaps morally to be regretted, but undoubtedly by means of the secret voting.

4033. Had the votes been open, do you believe that the result would have been otherwise?—I am inclined to think the result would not have been exactly the same; but I am not sure that the ministry would have had a majority even under a system of open voting; at this period the tendency to liberal opinions was so strong, that a great number of those who had every thing to hope and fear from the ministry, were determined to run all risks, that is to say, to lose their places if they should not succeed in turning out the ministry.

4034. Do you think that in that calculation of running all risks, the chances of being protected even in the event of the success of the Government by the secrecy of their votes, had any influence upon the minds of the electors in determining them to vote against the Government?—I think that a man perfectly master of himself is also master of his secret, but I also think that it is difficult during the period that precedes an election, and during the period of the election itself, and especially after the election, for an elector so to act as not to afford some reason for suspecting in what manner he is voting; he is almost sure to do something that will create suspicion enough to lead to the intervention of an authority so little responsible as the French authorities are in administrative matters; so that the elector in such a case must run great risk of losing his place; and the secret voting, though it is a security which may be employed, is not by itself infallible, it is certainly however a very great security.

4035. Do you think that in France the probability of the secret escaping is in any degree increased by that species of confidence between individuals which results from the equality of classes?—I think that in France there may be some greater danger in consequence of the equality of the classes, because men have very little distrust of one another; and I believe that, in general, the secret is kept as far as regards the agents of the Government; or of known friends of the Government, but that the secret is in general avowed in private communication, and although that communication is no evidence of the fact, yet there is a sort of current rumour, which is sufficient to induce public functionaries so irresponsible as they are in France, to injure the elector upon mere suspicion. This observation refers to the public functionaries who are electors, because it is difficult for the public functionaries to do any mischief to an elector who is not himself a functionary.

4036. Are not the shopkeepers, who are patentees to a certain degree, under the influence of Government?—To a very small degree, because there are very few patents which it is in the power of Government to refuse. For example, take the case of a printer; there are two ways of injuring a printer who does not comply with the wishes of Government with respect to an election. The first is to take from him his printing licence, because that is one of the few rights which the Government may refuse; however, I do not think there is a single instance of a printer being deprived of his licence; but suppose a printer is employed to print the Government Acts and advertisements, which is an important privilege for him, in that case there is no doubt that the least suspicion with respect to his vote would deprive him of that privilege.

4037. You have stated, that there are about 180,000 functionaries in France; what is the number of voters in France?— I do not believe the number of voters in France has ever been very positively ascertained, but the general opinion is, that it does not much exceed 200,000.

4038. Suppose that the agents of Government were to make it known that no man would be appointed to a situation under Government but those who voted for the Government, as you have said that every voter has the means of letting it be publicly known how he voted, would it not be the necessary consequence of that state of things, that every voter, who was a candidate for a place under Government, would take care that his vote was publicly known?—Yes, that may happen when an elector has any thing to hope or to fear from the Government.

4039. When the number of functionaries and the number of voters come to be so nearly equal, is not that almost a necessary consequence?—Up to a certain point it is; but I wish to observe, that the greatest portion of the 180,000 functionaries do not consist of persons belonging to the electoral body; many of those 180,000 situations are too unimportant to be an object of desire to the electors; at the same time I am bound to say, that it is by the aid of those hopes that the Government generally succeeds in determining the doubtful elections; but the power of Government in electoral matters has been constantly diminishing.

4040. Has the abolition of the law of primogeniture in France, by diminishing the amount and value of property as it goes on descending, materially diminished the number of voters?—I think it is extremely difficult, and perhaps impossible, to reply to that question. The law respecting the division of real property has two contrary effects; the first of those effects is to increase the number of electors by dividing the great fortunes in and among a greater number of proprietors in middling circumstances. The second effect is, to diminish the electoral body by reducing a certain number of the electors below the electoral qualification; but that question is one of the most difficult and the most important which can be agitated in the present state of France. Up to the present moment it has not been possible to ascertain, with certainty, whether the effect of the law of succession has been indefinitely to diminish the extent of inheritance, or only to break up the great territorial possessions, and still leaving untouched, or even recreating a great number of small properties. Many operations which have already commenced would induce the belief, that the effect of our law of succession is to make real property pass with immense rapidity from hand to hand, and that by this rapid transition from hand to hand, the number of the great properties is diminishing, and the number of the middling properties remains the same.

4041. Has not the qualification of voters been altered since 1821, as to the amount of tax to be paid to constitute a qualification?—Yes; in 1821 the electoral body was composed solely of the electors who paid 300 francs in direct taxes; but the law of 1831 lowered the qualification to 200 francs.

4042. Have you ever seen a statement that that diminution from 300 francs to 200 francs was made in consequence of the diminution of the number of voters?—The reason for lowering the qualification was not the diminished number of the electors, but a desire of increasing the then existing number.

4043. Was not it in the discussions of 1831 decided by facts that the number of voters taken in the different departments, during the several elections between 1821 and 1831, proved that a great diminution of electors had taken place?—I have not sufficient recollection of the discussions of 1831 to answer the question; but I think I can state positively that the principal object, if not the only object, was to bring in a new class of electors.

4044. If the fact were that, between 1821 and 1831, the number of electors had materially decreased throughout France, should you have the means, by reference to any authorities in France, to supply the Committee with the information as to that amount of decrease?—At this moment I do not possess those facts, but I think it would be possible to obtain them; but I believe that any accounts as to the number of electors in France would be incomplete before 1828, that being the period when the lists became permanent, and the electors became interested in the desire of increasing the partisans of their particular opinions; but my attention not having been particularly directed to this matter, I am not able to give such specific information to the Committee.

4045. Was not the number of voters decreased between 1821 and the Revolution in 1830, by some alterations made in the law of patents, and other laws relating to direct taxation?—Yes; the system of M. Villèle's ministry was to diminish as much as possible the electoral body; for this purpose a portion of the taxes which bore upon real property was repealed; the result of which was, that a good many electors were excluded from the list because they did not pay the amount required; the tax was reimposed upon landed property after the revolution in July.

4046. Is the voting for the president of the Electoral College, who was formerly named by the King, but is now named by the voters, taken in secret or in public?—I think that is also in secret, because generally in France every kind of voting is done in secret.

4047. You have stated that the French Government did not scruple to injure a voter who was in their employment, and who they suspected had voted against them, even although they could not be certain that he had done so; do not you think they would be very likely in that way to punish, without intending it, a man who might have voted in their favour?—It might sometimes happen, but I think very seldom.

4048. If it be impossible to arrive at certainty upon the matter, do not they run a considerable chance of injuring a friend as well as an enemy?—In general the Government does not injure an elector, except they know from other sources that his opinions are not favourable to them.

4049. Supposing such an elector, voting in secret, chose to vote in favour of the Government, contrary to his own opinions, he would not do himself any good by means of that vote?—If he could be prevented from voting publicly, I think the result spoken of might be obtained. Up to the present time we have not seen that it was, as I have said before, in the power of the law to prevent any one who wished to render his vote public from doing so. But I ought, however, to add that I believe the legislature have never tried to make the vote secret, in spite of the wish of the voter; at the same time I think that the object of the law was evidently that the secrecy should be kept, even although the voter did not wish to avail himself of that secrecy.

4050. But you have ground to think that the law does not take sufficient precaution in order to obtain that which was its intention?—Yes; I think that the French law has afforded great facilities of being disobeyed. I do not think it is known in France whether the legislature has any means of absolutely and completely preventing publicity. The law is manifestly imperfect, but we have no experience as to whether it can or cannot be made perfect.

4051. But the intention of the law was, that secrecy should be observed in spite of the wish of any voter to give publicity to his vote?—I think so. In examining the terms of the law, the law does not say that the vote may be secret, but that it shall be secret; it does not say that the elector may give his paper in folded, but that he shall give his paper in folded; from which I think it may be inferred, as it has been inferred in France, that the positive intention of the legislature was, that the vote should be secret, even although the elector did not wish to avail himself of it; and that the law considered the obligation of secrecy rather as a matter of public order than as a security to the interests of the voter.

4052. Then, in spite of the intention of the law, secrecy has not been successfully obtained in France?—Secrecy, as I have explained before, has been kept in a very great proportion, and the elections of 1827 proved it; but still all the electors who did not wish to avail themselves of the secrecy have easily been able to violate the law.

4053. Though the system of law in France enables the voter to keep his vote secret from those by whom he is employed, it is more difficult for him to conceal his vote from his neighbour and his equals in society?—That is the great difficulty, because in general men are not afraid of the influence of their equals in society, and consequently, in order to keep secrecy, he must not only look to the direct meaning of his words, but to the remote inference which may be drawn from them, which requires a greater effort of human prudence; and the result is, that they frequently keep the secret from the Government, and let it escape to their neighbours.

4054. But you attribute that to the fact of their not caring whether their neighbour knows it or not?—I think the thing is difficult in itself, but that it is more difficult in France than in a country where they would have to fear the immediate influence of a private individual.

4055. In the elections in France are the electors subject to any influence from the lower classes?—No, it is a very rare occurrence; I only know one or two cases.

4056. Having no opportunity of entering the Electoral College, do the lower classes in France attempt to exercise any influence over the individual electors as regards their votes?— I think they have never tried it, and I am sure they have never succeeded. There is not more than one or two instances of it which occur to my mind, and I think they are isolated cases.

4057. Will you state the nature of those cases ?—One of them was at the election of M. Berryer, at Marseilles; when the electoral body were assembled, as soon as they began to perceive that there was a decided majority in favour of M. Berryer, a certain number of individuals, who cannot be said even to have belonged to the lowest class, for the lowest class at Marseilles were favourable to M. Berryer, but at any rate enemies of that candidate, went in a body to the college, broke open the doors, and took possession of the urn and burnt the voting papers, and by this means the election was void. The next day it began again, and the friends of M. Berryer were afraid, and did not appear, and the opposing candidate carried the election. The second instance exactly relates to the question put to me, but I do not recollect either the place or the year, I only know that it was after the revolution of 1830. In one of the towns in the south, the populace were favourable to the legitimist candidate; that candidate did not succeed, and the friends of the opposing candidate ran some risks. It is possible that in the south of France, which is the part of the country in which the lower class of the people take the most ardent interest in politics, it is possible that in that part of France there may be some other instances, but I do not recollect any of them at this moment.

4058. Was not that the case in the year 1830, before the election at Montauban ?—I recollect perfectly that at that period M. de Presac, the deputy for Montauban, complained of violence almost personal, exercised by the populace of the town, but under what circumstances I do not know.

4059. But in those cases was not the force of Government always sufficient to put down such disturbances ?—Certainly.

4060. In the case which you cited of Marseilles, how did the people who forced the college gates, in consequence of the election going against their friend, ascertain that such was the case ? —That is very easy, because the names of the candidates are successively proclaimed, as I explained before, by the president, so that at the end of half an hour they begin to see what are the probabilities of the election.

4061. Then this violence was after the voting had ceased, but before the names had been proclaimed?—During the proclamation of the names.

4062. Had the declaration of the member who had been chosen been actually made, or was it merely in progress of being made? —It was in progress of being made; that is to say, suppose that the electoral body was composed of 400 persons, 200 of the voting papers had been already opened, and of those 200 papers, 150 bore the name of M. Berryer, and it was extremely probable that the same proportion would be found in the remainder which were not opened, and the enemies of M. Berryer ran to the Electoral College, and burnt the remaining unopened tickets, so that it was impossible to know on which side the majority was.

4063. Then the vote had been put into the urn but not all drawn out at the time the riot took place, and the riot took place while the votes were being examined?—Yes.

4064. You state that after that election was thus made void, the friends of M. Berryer did not venture to appear again; was that from a fear of personal injury, or from a fear of their votes being known?—It was a combination of two feelings on the part of those electors who did not come; on the one hand they considered that it was useless, because there appeared to be in the town a party who were supposed to be supported by the Government, and who seemed determined to defeat their efforts; and secondly, because I have no doubt that many of them were frightened at the idea of incurring personally the anger of those who had burnt the papers, because in the towns in the south of France the opinions of the electors are pretty well known beforehand, owing to the violence of the feelings that exist among them, so that when an elector presents himself at the college, they know beforehand how he will vote, so that in fact, in the south of France, it is almost as if a person voted openly, because the parties are so much in the presence of each other, that they know perfectly beforehand what the man's opinions are.

4065. A man's opinions being known, the presumption of every body is that he votes according to his opinions?—Certainly, till there is some proof to the contrary.

4066. Therefore it does not enter into the supposition of any body that he should vote contrary to his opinions?—No.

4067. When you say that the lower classes in France do not exercise any influence upon the voters, do you mean that they

P   225

take no interest in the election, or that they have not the power to influence the voters from the protection given by the secret voting?—There is a combination of both causes; generally speaking, for a long time past, the lower classes in France have taken very little interest in the result of the elections. In general the political feeling is concentrated among the middle classes; and moreover, I am convinced, that if the people had wished to influence the elections, they would have found the secret mode of voting a serious obstacle to their doing so.

4068. Do you think that if influence was exercised by the lower classes, secret voting would afford a perfect protection against them?—I would say complete protection; for if the electors became afraid of the populace, which has never happened yet, except in one or two cases, they would take still more effectual precautions to keep their own secret; I repeat again, that up to the present time, in the greater part of France, the only thing which has been feared in voting is the influence of the Government.

4069. Have you ever heard of the lower classes attempting to influence those voters, shopkeepers for instance, with whom they deal?—I have no knowledge of it, but I do not live in the south.

4070. Were not several elections annulled by the chamber in 1828, on the ground that the president had violated the secrecy of voting?—I do not perfectly recollect; I know that at that period many elections were annulled, but as far as my recollection extends, I think that the reason that was alleged was the introduction of false electors, which was subsequently rendered impossible by the law of 1828.

4071. Did it not happen even in 1830 that several elections were annulled, on the ground of false electors having been introduced?—I do not think so; I do not think much can be inferred from what passed after the election of 1830; there were many deputies excluded from the chamber, but I think that most of them were excluded rather by a spirit of reaction, as the friends of the Government which had just been overturned, than by any reason sustained by evidence.

4072. Suppose a proposition was made in the French chamber to alter the mode of voting now practised in France from what it is at present, to voting *viva voce*, would it or not be the general belief in France that the Government would acquire a very great increase of influence by means of that measure?—Up to the present time the public attention in France has never been turned to that question; secrecy of voting is in France what would be called here a matter of course; nobody of any consideration in the political world has hitherto expressed an opinion that the voting ought to be public, but my opinion is, that if the votes were given publicly, the power of the Government would be infinitely increased.

4073. Have you ever heard any case in the French elections, in which individuals had given money for votes?—The fact of giving money to obtain an election is a thing so rare that I do not think a single instance of it can be stated with any thing like proof. I know that in certain cases it has been said, that money has been given, but no inquiry has been made upon that subject, and I do not think that such proof ever was given of it as even to influence public opinion.

4074. Has there never been a case in which a complaint of an improper election has been made to the chamber, upon the ground of a candidate having obtained his election by bribery? —No, I do not know of any; but I may remark, that by the word 'bribery' I understand solely corruption effected by the giving of a sum of money, because it has constantly happened in France that the Government, by promising a place or by threatening the loss of a place, has influenced an election in a very notorious manner.

4075. In those cases where the Government has influenced the elections, do you apprehend that the electors have availed themselves of those provisions of the law which enables them to evade the secrecy of the vote, by making another person write their name for them?—In general, in France, if any party wishes to influence an elector, whether it be the Government or an individual, (the latter being a very rare thing) they rely either upon a promise given by the elector, or upon the impression which they think they have made upon him. It is very rare, excepting in the case of a man who is very low in condition and society, to dare to ask him to give you a proof that he votes as he has promised.

4076. Do you think that the infrequency of asking for such a proof arises from the known power which he has of keeping his vote secret?—It arises in part from that; it arises also from a more general cause. I think that in France, in election matters, the same feeling has not arisen which exists in countries where the custom of elections has prevailed for a long time. In election matters in France up to the present moment, the same ideas of honour and dishonour exist which are applied to all other human actions, and consequently the respectable persons who give their word keep it, and those who are not so, do not keep it; in the same way that some men steal and others have no desire to do so. I mean to say, that in election matters in France there have not yet arisen any notions of morality different from what apply to every thing else.

4077. Do you think that public indignation would be turned in France against any person who should publicly threaten or compel persons under his influence to vote in a particular way? —I think that in the present state of morals, it would be considered very bad, but still the thing has frequently been done.

4078. Is it done in general openly or secretly?—It is generally done in a very secret manner. A man who should be openly threatened, and who should act in consequence of that threat, would generally be considered as infinitely lowered in the opinion of society. I think that in general almost all those who wish to influence the electors, endeavour to persuade them that they are desirous not of forcing them but of convincing them.

4079. What do you think would be the public sentiment in France towards a landed proprietor, who stood at the place of election until his tenants had all voted at the poll, and who remarked to them as they voted 'Now take care how you vote', and other expressions indicative of an order, that they should vote according to his opinion and not their own?—I think it would be looked upon in a very bad light by the electors themselves, and by the population in general.

4080. Is there in France any sort of public opinion, that it is a matter of course that the votes of the tenants, or persons in the employment of powerful individuals, should go along with those who employ them, or have any authority over them?—I think it sometimes happens, but seldom, owing to a cause which is peculiar to France, that there are very few individuals who have a great number of tenants electors; it is very unusual for a landed proprietor and his tenant to be in the same Electoral College.

4081. Do the farmers in general vote?—There are a great number who vote.

4082. In those cases, where there are tenants voting in an arrondissement, suppose the proprietor resides not in the arrondissement, but at Paris, in the event of an election, is it customary for the proprietor to write down letters to his tenants, or to employ the influence of any land agent, so as in any way to direct the votes of the tenants who live upon his land?—That has sometimes happened, but it can only have happened upon a very small scale, because the number of the tenants who are at the same time electors and who belong to the same property is very small.

4083. When the Government procure a vote by the promise of a place, are they in the habit of requiring that the voter shall make his vote public?—That is very rare, and much more rare on the part of the Government than on the part of individuals, because the Government in asking a thing to be done which is considered so humiliating, would be obliged to conduct the investigation with a degree of publicity that would injure them more than the vote was worth.

4084. Is there any suspicion that individuals who are standing in the Electoral College during an election are spies and agents of the Government, walking about to watch how men vote?—That has sometimes happened when there was a public functionary of the arrondissement a member of the Electoral College, but in general the ostensible friends and supporters of the Government are regarded with suspicion when they are seen inside the Electoral College, and consequently they feel themselves to be in such a delicate position that they wish to remain there as short a time as possible; when I say this, I speak generally, but it must be always understood that there are exceptions.

4085. Do the Government, after promising a place to an elector, fulfil their promise, trusting to his honour to vote as he promised?—The Government, or rather the agents of Government, very frequently promise to two or three persons the same place, and I think that is a sufficient answer to the question, because, of course, they cannot multiply the places according to the promises.

4086. In fact, they confer the place without requiring the

voter to show to them how he voted?—Yes, very frequently; the Government must rely upon the word of the elector.

4087. You have visited the United States of America?—I have.

4088. Did you make any particular inquiry into the practice of secret voting there?—Before going to the United States of America I had not been in England, and I had not seen any other constitutional government than that of France. In visiting a foreign country I was naturally disposed to examine chiefly that which was different from what I had been accustomed to see in France; and as the secret voting had always existed, within my knowledge, in France, and as the political discussions had never turned upon that subject, I was led to regard the secret voting as a thing perfectly natural; therefore when, on arriving in America, I perceived in a great number of the States the practice of secret voting, my attention was not drawn to that point; and I examined only in a very slight and superficial manner every thing in America relating to the secret voting, considering it as a matter of course; consequently I cannot state to the Committee the details which they might otherwise expect from me. I can only give a general notion of the secret voting in America, and that notion is this, that I never observed in America that the secret voting was either objected to on the one hand, or praised on the other, with any degree of warmth, which I attribute to this circumstance, that, while the government in America is often weak, there is no individual, or at least a very small number, whose favour is to be courted, or whose power was to be feared.

4089. Supposing that, over and above the influence of the government in France, there was also a class of proprietors who had a very great power of either rewarding or injuring persons who vote; would not that be, in your mind, an additional reason for desiring the protection of secret voting for the general mass of French voters?—It is difficult to answer a question which is founded upon the supposition of circumstances which do not exist in my country, and which I can only conceive by an effort of imagination; but I am disposed to believe that, in the case supposed, the power of voting in secret would appear still more invaluable in the eyes of the electors of France.

4090. Do you conceive that the secret voting in America is necessary to protect electors against the strong state of popular feeling?—Yes; that is the greatest advantage which I ascribe to the secret suffrage in America. In America, tyranny can only come from the majority. Hitherto this tyranny does not appear to me to have been brought into action on a very large scale. I suppose, however, that the secret voting has afforded, and will afford, an important security against the tyranny of the majority, which I consider as the greatest evil and the most formidable danger that can attend a purely democratical government.

4091. Were you ever present at an election in America?—Yes; but I have never examined the details. The elections are so frequent in America that it is impossible to remain for any length of time in the country without passing through places where the elections are going on; but I confess I have not given to that subject all the attention which appears to me now to belong to it.

4092. Can you state whether, in point of fact, the voting is secret in America?—So far as I can judge, I believe that in America there has been too little danger in a man making his vote public, to create any great desire to conceal it.

4093. Are you aware that it is the practice in America to call meetings before the elections, and to get persons to sign papers in order to ascertain how they mean to vote?—No; the same sort of meetings take place in France, except, however, that the electors are not obliged to choose their candidates. In France almost all the electors meet together some days before the election; and the candidates, or the friends of the candidates, address them, and sometimes the feeling of the meeting is shown by a preliminary secret ballot.

4094. When the electors ascertain, by this preparatory operation, in whose favour the votes are likely to go, do not they always have recourse to the secret method of doing it?—I think they always have recourse to the secret ballot.

4095. You are not aware that in America a contrary practice prevails?—I have no knowledge upon the subject.

4096. Are you aware that in America, before the election, it is the practice to deliver coloured tickets?—I do not know. I know, from my own experience in America, that it is extremely rare for any election in the Northern States to be attended with any riot. I have heard that in the Southern States, in which I remained a much shorter time, the elections give rise to affrays; but I believe that in the Southern States the custom of voting publicly is more general than in the Northern States.

4097. When you say riots are rare in the Northern States, do you include New York?—I speak particularly of the New England States; but I think that the same thing applies to the State of New York, except the town of New York.

4098. In what year were you in America?—In the year 1831.

4099. That was before the last election of General Jackson? —Yes, that was in the year 1832. There is one thing which I was much struck with in America, and that was the extent to which they have gone in subdividing the electoral body, so as to obtain the votes of a very great number of electors in a very little time, and with very little trouble; the subdivisions of the electoral body is extremely great, especially in New England.

4100. How are they divided?—I believe that every township has its electoral body, and it is the results of those subdivided elections which give the general result.

[The Witness delivered in the following Paper]

Loi du 29 Juin 1820

ARTICLE 6

Pour procéder à l'élection du Député, chaque électeur écrit secrètement son vote sur le bureau, ou l'y fait écrire par un autre électeur de son choix, sur un bulletin qu'il reçoit à cet effet du Président. Il remet son bulletin, écrit et fermé, au Président, qui le dépose dans l'urne destinée à cet usage.

Loi du 19 Avril 1831

ARTICLE 48

Chaque électeur, après avoir été appelé, reçoit du Président un bulletin ouvert, sur lequel il écrit, ou fait écrire secrètement, son vote par un électeur de son choix, sur une table disposée à cet effet, et séparée du bureau; puis il remet son bulletin, écrit et fermé, au Président, qui le dépose dans la boîte destinée à cet usage.

ARTICLE 49

La table placée devant le Président et les scrutateurs sera disposée de telle sorte que les électeurs puissent circuler à l'entour pendant le dépouillement du scrutin.

ARTICLE 50

A mesure que chaque électeur déposera son bulletin, un des scrutateurs, ou le secrétaire, constatera ce vote en écrivant son propre nom en regard de celui du votant sur une liste à ce destiné, et qui contiendra les noms et qualifications de tous les membres du collège.

Chaque scrutin reste ouvert pendant six heures au moins, est clos à trois heures du soir, et dépouillée séance tenante.

ARTICLE 51

Lorsque la boîte du scrutin a été ouverte, et le nombre des bulletins vérifié, un des scrutateurs prendra successivement chaque bulletin, le dépliera, et le remettra au Président, qui en fera lecture à haute voix, et le passera à un autre scrutateur. Le résultat de chaque scrutin sera immédiatement rendu public.

ARTICLE 52

Immédiatement après le dépouillement, les bulletins seront brûlés en présence du collège.

6. ASPECTS OF BRITISH LOCAL GOVERNMENT

(8th June 1835)

Conversation with Mr. Sharpe[1]. (Mr. Sharpe is a very intelligent London lawyer.)

Political Conversation[2]

Q. Have you any general principles of administration?

A. One can hardly call rules subject to a multitude of exception 'general principles'. Nevertheless it is possible to indicate some main characteristics of English administration.

Q. What is the smallest political unit called?

A. The parish.[3]

Q. Are parishes *generally*[4] thickly populated?

A. No. There are three hundred thousand inhabitants in the London parish of Marylebone. But usually the country parishes are thinly populated.

Q. How do the parishes rule themselves?

A. All the taxed inhabitants, the poor rate payers, constitute a body called the *vestry*. This body represents the parish politically and exercises its collective rights.

In most parishes, especially the small ones, the vestry acts on its own without representatives.[5] But the occasions when it has to act are very few. The main function of the vestry is to appoint the various parish officers.

Q. Are they chosen annually?

A. Yes.

Q. Are all the vestrymen able to be elected?

A. Yes.

Q. Are these functions paid and sought after?

A. Most of them are unpaid, and the threat of fines is usually necessary to force men to fulfil them. Besides, the burden is imposed on each vestryman for one year only, until all have been elected in turn.

Q. Who are these officers?

A. Churchwarden, surveyors of the highways, constables, overseer of the poor.

Q. What guarantee is there that these officers should perform their functions, for hope of re-election is not their motive?

A. Fear of the Courts.

Q. Speaking generally, which Courts have competence in such matters?

A. The Justices of the Peace when it is a question of lapses in administration. The Court of King's Bench for crimes, misappropriation..

Q. Who can prosecute them before these Courts?

A. Any individual. No one but an individual. We have nothing like the French 'ministère public'.

Suppose that a poor man needed *relief*.[6] If the overseer refused relief and the man died in consequence, the overseer would be held responsible. If in order to help this poor man, the overseer deemed it necessary to levy a tax on the parishioners, and the latter considered it excessive or ill distributed, each individual among them has the right to appeal to the Justices of the Peace assembled *in quarter sessions*. If they think that the overseer has put some of the money in his pocket, any one of them can prosecute him before the Court of King's Bench.

Q. Which collective interests are the reponsibility of the parishes?

A. The church and the expenses of worship, local roads and the poor.[7]

Q. Do not the parishes own real property?

A. No.

Q. To whom then does the common land adjoining so many of your parishes belong?

A. To all the landowners in the parish and to them alone;[8] according to the extent of their holdings of land, these have the right to graze a certain number of beasts on the meadow.

Q. From what you have just told me, it would appear that there is a complete democracy at the basis of your social structure. But may I turn back to inquire what you mean by a *select vestry*?

A. In the large parishes it has become difficult to get the whole vestry to vote on the matters [9]that concern the whole parish. Hence the need for the *select vestry* or representative body for the parish. The select vestry is elected by the vestry, and *it is that body*[10]that appoints the aforementioned officers.

Q. To which parishes does this representative system apply?

A. Legally the parishes are free to choose either system. As I said just now, it is especially the large parishes that have chosen the select vestry or communal representative system.

Q. Is there a single official of the central government in the parish?

A. No.

Q. Does the central government exercise any supervision over the parish?

A. No.

Q. Before we go on to the counties, could you please explain one matter that muddles me. I see that there are parishes and there are *corporations*. I am confused to find that they are analogous but not alike as conceptions.

A. Corporations are exceptions within the communal system as I just explained it to you. A corporation is composed of a certain number of individuals enjoying certain political rights within a town. Some who are called freemen have such privileges as the choice of members of parliament for the town. There are others called mayor, aldermen and councilmen who are responsible for various details of municipal life. But it often happens that the main affairs are outside their sphere: some of these have been entrusted by *local acts* to special commissioners; others have always remained in the hands of the parish officers. For the parish often continues to exist within the *incorporated* town to a certain extent.[11] It is generally true to say that there are few considerable centres of population without original features in their government. For almost all have at one time or another secured from parliament local laws modifying their government. But it is fair to say that the parish organisation I have just described contains the general principles.

Q. Now let us turn to the Counties. Is there representation for the County?

A. No.

Q. Is it sometimes consulted?

A. No.

Q. Nevertheless it does have collective interests. What are they?

A. The County pays the expenses of criminal justice: sees to the building and maintenance of Law Courts and prisons. It has a duty to erect and repair bridges. Those are pretty nearly all its collective interests.

Q. Who looks after these interests?

A. The Justices of the Peace assembled in quarter session. The Justices of the Peace are appointed by the King at the instance of the Lord Lieutenant of the county.[12] The King can dismiss them, but that is an extremely rare occurrence. The Justices of the Peace tax, but do not represent, the County, which is a unique instance in our political system.

Not only do the Justices of the Peace administer the County within the sphere of the duties I have just outlined, but also, for the most part, guarantee the administration of the parishes: for most complaints against the parish officers must be brought before them, and so, while the form is judicial, their function is in truth administrative.

Q. I can well see what the Justices of the Peace do in their collective capacity, but I cannot so easily understand what duties they perform individually.

A. Individually their duties are entirely judicial: they receive complaints; take the first steps in proceedings, issue writs, and grant bail or insist on recognizances. Assembled in *petty sessions* they judge summarily slight offences and civil suits involving less than £5.

Q. What do you mean by petty sessions?

A. Each County is divided into a number of little districts. The Justices of the Peace of such a district come together in its main town; there must be at least two of them, and they decide such cases brought before them as fall within their competence.

Q. Apart from their administrative duties, do not quarter sessions have judicial functions to perform?

A. Most certainly. Aided by a jury quarter sessions try all crimes that do not entail the death penalty or transportation for 14 years.

Q. From what you told me, I have the impression that the Justices of the Peace control almost everything concerning the agricultural classes. As administrators they have an influence over the parish and manage the County; as judges in criminal cases they hold the whole of the poor rural population in their hands. I believe I have noticed, even among the upper classes, indications that the movement of reform will soon reach the institution of Justices of the Peace.

A. That is perfectly correct. Abuses of the organisation and, especially, of the functions of the Justices of the Peace have begun to arouse very many complaints. But various laws enacted within the last ten years have greatly reduced the extent of such abuses. And innovations in procedures have had even more effect than new laws. Formerly the Justices of the Peace usually met in closed session. Now all their proceedings are public (I must ask for further explanations about this.) The powers of the Justices of the Peace were at their height in the years between 1792 and 1825. Before 1792 the power of the aristocracy had never been put in question, and the aristocracy treated the lower classes with great condescension. After that moment, its rights have been contested, it exercised the greatest strictness in enforcing them. This tendency lasted down to 1815, when an opposite tendency began.

Q. So the use of force was the first indication of weakness. That is most often how it goes.

Not to interrupt the natural flow of ideas, I refrained from asking you about one particular point in administration which does deserve quite particular attention. I refer to the main roads. Of all material things there is no other perhaps that has so powerful an influence over the fate of nations as the roads. What have you to say about this?

A. As a general rule the central government never takes any responsibility for making or maintaining roads. But there are one or two exceptions to that principle. (I think a main road from London to Ireland is a national undertaking.)

The roads fall into two classes. The first is *local* roads, and the second main roads which cross several parishes and connect fairly distant places. The parishes are bound to keep the local roads in good repair; originally they were also responsible for the upkeep of the main roads.[13] But the planning and upkeep of the main roads have long since been almost completely withdrawn from their hands.

236

Q. Who then is responsible for the latter?

A. Suppose one is dealing with a twenty mile stretch of road. One chooses[14] a certain number of people dwelling on that stretch and so forms a sort of company with responsibility for maintaining it in good condition, and this company is given the right to levy tolls up to a fixed maximum for the use of that length of road. These individuals have a meeting and appoint a working agent who is called *the surveyor of the road*. They control and supervise him. Usually this body has the right to appoint its own members, but when a member resigns, they must appoint somebody living on the same part of the road. That is a necessary condition of eligibility. These people are called *trustees*.

Q. Are they obliged to accept these duties?

A. No.

Q. Are they paid either directly or indirectly?

A. No. The tolls have to be calculated as sufficient only for the upkeep of the road. If they are greater than the necessary expenses, they must be lowered. But usually things are arranged so that they are not more than the expenses.

Q. Is there a large number of individuals ready and willing to undertake these duties?

A. Yes. These little public occupations fill the lives of most of our small landowners and give them a certain importance in their district, which gratifies them.

Q. I always come back to the great question, namely how the parishes can be forced to keep up their communal roads, and the trustees to keep their road in good repair.

A. I shall repeat the answer I have already given to all analogous questions. The law almost always relies on individual self-interest.

Let us take the example of the parish first: each parish appoints a surveyor of the road, who has the right to levy the money, needed to keep the roads up, on the parish (I have already explained that those who think the levy excessive or arbitrary can turn to the Courts). Now every individual in the parish and anyone soever who suffers from the bad condition of the road, for instance a traveller who damages his carriage, has the right to bring a lawsuit and sue the surveyor for damages. Under this threat the surveyor has an interest in taxing the inhabitants for this purpose and he does not abuse this right because the inhabitants in their turn have the right to resist an excessive or ill distributed tax.

Now let us consider the *trustees:* we find the same system again. The trustees are responsible, subject to a fine, for keeping a part of the road in very good repair. Any man who sees that they are not fulfilling their duty, can bring a lawsuit against them and have them fined. Failing individuals, the grand jury may exercise this right and very frequently does so.

Q. All that is very ingenious. But I believe that much time is needed for such a system to be successful, and that success depends in part on habits and on a state of civilisation brought about by other factors besides that system itself. In your parishes there are almost always a certain number of prosperous individuals with horses and a carriage. The mass of your population is enlightened enough to see the practical use and agreeableness of good roads. It is natural for such a parish to expect great results from the *surveyor's* labours, and to be ready to attack him, if he does not do his job well and thoroughly. It is not just that private interest is armed with the power to create a public good, but that it has the will to act. The same comment applies to the main roads.

Perhaps in some country less enlightened, rich and advanced, it would be hard to find the support which is sufficient with you: one is told that England herself had abominable roads eighty years ago. But I appreciate that in the long run your system is infinitely preferable to ours. There are moreover entirely *political* advantages which would take too long to list now.

To make a unity of these ideas, I think I should add the information gathered from various sources about the Sheriff and the Lord Lieutenant of the Counties. They both, I believe, are appointed by the King, and, to some extent, represent him in the County. The Lord Lieutenant proposes the Justices of the Peace and commands the militia. I think his duties cover very few matters.

The sheriff's duties are very important, but they hardly make him depend at all on the central power. Usually it is he who receives the writs for the convocation of parliament, and who presides over the elections for the County. I think he supplies the list of jurors for quarter sessions and for the circuit Courts. He has to give effect to every judicial decision within the County. As in the case of other public functionaries, the execution of his duties is, I think, insured by the action in the Courts of individuals harmed. I do not know who are competent to do this. The office of sheriff, which only lasts for a year, is sought after by the richest landowners as the foundation of some public position in the County; for the sheriff's office is the only one that is a little bit central.

7. TWO LETTERS

Letter to Madame Ancelot[15]

London, April 28th 1835

I had only just posted my letter yesterday when I remembered that I had forgotten to give you my address. I hurried to retrieve it, but the post is like eternity—once in it, one may not leave it again. It is a matter finished for all time. I had only the one means of putting things right, which was, at the risk of boring you, to write you another letter. I have done this, lacking any better means, and I hasten to tell you, lest you cause me to forget yet again, that I am living at no. 101 Regent St.

After I had written to you yesterday I went out and walked about some of the London streets, which, seen at this time of year, seem at midday very like galleries lit by one lantern. When one enters into this thick damp air, one feels at first that one is in the midst of the homeland of spleen. So I walked about some of the streets and I renewed my acquaintance with several people whom I had already met on my first stay; everywhere I found the same reception: a great deal of insolence in the antechambers (since I was on foot), extreme kindness in the drawing room, and on returning to the antechamber most profound servility. Thus I covered all the degrees of the social scale in a quarter of an hour, I was a poor devil when climbing the stairs, a man like any other in the reception rooms and a great lord when coming down the stairs again. Unfortunately I became myself again, no more, no less, on coming back to the street. After I had returned home I started to philosophize (there is nothing so favourable to philosophy as fog), I found that society was arranged the wrong way round for my taste; I considered all classes, and I did not meet one which satisfied me entirely. There is, in what are called the higher classes—those enjoying hereditary wealth and leisure, a certain elevation of sentiment, a distinction in manners which please and attract me; but the atmosphere in which they live, their luxury, ostentation, great possessions, and affectation, all this bores and repulses me. In contrast, there is often to be found in the middle classes a simplicity, a reality of impression which pleases me, but the vulgarity of all kinds which is so often to be met with, ends up by making constant relations with the middle classes unbearable. Is there really no way of creating a society where external forms would have a more immediate bearing on essentials than is the case amongst us? Where manners would follow sentiments and would be more or less distinguished according to the greater wit, the greater elevation of the soul, the greater energy in the will, just as a pretty woman is always pretty whether she be dressed as the maidservant or the great lady? Here is a question which is truly difficult to resolve, but to whom may I turn more aptly than you, dear Madame, who do not need three footmen in an antechamber in order to express with ease and nobility witty ideas and distinguished sentiments?

Believe, dear Madame, in my very sincere attachment.

A. de Tocqueville

Letter to Comte Molé[16]

London, May 19th 1835

Dear Sir,

I would have written to you much earlier to let you know of the gracious welcome which your letters afforded me; but, first, the preparations which inevitably attend the start of a journey and later a somewhat lengthy indisposition prevented me from carrying out my intention. It would be a gross understatement to tell you that I was warmly greeted by the people you introduced me to. I was shown every consideration. The Marquess of Lansdowne in particular was clearly anxious to be agreeable to you and overwhelmed me with all kinds of favours. This proof of his esteem was all the more precious to me since I saw in it a reflection of the kindness which you yourself had been good enough to show me.

When I arrived in this country, I found the parliamentary battle suspended. The new Session was opened three or four days ago; but no important questions have as yet been discussed and the parties have not yet shown their true colours. It is therefore very difficult even for an Englishman to predict now what fate the new cabinet will meet with. It would be preposterous for a foreigner like me, so soon after my arrival, to make the attempt, so I have, up till now, only attempted to appraise the general changes which have occurred since my last stay by making a few points of comparison.

Eighteen months ago, I noticed that democratic ideas, which were progressing rapidly in everything related to political questions, seemed stationary in what concerned social problems; in other words, that the nation was preoccupied more with equal rights than with equal conditions. When I compared what I saw then with what I think I see today, it seems to me that the revolution continued its progress in the first direction, but that in the second direction it stayed at about the same point as I had left it. Eighteen months ago, the Whigs attacked the majority in the House of Lords, but respected the peerage. Today I hear ominous words echoing

240

through their ranks. According to many of them, the Reform Bill has completely changed the spirit of the English constitution. In the old days, the real government of society had its seat in the House of Lords; the Commons were inevitably swept along in the wake of the aristocracy. Today the contrary is inevitable. The consequences of the Reform Bill have been to place the government in the Commons. The Peers can still be used in the running of State affairs but they have lost the right to control them.

Others go still further, and ask why the rich alone can have access to the House of Lords. Some even question the privileges of heredity. Not long ago, all these doctrines were expounded in pamphlets which the Whig party does not oppose even though it does not officially approve of them. There is generally in the nation an obvious tendency to challenge the privilege of governing the State enjoyed by the wealthy classes.

If, from political opinions as such, we turn to opinions which I would call social, there is no evidence that similar progress has been made. Today I do not see more people in favour of equal conditions and of the sharing out of land than I could eighteen months ago. All those who are building up a fortune or have the opportunity of growing rich are in favour of the accumulation of wealth. The rest are not yet allowed to speak up. I can imagine easily enough the English people represented by two men, one of whom says to the other: *It is a matter of choice; would you like us to share out our common heritage equally; we shall then both have modest means.* To which the other replies: *Take everything and leave me the opportunity of taking your place some day.* In England, middle-class men still think in a double or quits fashion. In France, the same men prefer to share the stakes and, making a small allowance for the intervention of fate, to expect and fear less from the future.

When I consider carefully the situation in this country, I cannot help thinking that the same democratic revolution which took place in France must, sooner or later, happen in England. But it seems to me that it will not happen in the same way and will proceed along other lines. In France, indifference in religious matters has given an unusual amount of help in the reform of the old laws. Here, the revolution appears to have taken on a character as much religious as political. In France, people do not realise how ardent religious passions still are in this country, roused as these are by the party spirit, or how important is the influence they exert on human behaviour. The population is thus divided: on the side of the established religion are nearly all the rich; along with the dissenters go a large proportion of the middle classes and an important part of the lower classes. It is noteworthy that families which attain wealth hasten to join the established church while everyday a great many paupers join the dissenters. And if the tendencies and habits of the two doctrines are observed closely, the established religion will be found to lead naturally to monarchic and aristocratic ideas and that of the sects to republicanism and democracy.

Republican and democratic theories do not occur in an atmosphere of unbelief in England as they do in France. On the contrary, they enlist the help of beliefs. They successively become their tools or use them as tools. Following the probable course of events, the dissenters will win in the end and they will be seen to overturn the State, after having destroyed the Church, as they did in 1640. One instance is enough to show the difference which exists between the two countries in religious matters. Last year, a bill would, but for a few votes, have gone through the House of Commons; it would have made the already very severe Sunday observance much stricter. The Reform movement is thus pushing towards puritan austerity, as it does in France towards weakening religious discipline.

In France the number of small land-owners has always been very considerable and the taste for land ownership widespread among the people. The revolution has only generalised this state of affairs. Here, not only is land very undivided, but it becomes everyday more concentrated in a few hands. I think that this stems mainly from the huge proportions which the development of trade and industry is taking.

I believe that it is an acknowledged fact that, as a nation becomes more civilised, men move from the fields to the factories. This natural movement of the population is particularly noticeable in England, where they make almost all articles necessary not only for English consumption, but for world consumption as it were. Besides, the land in England was always little divided and never provided for the poor as well as it does in France; it never occurred to the common man that land was the most natural end of industry. The English peasant thus has very different habits and instincts from ours. As soon as he has acquired more knowledge, or more capital than his neighbours, he tries to convert these advantages to trade; the idea of becoming a landowner does not occur to him. For the English, land has therefore become an object of luxury; it gives honour, pleasure, but relatively speaking, little money. Only very wealthy people try to secure it. So, while in France the big landowner sometimes sells his land piece by piece for speculation, here the small landowner tries to rid himself of his to acquire wealth. The large estates thus grow larger every day at the expense of the small ones and the taste and habit of cultivation on a large scale become more widespread. Among other things, this has the following effect: cultivation on a large scale requiring comparatively less workers than cultivation on a small scale, every year a great many small farmers find themselves without work. So, while industry and trade attract them, land discourages them.

I do not know whether you will think, sir, as I do, that such an abusive use of the aristocratic principle leads almost as certainly to a revolution as the natural development of democracy does in France. England already exhibits a strange phenomenon: nearly two thirds of the population have left the land and have taken up an occupation in industry. Such an emigration, which goes back a long time and continues at an ever increasing pace, can only lead to an unnatural state in which I believe society could not maintain itself. There is already one complaint in this country against the excess population and the lack of work. The population seems excessive because it is unevenly spread out and there is a lack of work because the workers are all orientated the same way. Opposite a minority of haves is a hugh majority of have-nots; and nowhere else is the question put in a more daunting manner between those who have everything and those who have nothing. I know that all the rich are beginning to agree very well among themselves, but the poor also are in better agreement than in any other country in the world. So there is a lack of agreement only between one side and the other.

It is true that democracy, which already possesses a huge army in this country, does not, strictly speaking, have any leaders. The men democracy succeeds in sending to Parliament represent it very inadequately; most of them want to attain political equality whilst respecting social inequality. But it seems obvious to me that, in a given period of time, they will be pushed from one to the other in spite of themselves. The general unease will draw them to it. When the aristocracy is deprived of most of its political influence, its leaders will still lead a good life, because they are rich; but, in its lower ranks, the troubles which will follow this change will seem intolerable. What makes up the rearguard of the aristocracy will become the vanguard of democracy and, when the effects of the unrest are widely felt, someone will see to it that the idea of the remedy comes to the mind of the people.

In short, one could say that, if the taste for land in the people and the habit of cultivation on a small scale have helped equal conditions in France to an uncommon degree, one would think that the excess of opposite causes will necessarily bring the English to the same end. Many other differences could be pointed out between this country and France, but I must stop here and indeed it is high time I apologised for the ridiculous length of this letter. I realise that I have allowed myself to write half a book but I have not yet said anything of the thousand and one obstacles which accompany the daily running of affairs; and while I talked much about the future, I forgot the more important chapter, the present. You probably wanted me to give you facts, and I only send you speculations. But I hope, sir, that you will kindly notice in this letter, not its contents, but the intention with which it was written, and that you will see in it the wish to do something which you might find agreeable.

Please believe me...

Alexis de Tocqueville

p.s. I hope that you will be so kind as to remember me to Mme. d'Aguesseau.

1 See Footnote 3 on page 92.

2 Note by Tocqueville in the margin: General principles. Little change following demand for change. Personal activity of individuals. No hierarchy. Administrative functions of the judicial power. *The importance of this which in my view is increasing.*

3 For a full historical treatment of the British parish, its legal and administrative aspects, the reader should consult: Sidney and Beatrice Webb, *English Local Government from the Revolution to the Municipal Corporations Act: The Parish and the County,* London, 1906. There is a reference to the *Correspondence and Conversations of Alexis de Tocqueville with William Nassau Senior* on page 604. To Maitland's *Constitutional History of England* we have already referred. A *comparative* historical perspective can be gained by the study of John P. Lawson's admirable work, *A History of Lay Judges,* Cambridge, Mass., 1960.

4 Note by Tocqueville: I ought to say once and for all that the word 'generally' is to be understood in every question and answer. The exceptions are *always* very numerous.

5 Note by Tocqueville: Form of these meetings. Way of coming together and procedure. (Need to enquire about them.) Other doubtful points: accounts of their expenses: lawsuits.

6 Note by Tocqueville: This example is based on the way the old poor law functioned. The matter would be organised slightly differently now.

7 Note by Tocqueville: I did not ask about the *local police* or about the schools. I know that schools are private undertakings.

8 Note by Tocqueville: This is not correct: the common almost always belongs to the *Lord of the Manor.* The landowners only have right to graze their beasts proportionate to the size of their estates.

9 Note by Tocqueville: I need to know that these *matters* are.

10 Note by Tocqueville: I am not sure that I understood this correctly.

11 Note by Tocqueville: All this requires further explanation. I imagine the position is like this: Let us call the town A. It has a corporation which administers justice, is responsible for the police, and manages a certain amount of property. There are also some special commissioners appointed under local laws who see to the paving and lighting of the streets. Finally the various districts of the town appoint their churchwarden and fix the tax necessary to repair the church and defray the expenses of worship. So one finds there three distinct orders of local government.

12 Note by Tocqueville in the margin: Ask for more details about the *High Sheriff* and the *Lord Lieutenant.*

13 Note by Tocqueville: I am not quite sure that I understood that correctly.

14 Note by Tocqueville: I do not properly understand how or by whom these individuals are chosen.

15 Virginia Ancelot (née Chardon), 1792-1875, was the wife of Jacques-Arsène François Ancelot (1794-1854) who was a sucessful playwright. His wife collaborated with him, but she herself wrote also plays and published several novels, all of which are now forgotten. Her husband became a member of the Académie française in 1841. Mme. Ancelot published the memoirs of her Salon in the book from which the above letter is taken: Mme. Ancelot, *Un Salon de Paris,* 1824-1864, Paris, 1866, p. 79ff.

She met Tocqueville, as she writes in her memoirs, "soon after his return from America, that is to say, around 1832. He published then a work on the penitentiary system in the United States with his friend Gustave de Beaumont.

Shortly afterwards M. de Tocqueville published his great work on *De la Démocratie aux Etats-Unis d'Amérique,* of which he had read me fragments from his manuscript."

She remained Tocqueville's friend until June 1858, when she saw him for the last time in Paris. "Nothing made me anticipate the danger and yet one of these presentiments which have never deceived me tore at my heart when he left. We spoke much of his returning and his work in the future. And then he didn't come again! He had no future." (*op. cit.,* p. 88). Tocqueville died in Cannes in 1859.

16 Louis-Mathieu, Count Molé, 1781-1855, statesman, relative of Tocqueville, was appointed Minister for Justice in 1813. He was made a peer during the Hundred Days; his peerage was confirmed by Louis XVIII. Comte Molé was Minister for Foreign Affairs and President of the Council of Ministers twice, in 1836-7 and then again from 1837-9. He was elected to the French Academy in 1840 and he was a member of Parliament from 1848-51.

In 1837 he attempted, in his official capacity as Prime Minister, to support Tocqueville's candidature for Parliament in the constituency of Valognes, but Tocqueville refused his support and was, of course, not elected. However, he succeeded triumphantly, without government support, during the elections in 1839 and remained Deputy for Valognes until 1851. Cf. the revealing correspondence between Molé and Tocqueville in *Oeuvres Complètes,* ed. Beaumont, vol. VI, pp. 73ff. See also: *Le Comte Molé, Sa Vie, ses mémoires 1781-1855* published by the Marquis de Noailles, Paris 1922-30, 6 vols.

Index[1]

[1] I wish to thank Mrs. N. H. Feeny who kindly compiled this Index.

Index